C Tools for Scientists
and Engineers

D0905868

Other McGraw-Hill Books in Mini and Mainframe Computing

ISBN	AUTHOR	TITLE
0-07-056578-3	Sherman	*The CD-ROM Handbook*
0-07-039006-1	Lusardi (hardcover)	*Database Experts' Guide to SQL*
0-07-039002-9	(softcover)	
0-07-016609-6	DeVita (hardcover)	*Database Experts' Guide to FOCUS*
0-07-016604-8	(softcover)	
0-07-036488-5	Larson (hardcover)	*Database Experts' Guide to Database 2*
0-07-023267-9	(softcover)	
0-07-000474-9	Adrian	*The Workstation Data Link*
0-07-057336-0	Simpson, Casey	*Developing Effective User Documentation*
0-07-007248-5	Brathwaite	*Analysis, Design, and Implementation of Data Dictionaries*
0-07-035119-8	Knightson	*Standards for Open Systems Interconnection*
0-07-044938-4	McClain (hardcover)	*VM and Departmental Computing*
0-07-044939-2	(softcover)	
0-07-046302-6	Nemzow	*Keeping the Link*
0-07-038006-6	Lipton	*User Guide to FOCUS™*
0-07-057296-8	Simon	*How to Be a Successful Computer Consultant*
0-07-016188-7	Dayton (Ranade, Ed.)	*Integrating Digital Services*
0-07-002673-4	Azevedo (Ranade Series)	*ISPF: The Strategic Dialog Manager*
0-07-050054-1	Piggott (Ranade Series)	*CICS: A Practical Guide to System Fine Tuning*
0-07-043152-3	Morgan, McGilton	*Introducing UNIX™ System V*
0-07-050686-8	Prasad (Ranade Series)	*IBM Mainframes*
0-07-065087-X	Towner (Ranade Series)	*IDMS/R Cookbook*
0-07-062879-3	Tare (hardcover)	*UNIX™ Utilities*
0-07-062884-X	(softcover)	
0-07-045001-3	McGilton, Morgan	*Introducing the UNIX™ System*
0-07-062295-7	Su	*Database Computers*
0-07-041920-5	Milenkovic	*Operating Systems Concepts and Design*
0-07-010829-3	Ceri/Pelagatti	*Distributed Databases*

C Tools for Scientists and Engineers

Louis Baker, Ph.D.

McGraw-Hill Publishing Company

New York St. Louis San Francisco Auckland
Bogotá Hamburg London Madrid Mexico
Milan Montreal New Delhi Panama
Paris São Paulo Singapore
Sydney Tokyo Toronto

To Jennie

Library of Congress Cataloging-in-Publication Data

Baker, Louis.
  C tools for scientists and engineers/Louis Baker.
    p.   cm.
  Includes index.
  ISBN 0-07-003355-2:
  1. C (Computer program language)   2. Algorithms.   I. Title.
QA76.73.C15B34 1989
510'.28'55322—dc19   88-39703
                                                                             CIP

    34567890   DOC/DOC   9543210

ISBN 0-07-003355-2

The editor for this book was Theron Shreve.

Printed and bound by R. R. Donnelley & Sons Company.

Contents

4. Eigenvalue and Discriminant Analysis

5. Singular Value Decomposition: Robust Least-Squares Estimation, Factor Analysis

6. Newton-Raphson and Related Methods

7. Complex Arithmetic. Muller & Jenkins-Traub Methods

ABOUT THE SOURCE CODE

The source code for the programs contained herein is available on an IBM-PC-compatible double-sided diskette by mail order. Send $9.95 (New Mexico residents add applicable gross receipts tax, 5.25%) to:

Dagonet Software
2904 La Veta Dr. N.E.
Albuquerque, NM 87110

Write for information on other disk formats.

Preface
What's in It (This Book) for You

This book is intended to provide a collection of tested algorithms which may be immediately applied to real-world problems encountered by scientists (physical and social), engineers, and programmers. All codes have been tested and are supplied with "driver" programs that provide test cases to benchmark the codes on problems with known answers. The reader will easily become a user who does not have to reinvent the wheel.

The word "tools" in the title might wrongly suggest that only fragments of programs are provided, and that users must be experts to employ those building blocks in constructing their programming edifices. While many of the programs found in here can serve with or within larger codes, many are complete programs. Others may require a minimal amount of scaffolding for specific problems.

All of the methods used are explained and documented. Users do not have to take the author's word that the method presented is valid; they will be given the information to use it intelligently and knowledgeably. Much of "computer science" is still an art. Therefore, it is desirable that readers understand what programs are doing in order to avoid any possible pitfalls. Users should not only run the test problems to convince themselves the programs are working as they should; users should also critically examine their working runs to be sure the results are reasonable.

How to Use This Book

There are a number of ways to use this book. One is to lift a program bodily, run the test case, and then apply it to the problem at hand. Most of the methods presented in this book could conceivably be used with little or no modification on common problems. I do encourage readers to read the discussion and understand the methods discussed. This will help to avoid embarrassments later. Another use for this book would be as a set of examples of working C code. Readers uncomfortable with pointer variables, for example, will see many applications of them and could learn how to use them from seeing them in action. The numerical methods used could be a useful supplement to texts on numerical analysis, and the non-numerical algorithms should be of interest to programmers. The statistical methods will be of interest to statisticians, social scientists, or students in such courses. Similarly, engineers and physical scientists, researchers, and students should all be able to find useful programs in this book.

C for Scientists and Engineers

This book is written in C for a number of reasons. This language is rapidly becoming the lingua franca of the computer world. It is on machines from microcomputers to supercomputers, PCs to Crays. It is a structured, high-level language. Algorithms written in C should be very portable, and easily converted with reasonable readiness into other high-level languages.

What This Book Contains

The algorithms are grouped by method rather than by application. The selection is intended to provide useful methods for a broad variety of disciplines. Possible applications are discussed.

The first two chapters provide an introduction for users new to numerical analysis or to the C language. Particularly noteworthy is a discussion of pitfalls and hints for programmers whose background is in FORTRAN. Tips are given for the conversion of FORTRAN programs to C. Because much scientific and engineering code is written in FORTRAN, this should be of interest.

The next section includes chapters containing routines for linear algebra. These include solving systems of simultaneous equations, inverting matrices, eigenvalue analysis, and performing multivariate regression (least-squares fits) with the Singular Value Decomposition. In different disciplines, these methods may be known under different aliases; for example, statisticians use the term "factor analysis" for what is an eigenvalue analysis. The Singular Value Decomposition (SVD) has many additional uses in statistics which are discussed in Chapter 5 below. Converting a FORTRAN code to a C code is discussed, and a special C header file to ease this process is given.

The next section, of two chapters, turns from linear to nonlinear systems of equations. The Newton-Raphson method is developed in the first for systems of real equations with real roots. For complex roots, Muller's method is presented, along with the Jenkins-Traub iteration for polynomial roots. Of particular interest is the implementation of complex arithmetic in the latter, again facilitated by a tool in the form of a header file.

The following section builds tools for the numerical solution of differential equations. First, interpolation, specifically the use of B-splines, is discussed. Interpolation is applied to integration in the adaptive quadrature program of the next chapter. A very important special integral, the Fourier Transform, is treated next. A Runge-Kutta-Fehlberg method, which is used for initial value problems, and an implicit method for "stiff" problems, are presented to complete this section. Stiff system solvers are often omitted from books but they can be very important for treating, e.g., chemically reacting systems.

The final section presents a chapter on graphics, which is a topic often slighted in collections of programming tools. A simple, ready-to-use plotting program is given.

Rarely is one algorithm better than all others for all cases. For this reason, alternative methods for the various cases that may appear are discussed where appropriate. While every effort has been expended to use methods that are "state-of-the-art," computer science changes at a rapid pace, and it is possible that improvements will be discovered. I would appreciate hearing from readers with improvements, corrections, better algorithms for some problems, etc.

It is my sincere hope that readers will save themselves much grief by being able to use the routines presented here with a minimum of effort. I also hope that students and others will take the opportunity to learn from the methods presented here. They are not perfect, but most derive from a long series of efforts by workers in the fields of programming and numerical analysis. They, therefore, represent the distilled effort of many people. I apologize to those workers whose contributions I fail to adequately cite, through ignorance or error. Readers of this book might justly feel that they are standing on the shoulders of many giants when they use some of the methods contained herein; they will almost certainly "see" further by doing so than by relying only on their own legs.

Acknowledgments

I'd like to thank many colleagues for help, especially W. Zimmerman and B. S. Newberger for contributing FORTRAN programs they had written, B. Stellingwerf for advice on solving ODE's, and A. Giancola for much critical advice. K. McGuire drafted the figures. The book was typeset with Ventura publisher (excluding program listings), the figures scanned with a Princeton LS-300, and camera-ready copy was produced with a PS Jet +. Stephen Parks helped proofread the manuscript.

A Word to the Wise

While every effort has been made to test and ensure the correctness of the methods presented here, final responsibility rests with the user for assuring their results are correct. The programs presented here are without warranty, and no liability shall be incurred by the author or the publisher for any loss or damage caused directly or indirectly by the programs or algorithms described in this book (please read the full disclaimer which precedes this Preface). Please check all programs and results carefully. In addition to running the test problems contained in this book, generate your own to confirm that you fully understand the calling conventions and data formats. To paraphrase John Philpot Curran, the condition upon which freedom from errors depends is eternal vigilance.

Louis Baker

CHAPTER 1

Overview of Numerical Analysis

Chapter Objectives

This chapter is an introduction to numerical analysis. It will discuss the topics of finite-precision arithmetic, error analysis, robustness, and complexity analysis.

Introduction

Computers enable us to solve problems beyond the scope of analytic methods by making the application of numerical methods feasible. Some problems, e.g., highly nonlinear problems, may simply be impossible to treat analytically. Others might be too large or cumbersome.

There is a price to pay, however. One is that, by delegating the problem to a computer, insights that might be made along the way toward the solution, as well as invalid assumptions or errors, can be missed. Furthermore, the computer is not a perfect calculator with infinite precision. Even if it were, limitations of time and memory would insure that answers would generally be inexact. Neither are the algorithms embodied in programs "perfect." It is therefore valuable to understand something of the computational process. Scientific computer users can never afford to take themselves "out of the loop."

Finite-Precision Arithmetic

The major difference of computer arithmetic from "ideal" analysis is that numbers are computed to finite precision. We assume that scientific and engineering computations are done using floating-point arithmetic, and that the reader is generally familiar with this method of representing numbers and a mantissa or fractional part which multiplies a standard base raised to an exponent. By storing the mantissa and exponent only, we can represent numbers of widely varying magnitude with the same fractional precision. There are various standards, but typically C uses type double arithmetic (even if the results will ultimately be stored in variables of type float), which generally occupies 64 bits of storage and will provide a precision of about one part in 10^{-20} in computation, and a similar precision of the variable is stored as type double.

Generally, such precision is more than sufficient. The danger is loss of precision. The rules for "significant figures" you probably have encountered when taking a laboratory course as a student govern the numerical analyst as well. Generally, multiplication and division do not cause any loss of precision. Addition and subtraction are dangerous, however. If we subtract two approximately equal numbers, we can lose precision (significant digits). Assume we have 3 digits of precision (significance). Then $1.00 - 0.99 = 0.01$ is a classic example of how we can lose most of our precision (2 digits) in one simple operation! A similar danger in floating-point arithmetic is a situation in which $1.00 + 10^{-3} = 1.00$. Here no precision has been lost, but the result can be disaster if the users have not protected themselves.

To illustrate the last point, consider the fairly common problem of the solution of the quadratic $x^2 + bx + c = 0$. Assume that $a, b > 0$ and that we desire the solution with $x > 0$ ($c < 0$ is implied). Then

$$x = [\sqrt{(b^2 - 4ac)} - b]/2a$$

is the desired answer. Or is it? Assume $b = 1$ and a is small. Then $x = [\sqrt{(1 - 4ac)} - 1]/2a$, which for small ac will be roughly (by Taylor series expansion of the square root) $x = -c$ (recall that $c < 0$, so $x > 0$). But if ac is sufficiently small that $1 - 4ac$ is roughly 1, we find that $x = 0$. Note that $|c|$ might be quite large and still have $|ac| < 1$ in some problems, thus finding $x = 0$ when in fact it should be quite large! The reader will encounter this problem in the analysis of ionization equilibrium discussed in the chapter on the Newton-Raphson method. Such problems are therefore not "cooked" but occur commonly.

One solution to this difficulty is to multiply the numerator and denominator by $(\sqrt{(b^2 - 4ac)} + b)$, giving

$$x = -2c/(\sqrt{(b^2 - 4ac)} + b)$$

as an answer which is well-behaved for small $|ac|$. Of course, it will have other difficulties (e.g., were $b < 0$). (See the chapter below on the Newton-Raphson method for another approach.)

The loss of precision as illustrated here is often called "roundoff" or "truncation" error. These terms refer to how the computer does its arithmetic, i.e., if we multiply 1.23 by 4.56 do we truncate the exact answer (5.6088) to 5.60 or round (by adding .005 before truncation) to get 5.61? Typically, machines do the latter to get somewhat more accurate results, but this should never be relied upon. The term "truncation error" is also used to describe the error resulting from retaining only a finite number of terms in an infinite series, or continued fraction, or iterating a finite number of times where an "exact" answer would require an infinite number of terms.

The moral of this story is that there will probably never be perfectly "canned" programs which allow the user to take for granted the results. Numerical analysis remains an art.

Error Analysis

Given the imperfection to be expected of results, it is useful to be able to estimate how good they will be.

There are two approaches: forward and backward. The former seeks to tell users what they most desire: just how accurate is the answer, given the imperfections of the method. This is often quite a difficult task. Consequently, backward error analysis is often used. This method asks the question: given my computed solution, what problem is it the exact solution to? This is often a much easier question to answer. If that problem is "close" in an appropriate sense to the problem you wish answered, then you can relax.

For example, suppose you have computed the value z for the root of a polynomial $P(x)$. Then z is an exact root of $P(x) - P(z)$ where $P(z)$ is the constant value of the polynomial evaluated at z. The forward analysis of this problem, by contrast, is extremely difficult.

Many problems can be "ill-conditioned," that is, give rise to situations in which small changes in the problem to be solved (as might arise through finite-precision arithmetic) cause large changes in the answer. The determination of the roots of a polynomial of high degree is one such problem, and there are famous examples (one is given below in Chapter 7) of how a minuscule change in one coefficient can alter the character of the roots drastically. Another example is solving the linear system $Ax = b$ where the matrix A has a small determinant (another measure is the "condition number"—see Chapter 3 on linear systems below). In both these cases, the problem is not easily solved by a "good" numerical scheme, because the difficulty is in the problem itself, not the method of solution.

Robustness

This brings us to the issue of "robustness," the ability to get a good answer (or at least know when the answer might be poor). One should generally try to "bulletproof" programs, especially those intended as canned library routines, to check for parameters out of their range of validity, for example. Robustness goes beyond this to ask for methods that are relatively insensitive to error. For example, in the solution of linear systems, the "pivoting" scheme is an attempt to avoid potential problems which may be caused by small coefficients. Partial rather than complete pivoting is used as a compromise between efficiency and robustness. This tradeoff is always with us in the choice of numerical methods.

A few hints might be appropriate here on robustness. First, avoid, if possible, high degree polynomials. When interpolating, use low-order polynomials over portions of the region to be fit (see Chapter 8 on spline fits below), or use rational approximations.

In general, try to avoid ill-posed or ill-conditioned problems. One class of such problems which often can't be avoided are so-called "inverse" problems. These arise in inverting integral transforms, or determining the nature of a scatterer from the scattered signal. The scattered signal is often an integral over the scattering distribution. The poor conditioning of the problem is due to the fact that the integral transformation is a smoothing operation. Consequently the inverse operation is an "un-smoothing" operation, and is, therefore, quite sensitive to noise, either numerical or the kind that is ever present in data taken from the real world. When the inverse problem is approximated as a linear system, $Ax = b$, the result is often a matrix A with poor condition number (see Chapter 3).

The best way to deal with such difficulties is not to solve the ill-conditioned system $Ax = b$. Rather, solve a related system in a least-squares sense (or some other "goodness" criterion if least-square error is not appropriate) while imposing some constraints to avoid bad solutions. One way might be to constrain the solution's variation. A generally useful approach is to write the desired solution as the superposition of a number of terms with undetermined coefficients, each of the terms being well-behaved. The coefficients are the solved for by applying the Singular Value Decomposition (SVD) method to an appropriate least-squares problem (see the chapter on the SVD). The SVD is a very robust method for treating least-squares problems.

There are other methods for inverse problems, such as "filtering" or "regularizing the kernel." These are often equivalent to the least-squares method discussed above. Once again, the analysis is an art requiring "audience" participation.

Complexity Analysis

No matter how robust the method, no matter how good the solution, we must be able to solve the problem with our resources. Therefore, the method must be sufficiently fast and efficient in its use of memory. The former is usually more of a concern than the latter. It is for these reasons that complexity analysis is of interest.

There are some methods that are clearly losers, e.g., Cramer's rule for solving linear systems. It is far more expensive to calculate determinants than to use Gaussian elimination, and the results are often less accurate to boot.

However, care must be used in applying complexity analysis. For example, multiplying two matrices of size N x N each requires N^3 floating-point operations, if we define such operations (as is common in such complexity analyses) as a multiplication (or division) followed by an addition (or subtraction). There is a method, due to Strassen, which reduces the number of floating point operations by carefully saving the results of some intermediate results. However, the "bookkeeping" of storing and retrieving these results is such that the method is of little practical interest.

Complexity analysis is usually done for the typical sequential "von Neumann" architecture machine. When "pipelined" or vector machines, array processors, or more advanced parallel processing machines are used, the analysis must be rethought. The comments on Strassen's method are amplified for a vector machine, which would very efficiently perform the scalar products of the "dumb" method and choke on the irregular memory references required by the "sophisticated" method of Strassen. On the other hand, an interactive method suggested by Pan and Reif for solving linear systems and which uses order N^3 operations per iteration for a system of N unknowns, is clearly not competitive with Gaussian elimination on a sequential machine, as the latter requires one-third as many operations to achieve the solution. However, the Pan-Reif method allows the iterations to be done in parallel on multiple processors, while Gaussian elimination requires the results from one row operation before the next row can be processed. Therefore, on a suitable machine, the Pan-Reif method could finish well ahead of Gaussian elimination.

When the methods used are not deterministic, i.e., when the nature of the data determines how many iterations or other operations are needed, care again must be exercised. Worst case analysis can be overly pessimistic. The worst case might be a laboratory curiosity which would be difficult to find in the real world if one were not looking for it. R. E. Tarjan has developed the concept of "amortized" complexity to appropriately weight the likelihood of worst cases, for example. He has used this analysis to explain why some data structures which adapt themselves to the data, such a the "splay tree," can be quite effective even though less subtle complexity analysis might suggest that they should be avoided.

Given the tradeoff between algorithm robustness and complexity, the most robust method which permits the problem to be solved within the allowable resource should be used. Thus, complexity holds the upper hand; it does not matter how good the answer would be if we can't have it in time or with our computer. The size of the problem can then determine if the most robust method is affordable or if we should use a more economical method. Consequently, there may not be one unique best method for all problems of a given type. In this book, because we expect that the code will be used as a library routine, a high premium is placed on robustness. Alternatives are given where appropriate, however.

CHAPTER 2

The C Language for Scientists and Engineers

How to Use This Book

This book contains programs which solve the problems of greatest interest to scientists and engineers. Some, such as the statistical function calculator of Chapter 13, may be used exactly as listed. Others, such as the differential equation system solvers of Chapters 11 and 12, will require some changes in the "driver" routines to specify the problem to be solved. Still others will be tools to be incorporated in libraries and called as needed.

All the source code is presented here—there are no cards up anyone's sleeve. The user can, therefore, see exactly what is supposed to happen. There can be no more complete, detailed presentation of an algorithm than the code listing.

Numerical analysis has traditionally been done in FORTRAN. For this reason, there is a great deal of FORTRAN code, in libraries personal and public, of interest to scientists and engineers. Methods which ease the conversion of FORTRAN code into C code are to be found throughout this book. Chapter 3 contains a generally useful header file for such purposes, and Chapter 7 presents another header file to facilitate the use of complex arithmetic in C.

As B. W. Kernighan and P. J. Plauger state in *Elements of Programming Style*, programming cannot be taught by preaching generalities but must be done by presenting actual code. I hope that this book may be of use to those scientists and engineers who may be learning C or numerical analysis and desire examples of C programs that treat significant problems encountered in these disciplines.

Why C?

No computer programming language is perfect. FORTRAN, the oldest of the "high-level" languages, was specifically tailored to scientific and engineering applications and continues to be popular among this group of users. It has been updated and standardized a number of times, with at least one more version in the offing in the not-too-distant future. So why abandon this old friend for an upstart language such as C?

There are a number of reasons. First, C is readily available on a wide range of machines, from personal computers to supercomputers. Wherever the popular UNIX operating system (or clones such as XENIX) goes, C comes along (since UNIX is largely written in C). C is perhaps the most portable language in existence today. Perhaps Ada will take that crown away, but at present Ada is not universally available, and Ada compilers are expensive when they can be had. A program written (with an eye toward portability) in C is a program that, with minor touches, should run almost anywhere. Scholars or professionals who find themselves on the move can (almost) relax about "porting" their codes. Porting FORTRAN can often be quite a chore.

The situation is different with FORTRAN or Pascal, to name the most popular alternatives to C. It took a number of years for a FORTRAN compiler to appear for the IBM PC. The principal reason for the difficulty was the freedom of FORTRAN syntax. As there are no keywords and blanks are ignored, statements such as

DO1I=1

and

DO 1 I=1,27

are not easily distinguished. The use of lexical analyzer generator programs such as LEX, with compiler-compilers like YACC, is not possible, due to the inability to recognize language tokens easily. Of course, FORTRAN compilers can be written in a portable form of C, but this would generally still require a reasonable amount of effort to achieve acceptable performance. They also tend to be expensive compared to similar compilers for personal computers.

Pascal suffers from a number of difficulties. The input/output operations, including file handling, are not standardized and therefore not portable. Programs must be compiled completely anew any time any portion is changed—libraries of compiled object code cannot be "linked." Modula-2 was developed to redress the second complaint against Pascal, but has not become a popular and available substitute.

Another reason for the use of C is that it allows a natural linkage with the operating system and, through the operating system, peripherals, hardware, etc. (try accessing command line arguments in FORTRAN). This feature alone can result in great convenience and time-savings, especially if the program is running in "batch" mode. Non-numerical functions, such as file manipulation, input-output functions, access to ports and busses (e.g., the IEEE-488 GPIB or VME busses) data communications and real-time applications are naturally written in C. Engineers especially use computers, including personal computers, to monitor experiments, take data in real time from sensors, and often to process the data in a preliminary manner. This processing can involve significant numerical "massaging" of the data. The use of C enables the interfacing of these two forms of programming, numerical and non-numerical, with a minimum of tears. Some of the examples in this book are primarily non-numerical. The enumerated types preprocessor is one such program. It should be of value to those readers whose C compiler does not support enumerated types (or the "void" identifier for procedures) but who wish to use C programs which employ such variables. The program should also be useful to those readers who need to do lexical analysis for some application.

The power of C to handle recursion, which is often not supported, is exploited in some of the programs in this book.

The C preprocessor is often a powerful tool to reduce the redundancy in many codes. Its use will be illustrated below in handling complex arithmetic or facilitating the conversion of FORTRAN programs to C. The preprocessor goes a long way toward making the C language "extensible" by allowing users to define their own operators, conditionally substituting different code for the same symbols depending upon the setting of various flags, etc. FORTRAN has nothing like it.

There is no such thing as perfect portability, although C is among the most portable languages that exist today. Most of the programs contained in this book have been run on a number of machines and compilers, generally DeSmet C on an IBM PC clone and Aztec C on a Kaypro II CP/M machine. The programs have been written to avoid the idiosyncracies of C compilers and should generally run without modification in almost any environment. As an example, a while loop statement of the form while() should result in an infinite loop. Aztec C version 1.05g (for CP/M machines) treats the statement as a while(0) and does not execute the loop at all! Therefore, you will see the code used in this book use statements such as while(1) or even while(1==1). As another example, DeSmet C requires functions to end with a statement of the form return (x), where x is a variable of the same type as the function. In some of the programs contained in this book you will find statements of this form which are unreachable, but which must be present to satisfy the compiler. Typically, if the C program is written to be portable and to avoid machine-dependencies and compiler idiosyncracies, the only changes needed are in regard to the standard libraries. To convert from Aztec C to DeSmet C usually requires removing the #include specifications for the libc.h and math.h header files. There is also the need for a #define statement for EOF and a "missing" function which is in the Aztec library but not the DeSmet library. The library demands of the programs below are such that most any C will have all the functions called. The most insidious problems can be caused by library functions that behave differently on different machines. Some use a different definition of EOF (− 1 is the usual return value, but in some environments the return from getchar for an end of file can be zero), or handle files in a different manner. These kinds of problems should not affect the programs in this book.

In summary, there are no ideal languages. C has its strong points and weaknesses, as do all the other languages. Because it was not specifically designed for the types of analysis performed by scientists and engineers, which are largely numerical, but was adapted more toward systems programmers and operating system concerns, it is in some ways awkward for use in such problems. This book will try to explore the easier routes around that awkwardness. It should serve as a guide to those looking for those paths. Along the way, the reader should find the path strewn with useful programs.

Table 2.1

Merits of C vs. FORTRAN

C Superior	FORTRAN Superior
system interface	COMPLEX data type
recursion supported better	NAMELIST input convenient
preprocessor	Precision control by user
portability	Optimizing compilers
command-line access	

The summary in Table 2.1 compares the virtues of C and FORTRAN, from the point of view of a scientist or engineer.

Number Crunching with C

The emphasis of this book is on numerical methods. There are many books available which treat aspects of C of most interest to systems programmers, mostly file manipulation, screen handling, etc. Engineers and scientists have applications involved which require more numerical analysis. They might be tempted to just try to translate such codes into C. It is not trivial to translate FORTRAN code directly into C, as writing this book has taught me! The programs in this book should serve as illustrative examples to aid those doing similar conversions.

One instance would be the problem of performing complex arithmetic. FORTRAN has the COMPLEX data type, which electrical engineers come to appreciate easily. Ada allows a complex data type to be defined. In Pascal, one has to use clumsy subroutines to effect complex arithmetic. In C, one can use the preprocessor feature to make complex arithmetic reasonably efficient (it is performed "in-line" without subroutine calls), if unaesthetic. The programs in this book which rely on complex arithmetic should not only be useful in their own right but useful as a guide to those who need complex arithmetic in C in their own codes.

The C language was developed at Bell Telephone laboratories for use on a PDP-11. This explains peculiar features, such as a statement of the form:

```
i++;
```

which would compile directly into an instruction on the PDP-11 (that is, assuming i were a register integer variable). Because of this and other "features" of the language, C has been called a "write-only" language. It is difficult to read someone else's code and easily understand what is happening. Comments help, of course. Despite claims for Pascal, there is no such thing as "self-documenting" code. The programs in this book tend to be liberally supplied with comments, as well as being described in the text. Variable names can be more descriptive than in FORTRAN. Loop indices will often be called i,j,k, etc., in keeping with FORTRAN custom, as well as a desire to avoid long-winded names for such indices that would have to be typed many times. Integer variables do not in general start with i through n as in FORTRAN in this book.

The C language permits recursion naturally. This is not often used in numerical analysis. When functions are defined recursively, it is often a simple "tail-end" recursion which can be converted to a loop relatively easily, giving a more efficient computer implementation. Recursion does come in handy for implementing the adaptive quadrature program discussed below.

Converting FORTRAN Programs to C

Much of numerical analysis centers on linear algebra. This encompasses vector and matrix algebra, including solving simultaneous systems of equations. FORTRAN and Pascal support the very natural convention of calling the first element in a vector A A(1). In C, this would be A[0]. If the array had twenty elements, we would have a declaration statement such as:

> float A[20];

but the last element of the array would be A[19]. This can be a source of confusion and difficult-to-locate bugs. Matrices are even more problematical. FORTRAN allows one to pass a matrix (two-dimensional array) as an argument to a subroutine, with the dimensions as arguments as well:

> SUBROUTINE X(A,N)

> DIMENSION A(N,N)

whereas c has no such facility. We must pass a pointer to the array

> x(a,n)

> float *a;int n;

and handle the subscript generation, based on the value of the dimension n, ourselves. Note that a vector can be declared as

> float *v;

or

> float v[];

but C does not let us pass the dimensions of an array in such a manner that we can just use the array as a matrix, e.g., a[5][7]. We shall illustrate below how the use of the C preprocessor eases this burden somewhat. The preprocessor can also be used to make writing the loops easier.

Matrices are stored and accessed differently in C and in FORTRAN. In FORTRAN, they are stored by column, in C by row. In FORTRAN, the first element in storage is A(1,1), followed by A(2,1), etc., whereas in C the first element a[0][0] is followed by a[0][1]. This can be important, particularly for problems involving large matrices on mainframe machines.

Row operations would be more naturally done in C, as the next element in the row would be the next element in the storage address space. Column operations might be more natural in FORTRAN. Sometimes FORTRAN algorithms for dealing with large matrices are specifically designed to accommodate storage by columns, to minimize data transfer from secondary storage. If one is dealing with large matrices, these considerations should be kept in mind. If one is using a microcomputer, one can probably forget about them, unless very large matrices are being used.

Conversion of most FORTRAN and Pascal programs to C is rather straightforward, if the programmer does not attempt to take advantage of the special features of the C language. For example, in FORTRAN DO loop indices must increase, requiring somewhat awkward constructs to have a working index decrement. We have illustrated both conversion methods, in Chapter 2 staying very close to the FORTRAN implementation while illustrating the alternative in Chapter 4. The preprocessor is used to aid the conversion as mentioned above and illustrated primarily in the chapters that deal with complex variables and matrices. Pascal translates relatively easily to C, with the exception of variant records.

Eight Hints for Debugging C Programs

The usual pitfalls in C code, particularly for programmers experienced in FORTRAN, are the following (many relate to arguments in function and subroutine calls):

1) *Array Indices Start at Zero·*

Remember that an array declared as, say, array[10] extends from array[0] to array[9]; attempting to reference array[10] could have unpredictable results, at best. Recall also that multi-dimensional arrays are quite different in C than in FORTRAN or Pascal, and that what does resemble them in C is quite different from the FORTRAN analog. In FORTRAN, the first two elements of a two-dimensional array will be a(1,1) and a(2,1), whereas in C they would be a[0][0] and a[0][1].

2) *Function Arguments Cannot Be Altered by the Called Subroutine*

Remember that function arguments are passed by value. The argument is evaluated and that value pushed onto the stack. Do not try to modify these values or to return answers through them. Pointers must be used if the calling program needs to have information returned to it through the variables.

3) *Different Syntax May Be Required in Declarations for the Same Object*

Arguments sent to a function are declared differently in the sender than in the called function. The simplest example would be an integer, declared, say:

    int i;

in one program, which passes a pointer to a subroutine as:

    subr(&i);

which then declares:

    subr(i) int *i;

and assigns integer values to i via statements like:

    *i=7;

If the called subroutine had a statement such as i=7; unpredictable or disastrous things could happen.

If a function name is passed as an argument, say:

    subr(f)   float (*f)();

then we know that a usage such as:

    x= (*f)(z) ;

within the body of subroutine subr will set x to a floating point value. The calling program should have a declaration of the form:

    float f();

and call the subroutine with

    subr(f);

Again, disaster will likely result if the calling program has a declaration of the form:

    float (*f)();

Arrays can be especially tricky. Remember that a level of indirection is lost when a subscript is supplied. That is, when we have a declaration of the form

    float array[10];

in the calling program, array[i] will be a floating point number, but that array , as in

    subr(array);

will be a pointer. It will then be declared as such:

    subr(array) float array[];

by the subroutine. The subroutine can use array as a pointer (e.g., in passing the array to further subroutines), or as a floating point number in

    array[5]=1.0;

As a more complicated example, consider an array of structures:

    struct complex a[10];

The pointer is again passed in a call as:

    subr(a);

with the called subroutine declaring:

    subr(a) struct complex a[];

Within this subroutine the variable a will be a pointer to the array of structures. However, a[3] will be an element of the structure, not a pointer to the FOURTH element in the structure; for that we would need &(a[3]). (We capitalized the word "fourth" to remind you that in C arrays are based at index zero not one as in FORTRAN.) The chapter on Muller's method contains examples of passing structures of the form discussed here.

4) *Pointer and Array Declarations Are Not Interchangeable*

The declarations:

    float array[];

and

    float *array;

are not interchangeable, even though they both declare the variable array to be a pointer to a variable of type float. The former can cause problems unless it is for an argument of a function. Note also that int a[10][10] and int *a[10] are very different in their effects (see Kernighan and Ritchie, *The C Programming Language*, Englewood Cliffs, NJ:Prentice-Hall,1978, p. 110).

5) *Don't Get Too Fancy*

There are many subtle pitfalls. For example, what would you expect as the result of program code:

    x[i]= i++;

According to page 50 of Kernighan and Ritchie, almost anything! C does not constrain the compiler as to the order of evaluation of function arguments, or whether the location of x[i] is determined before or after i is incremented by the i++ statement!

6) *getc() and getchar() Return Integers, Not Characters*

Remember that getc() and getchar(), although intended for character input, return integers and not characters. This is important when an end of file may be encountered.

7) *Subprograms Forget Local Values between Calls*

Unlike "old" FORTRAN, subroutines will lose the values of local variables between calls. In more recent standards of FORTRAN this forgetfulness occurs as well, although one can force recollection via the FORTRAN SAVE statement. In C, a similar effect can be had by declaring the variables static, or by making them globals.

8) *Don't Trust scanf()*

The scanf() function can be unreliable. It generally does not work for reading type double, for example. Always "echo" the results of such input to be sure the program has received the correct value. As a general "user-friendly" gesture, echo input to allow the user to be sure the program will attack the desired problem—it is preferable to allow the user the option of correcting or starting over at points, although doing this for every input parameter can quickly become tiresome. It is also sometimes useful to remember the parameters of a previous case if they may be re-used as defaults for further input—the "pocket calculator" for statistical functions discussed below has this feature.

Program Selection

The programs selected for this book were chosen primarily for their utility but also for their illustrative value. Tried-and-true programs have been adapted wherever possible for greater reliability.

In general, the algorithms selected have been state-of-the art methods with maximal robustness and utility.The methods presented are compact and generally perform quite well. While some people might quibble about their favorite method being superior to another presented here, with this one exception, the methods presented here are as robust and useful as any other for the problems presented.

Chapter 3

LU Decomposition

Chapter Objectives

This chapter contains tools to:

-perform the LU decomposition of a general matrix

-solve a simultaneous system of linear equations

-invert a general matrix

-calculate the determinant of a matrix

-facilitate the conversion of a FORTRAN program involving arrays into an equivalent C program.

These tools will be used in this chapter to solve a simple linear system. They will also be applied in subsequent chapters where such systems arise, such as in the implicit stiff differential equation system solver of Chapter 12 and the Newton-Raphson solver of Chapter 6.

Linear systems arise in many problems as a result of the application of techniques such as "Galerkin's Method" or the "Method of Moments." How linear systems may be obtained using these methods is discussed below.

Simultaneous Linear Equations

One of the most common numerical problems encountered is the solution of a set of simultaneous linear equations. This problem may arise as part of another problem—for example, we will use the subroutines given here in solving stiff differential equations. The sample problem we will solve will be:

$$2x + 3y - z = 5$$
$$4x + 4y - 3z = 3$$
$$-2x + 3y - z = 1$$

which has the solution $x = 1, y = 2, z = 3$. This problem may be expressed in the language of linear algebra as $\mathbf{Ax} = \mathbf{b}$, where $\mathbf{A}$ is the matrix:

$$\begin{pmatrix} 2 & 3 & -1 \\ 4 & 4 & -3 \\ -2 & 3 & -1 \end{pmatrix}$$

and $\mathbf{b}$ is the vector $(5,3,1)$. The vector $\mathbf{x}$ contains the unknowns formerly denoted x,y,z and now, using the natural notation for C, we will denote these unknowns as x[0],x[1], and x[2]. Similarly, A[0][0] is the element 2 of the $\mathbf{A}$ matrix, while a[2][0] $= -2$. These values for $\mathbf{A}$ and $\mathbf{b}$ are chosen because they give an integer solution vector, which can serve as a check on machine accuracy. We will also use this matrix to illustrate matrix inversion and solve the linear system involving the transposed matrix $\mathbf{A}^\wedge$ (the transpose is a matrix in which the columns of $\mathbf{A}$ have become the rows of $\mathbf{A}^\wedge$, i.e. A[i][j] $= \mathbf{A}^\wedge$[j][i]).

How Linear Systems Arise

Problems Which Give Rise Directly To Linear Systems

Simultaneous linear equations often arise naturally in problems of science and engineering. Very often an equilibrium or steady state of a physical system can be described by a set of linear equations. An AC or DC electrical circuit is an example. The currents in each branch and the voltages at the nodes (where branches meet) are the principal variables of interest. In a steady state these are all related by Kirchhoff's and Ohm's laws. For AC circuits, similar equations with complex coefficients arise in the steady state. There are a number of ways of formulating the set of linear equations actually solved, such as the nodal, branch, and cutset formulations. These differ in which variables are chosen as the independent variables to be solved for. Some formulations give rise to systems with a larger number of variables (and equations), but which are still "sparse" systems in which many of the coefficients are zero. Some are not capable of treating a general branch, say of a battery with zero resistance in series. A typical "textbook-problem" circuit is shown in Fig. 2.1. It is a DC circuit with batteries and resistors. In the first case, we use the Kirchhoff or branch analysis method. By Kirchhoff's current law, I[3] $=$ I[1] $+$ I[2]. By his voltage law, the voltage sources (batteries) along any loop must be balanced by the voltage drops due to the current flow in the resistors. By Ohm's law, the voltage drop is the product of the current and resistance, IR. Thus, we arrive at the system to be solved:

$$
\begin{pmatrix}
-1 & 1 & 1 \\
R[1] & 0 & R[3] \\
0 & R[2] & R[3]
\end{pmatrix}
\begin{pmatrix}
I[1] \\
I[2] \\
I[3]
\end{pmatrix}
=
\begin{pmatrix}
0 \\
V[1] \\
V[2]
\end{pmatrix}
$$

In an alternative method called loop or Maxwell analysis, we define the currents as shown in the second half of the figure. The currents are associated with loops, not branches, and any branch may carry the current of a number of loops. Kirchhoff's current law is automatically satisfied, and we need only write two equations (setting I[3] − 0):

$$
\begin{pmatrix}
(R[1] + R[3]) & -R[3] \\
-P[3] & (P[2] + P[3])
\end{pmatrix}
\begin{pmatrix}
I[1] \\
I[2]
\end{pmatrix}
=
\begin{pmatrix}
V[1] \\
V[2]
\end{pmatrix}
$$

Note the typical trade-off in formulations: the first matrix is sparse, but order 3 x 3, whereas the second is dense (no zeros) but only order 2 x 2. Structural mechanics is another good example of a source of linear systems. The forces and torques at any joint must vanish. This gives rise to a problem involving a system of constraint equations at each joint, relating the components of forces and the torques transmitted by the structural members. If there are N such equations and N unknowns, the problem reduces to solving a simultaneous linear system of equations. Such a structure is called statically determinate. Sometimes (often in "real world" problems) the structure is "statically indeterminate," and additional constraint equations must be created by assumptions about the elastic properties of the beams. The

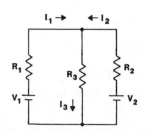

*Fig. 3.1: Simple Circuit.
Above, branch analysis;
below, loop analysis variables
shown.*

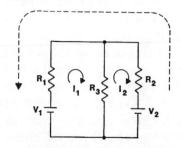

problem still devolves to the solution of a set of linear equations for the stresses in each beam. In "textbook" problems, various simplifications are introduced so that students do not have to get their hands dirty solving a linear system. For example, in the typical "truss" problem the beams are all joined with hinges or pins, so that the torques are all zero automatically at any joint. Typically, one end of the truss is supported by a roller so that there is no horizontal constraint at this end, making the structure statically determinate. In the real world, of course, beams are often cantilevered (the direction of the beam as well as the end point is constrained), and joints are not hinged. Consequently, simultaneous systems have to be solved more often than the simplified textbook problem might suggest.

Problems which Require the Solution of a Linear System as an Intermediate Step

Another manner in which linear systems arise is in approximate methods for continuous problems, such as the solution of integral and differential equations. There is a large class of numerical methods with names like the "Method of Weighted Residuals," "Method of Moments," "Galerkin Method," "Collocation Method," "Rayleigh-Ritz," etc. These methods all have a common core idea, namely, to expand the unknown function or functions as a linear super-position of known functions. The coefficients in this expansion are the unknowns which are to be solved for. These methods give rise to a linear system of simultaneous equations for these coefficients when the original problem to be solved is itself linear. Such linear problems frequently arise in problems of interest in elasticity and antenna theory, as two examples. Such methods are the numerical equivalent of the "Method of Undetermined Coefficients," a term which is generally applied to analytic methods.

These methods differ in how the expansion functions are chosen, and how the equations for the coefficients are generated from these functions and the original differential and/or integral equation(s). It is easiest to explain with a concrete example, so consider solving a problem for a function $F(z)$ of a single independent variable z in the range $0z$. We will assume that F is expanded as:

$$F(z) = \sum_{i=1}^{N} c[i] \; f[i](z)$$

In addition, it is useful to introduce another set of functions, $w[i](z)$, which are weighting functions. Suppose now the equation to be solved is of the form $E(F) = 0$. We form N equations by multiplying successively by the N $w[i]$. We then integrate over z in the allowed interval.

In the collocation method, the $w[i]$ are chosen to be Dirac delta functions of the form $\delta(z - z[i])$. Thus the integral results in evaluating the values of F at the collocation points $z[i]$. We are constraining the approximation to the function F to satisfy the equation at selected points. Obviously, the collocation method can be dangerous, i.e., give very poor results if those points are badly chosen. On the other hand, it is one of the most economical methods.

Often, the requirement that w[i] = f[i] is imposed. This gives rise to Galerkin methods. If there are boundary conditions, as at $z = 0$ and $z = 1$ in our example, it is almost always desirable to have the f[i] satisfy these. Otherwise, we would have to treat these boundary conditions as collocation points or by some other means. Often, the f[i] are chosen from some complete set, e.g., sin nz and cos nz for $n = 0,1,M$. This is actually more subtle than one might think. Depending upon what the operator F is, such a "complete set" might not span the range of the operator, and some solution terms might be missed. Consequently, the selection of the f[i] and w[i] require some knowledge of what the solution ought to look like. Intelligent choice of the f[i] can give excellent results with a very few expansion terms. In antenna theory, for example, it is well known that a sinusoidal current distribution is a good approximation for thin antennas, and this is often used in moment method calculations.

Table 3.1

Forms of the Method of Weighted Residuals or

Method of Moments

Name	*Weighting Function*
Collocation	Delta functions
Galerkin	Same as expansion function
Rayleigh-Ritz	Adjoint to expansion function

The Rayleigh-Ritz expansion can be considered as a special case of the Galerkin method when the system to be solved is self-adjoint. Even if the system is not self-adjoint, adjoint functions can often be determined and these may then be used for the weighting functions.

The various forms of the weighted residual or moment methods are summarized in Table 3.1. One can generate any number of equations for a given number of expansion functions. For example, the number of collocation points can be chosen as a number M which is greater than N. If M exceeds N, there are more equations than unknowns, so that not all equations can be satisfied simultaneously. What is then most appropriate is a least-squares solution, which minimizes the sum of the squares of the error residuals of the equations. (There is no obvious point in choosing M < N, which will give us an infinitude of possible solutions.) Least squares solutions are discussed below when the Singular Value Decomposition method is discussed. This method is computationally more expensive than a straightforward solution of a linear system of comparable size. Therefore, it is probably best to use M = N in most circumstances.

Table 3.2 list many of the ways (of interest in science and engineering) linear systems can arise.

Table 3.2

How Linear Systems Can Arise

Directly:

Equilibrium or Steady-State Problems

Statics Problems in Structural Mechanics

Electrical Circuits

Indirectly:

Discretization of Continuous Problems

Method of Weighted Residuals (MWR) and Related Methods

Method of Moments (another name for MWR)

Method of Undetermined Coefficients

Collocation

Galerkin's Method

Rayleigh-Ritz Method

Stiff Ordinary Differential Equations (Implicit Methods,Chapter12)

Partial Differential Equations

Boundary Value Problems

Data Fitting:
      e.g., B-Splines (Chapter 8)

Finally, systems of linear equations can arise from the discretization of continuous differential operators into finite-difference operators. The resulting systems almost invariably have a sparse, repetitive structure. The savings resulting from taking advantage of this structure can be very substantial.

The routines developed here will be used as tools by a number of later chapters. The stiff system solver and B-spline routines must solve linear systems.

How to Solve Linear Systems

The LU Factorization

What is the best way to solve the general linear system? There are two approaches: "direct" and iterative. The iterative methods have the advantage that they are not troubled by "fill-in," i.e., loss of sparseness. In general, when direct methods are used, matrix entries which had been zero become nonzero. This can easily lose any advantages of the initial sparseness of the matrix

At present, for computers with present-day ("von Neumann") architectures, the LU factorization with partial pivoting is the consensus choice. We will see below, when discussing the QR factorization, that this method may have advantages for use with parallel processing arrays of computers.

The LU factorization (often called a "decomposition") is very closely related to Gaussian elimination. In Gaussian elimination, we take a problem of the form

$$\mathbf{A}\mathbf{x} = \mathbf{b}$$

where **b** is a vector of right-hand sides, **x** is the unknown solution vector, and **A** is a matrix, and convert it into a problem of the form

$$\mathbf{U}\mathbf{x} = \mathbf{b}'$$

where the matrix **U** is upper triangular, i.e all of the sub-diagonal elements are zero:

$$
\begin{pmatrix}
u(1,1) & u(1,2) \\
0 & u(2,2) \\
0 & 0
\end{pmatrix}
$$

{Here we have used standard mathematical notation, similar to FORTRAN conventions, in calling the first element of the first row u(1,1), etc. In C, that element would be addressed as u[0][0], for example.} This transformation is achieved by using "elementary row operations." One multiplies a row of the matrix (and the corresponding element of **b**) by any desired constant, and subtracts it from underlying rows to zero out desired elements. One uses the first row to zero out the first column. Then the second row, whose first element is now zero, is used to eliminate the coefficients below it in the second column, etc. The resulting system, $\mathbf{U}\mathbf{x} = \mathbf{b}'$, is easy to solve. The equation for the last variable $x[n]$ is $u[n][n] \; x[n][n] = b'[n]$, whose solution is $x[n] = b'[n]/u[n][n]$. The next equation above this for x[n − 1] includes the now known x[n], and so may be simply solved. One continues to proceed upward.

There is one possible fly in the ointment—when we have gotten to the mth row, the diagonal element, called the "pivot," which we will use to eliminate the remainder of the mth column, could be small (in absolute value) or zero. If it were zero, there is nothing finite we could multiply the mth row by in order to eliminate other elements in the mth column by subtracting the multiplied row. A simple solution is to exchange the row with any of the underlying rows, exchanging the identity of the associated b as well. The clear choice is to pick the row with the largest magnitude element. This method is called "partial pivoting by rows." One could also exchange columns, switching the identity of the variables in x, to move the largest element to the pivot, and one could use "complete" pivoting in which both column and row are searched for the largest element, and this element is used as the pivot. The need for changing the sequence of the variables is an excessive overhead burden, and is almost never done; partial pivoting, as described here, generally suffices.

Consider our model problem. Pivoting is required (and hence tested by this example), the first and second rows being interchanged because A[1][0] = 4 is of greater magnitude than either of the other elements in the first column. The "packed" LU factors to be found in the A matrix are printed out as:

$$\begin{pmatrix} 4 & 4 & -3 \\ -.5 & 4 & -2.5 \\ .5 & 2 & 1 \end{pmatrix}$$

which means that:

$$U = \begin{pmatrix} 4 & 4 & -3 \\ 0 & 4 & -2.5 \\ 0 & 0 & 1 \end{pmatrix} \quad L = \begin{pmatrix} 1 & 0 & 0 \\ -.5 & 1 & 0 \\ .5 & .2 & 1 \end{pmatrix}$$

The LU decomposition does not touch b at all. Instead, it accomplishes the same effect by factoring the matrix A as the product LU, where U is upper triangular as described above, and L is lower triangular, with all of its diagonal elements 1. This factorization may be done "in place," i.e., without any additional storage space, except for an integer array to keep track of the pivoting exchanges used.

Given the system LUx = b, one solves first the system Ly = b, and then Ux = y. The latter is identical to the back substitution stage of Gaussian elimination. The former is like the latter, except that it proceeds from the top down.

A great advantage of the LU factorization is that, once the LU factors have been obtained, the system may be solved for different **b**'s without starting all over again. The cost of computing the LU factorization is approximately $n^3/3$ floating point operations (each is taken to be a multiplication followed by an addition; typically, multiplications take much more time than additions, although there are exceptions to this rule on some hardware.) The cost of the back substitution is of order $n^2/2$ floating point operations. The savings can be substantial over other methods, if there are multiple right-hand sides.

The Inverse Matrix; Gauss-Jordan Method

Curiously, one sees articles and books recommending the Gauss-Jordan method. Gauss-Jordan uses elementary row operations to eliminate both above- and below-diagonal elements, giving a diagonal matrix **D** for the system **Dx** =**b**",which may be easily solved. This method requires n^3 operations, so it is more costly, and more prone to numerical errors. It does generate the inverse of the matrix **A**. This is rarely useful, however. If there are a number of right-hand sides, it is still cheaper to use the back-substitution than to multiply **b** by the inverse of **A** to generate the solution. If an inverse is to be obtained, the LU decomposition may be used to do so. One way to do this is to set **b** = (1,0....) and solve for **x**. This x is the first column of the inverse. The next column can be found by setting **b** = (0,1,0...), etc. This method is more computationally expensive than necessary, as it does not take account of the the especially simple structure of **b** in these cases—all of the multiplications by zero and subsequent operations that may be omitted, and all of the multiplications by one which are unnecessary as well. An optimized method which takes account of these special features can compute the matrix inverse as economically as the Gauss-Jordan method and be less prone to numerical difficulties in the process. We said above that many times there are a number of competitive methods without one being clearly superior in all cases for a class of problems. That does not, however, preclude the possibility of methods that are clearly inferior in all cases and should never be used. Gauss-Jordan is clearly one such method. Cramer's rule, in which many determinants are computed, is another.

The C source listing shown below solve a simple test problem for n = 3. The matrix, which now contains the **L** and **U** matrices, is printed out. The solution vector is printed out following back-substitution. The solution overwrites the contents of the **b** vector, but the LU factors are unchanged, as the printout shows. Finally, the inverse of the matrix is calculated. This overwrites the LU factors. Note carefully that what used to be the **A** matrix now contains two matrices, **L** and **U**. This is not one new matrix, **LU**, but two matrices. The matrix equation **A** = **LU** holds (taking care to remember that pivoting may have taken place, resulting in the exchange of rows). Indeed, the factorization is often written as **A** = **PLU**, where **P** is the permutation matrix, whose entries are all 0's and 1's, with one nonzero entry in any row or column.

Determinants

The determinant of the matrix **A** is the product of the determinants of L and U. For any triangular matrix, the determinant is the product of the diagonal elements. The determinant of **L** is therefore one. One can easily calculate the determinant and the product of the diagonal elements in the overwritten **A** matrix. There is one trap for the unwary, however: we have permuted the rows, and this can alter the sign of the determinant. To correct for this is not difficult. We simply count the number of times that pivot[k] does not equal k, which tells us how many such interchanges have taken place. If the result is odd, the we multiply by -1 the product of the diagonal elements.

Two programs are included to calculate determinants. One produces the determinant by determining $a \times 10^n$ where n is an integer and $.1 < |a| < 10$. This form is useful if the determinant is very large or very small.

Condition Number

Often, numerical analysis books discuss a parameter called the "condition number." This may be used to estimate how accurate the solution will be.   If the system is ill-conditioned, i.e., if small pivots had to be used, then the condition number will tell us. It is a very pessimistic estimate. As it has no way of taking account of the structure of the **b** vector, it must assume the worst case for it. I had occasion to write a circuit solver. To treat current sources, a branch had to be modeled as a current source in parallel with a large resistor. Those large numbers for the resistance had effect on the answer so long as they were large enough, but the condition numbers were grossly affected by the choice of the non-existent resistor value. The variable info, if nonzero upon return from the LU factorization, indicates trouble. The determinant may also be calculated if desired, and if small indicates trouble. Generally, in most problems of interest to scientists and engineers, a zero or ill-conditioned system means an error in coding rather than a genuinely ill-conditioned problem. In systems arising from weighted residual methods, it could mean poorly chosen collocation points or expansion or weighting functions. If two collocation points are such that they are too close or otherwise fail to give independent information about the solution, the resulting system can be ill-conditioned, as the two equations (rows) will be quite similar.

Tools for Converting FORTRAN to C

The header file, FTOC.H, has a number of preprocessor definitions designed to ease the translation of FORTRAN codes to C. These are employed to ease the translation of DO loop structures involving arrays and to convert matrices from one language to the other.

The package to solve linear systems, including LU factorization, back-substitution, and matrix inversion, are based upon the FORTRAN routines in LINPACK. The LINPACK routines are in fact based upon the routines in Forsythe and Moler and in Forsythe, Malcolm, Moler (see references at the end of the chapter). The LINPACK routines use some auxiliary routines for row and column operations, from the Basic Linear Algebra (BLAS) package of R. Hanson. All of these routines have been simplified here. For example, the BLAS routines use "unrolled" loops which are not used here. Unrolling is useful only if the computer has a "pipelined" or "vector" architecture and the compiler is not smart enough to vectorize loops well. On some compilers, unrolling will inhibit optimization. The BLAS routines are contained in file LUS.C.

The LINPACK routines compute determinants in a manner similar to our second method, except that they use floating-point arithmetic exclusively. The C routines presented here should, all other things assumed equal, be faster. The major changes have been to account for the differences in C's storage of vectors (the first subscript being 0, not 1), and the use of preprocessor #define statements to simplify coding. The location of a[i][j], where i = 0,...(rown − 1), j = 0,...(coln − 1) is a[j+coln*i]. This is simulated by the function INDEX. The various in-line functions DOFOR, DOBY, etc. simplify the coding of loops. For example, the FORTRAN loop produced by a statement such as:

    DO 27 I=1,N

and designed to work with a vector (or row or column of an array) whose subscripts range from 1 to N is most easily mapped into C with a loop of the form:

    for (i=0; i<n ; i++)

    {

We use the preprocessor's #define statement to produce a DOFOR statement which generates this **for** loop with:

    DOFOR(i,n)

    {

Other statements handle situations where the increment is not 1 (typically, when the increment is coln, the number of columns, as we loop through the rows of a matrix with the C ordering convention), for example.

FORTRAN does not permit DO indices to decrease. Consequently, when one wants to go backwards through an array or vector, a "dummy" index must be used, which is incremented. C allows greater generality. To illustrate the options, subroutine backsub() is implemented carrying over the use of dummy variables, while subroutine backt() uses a loop index which decrements.

Implementation Details

The test case in this chapter checks only the rank three case, n = 3. Subsequent chapters use the routines of this package and test other cases. A larger n case is treated in the Chapter on B-splines. The stiff ODE system solver also uses the package of linear system solvers given in this chapter.

The test driver, LUD.C, solves the problem $Ax = b$, printing the solution vector (which overwrites the vector **b** of equation right-hand sides) and the LU factors (which overwrite the **A** matrix). This is done in two steps: by calling lufact() to determine the factors, and backsub() to solve the system involving the right-hand side **b**. Because backsub() does not alter the LU factors, additional solutions for different **b** vectors could be found without factoring the matrix **A** again. We then use these factors to solve the transposed problem $A^\wedge x = b$, with a call to backt(). We have to reconstruct **b**, which has been overwritten. If $A = LU$ then $A^\wedge = U^\wedge L^\wedge$, where the transpose $U^\wedge$ of U is now a lower-left hand matrix and $L^\wedge$ is now an upper-right hand matrix. Thus backt() does the same job as backsub(), except that it has to look in different locations of **A** to find the appropriate elements of the factor matrices. Next, invm() is called to determine the inverse of the matrix. This overwrites the **A** matrix. Finally, as a check on backt(), we construct the transpose of **A** "by hand" and solve it using lufact() and backsub().

File LUS.C contains support routines, including versions of the BLAS functions. Also included is a general routine for printing matrices in a readable fashion, no matter how many columns are present. This routine can be easily altered depending upon how many columns your line printer or display supports—it currently is conservative and assumes an 80 column display and typical C formatting.

The LINPACK collection has other routines to compute the condition number, which we have not attempted to reproduce as we do not believe that the condition number is of significant value for most problems. Although not part of the LINPACK routines, the LINPACK document and other books (see Forsythe and Moler, for example) discuss iterative improvement of the solution. This requires the use of higher-precision arithmetic, and requires that copies of the A matrix and the b vector be kept. Once a solution x is found, one computes in double precision the residual error b −Ax. The correction to x is then computed using the LU factors found previously with the residual error as the right-hand side. This method is clearly useful only if the LU factors are accurate. It turns out (Wilkinson, 1965, or see Stewart,1973) that if the A matrix is "somewhat" ill-conditioned, the LU factors might be reasonably accurate although the solution vector x obtained without iteration is poor. In this case, iteration will improve the solution vector. If the A matrix is not ill-conditioned, there is probably no point to iteration. It is pointed out in Wilkinson (ibid.) that a matrix can be ill-conditioned without small pivots and a small determinant resulting to give a warning. Such pathological cases are very rare and not ordinarily encountered. In the usual implementations of C, there is only one precision, double, at which calculations are done, so iterative improvement has little point in such an environment.

In Chapter 4, it will be found necessary to determine the solution of the transposed system $A^{\wedge}x = b$ in order to determine the eigenvalues of a nonsymmetric matrix. This is done using the same LU factors of A with routine backt().

Chapter 4 contains a number of routines for matrix algebra that may be of interest with regard to linear systems. LINPACK and other packages have routines which take advantage of special matrix properties such as symmetry, positive-definiteness, bandedness, etc. Positive-definite matrices never need pivoting, for example, and the workload for symmetric matrices (i.e., those for which $A(i,j) = A(j,i)$) can be halved compared to general matrices. The references given below and at the end of this book consider such special cases. Note that taking advantage of the special structure of a matrix, such as its bandedness, precludes the adoption of pivoting, because

---

Table 3.3

Programs of Chapter 3

Name	Purpose
FTOC.H	Facilitate conversion of FORTRAN Code to C
MAIN (LUD.C)	Test LU system routines
ISAMAX	Find maximal element of a vector
SAXPY	Elementary Row Operation involving vectors
SDOT	Dot Product of two vectors
SSWAP	Swap vectors
SSCAL	Scale a vector
SASUM	Sum the absolute values of a vector
PRINTM	Print out a matrix (by rows)
LUF.C	Perform LU factorization of a square matrix
BACKSUB.C	Use LU factors of A to solve $Ax = b$
BACKT.C	Use LU factors of A to solve $A^{\wedge}x = b$
INVM.C	Use LU factors of A to find inverse of A
DET.C	Return as double the determinant
DETI.C	Use if very large/small determinants expected

pivoting generally will destroy the special structure. Consequently, solvers that rely on the special structure pay a price in robustness for their efficiency.

The subprograms and functions are listed in table 3.3. backsub, backt, inv, det, deti all require the LU factorization to have been determined by LUF.

REFERENCES

J. J. Dongarra, C. B. Moler, J. R. Bunch, G. W. Stewart, *LINPACK User's Guide*, (Philadephia, PA: SIAM, 1979).

G. B. Forsythe, M. A. Malcolm, C. B. Moler, *Computer Methods for Mathematical Computations*, (Englewood Cliffs, NJ: Prentice-Hall, 1977).

G. B. Forsythe and C. B. Moler, *Computer Solution of Linear Algebraic Systems*, (Englewood Cliffs, NJ: Prentice-Hall, 1967).

G. W. Stewart, *Introduction to Matrix Computations*, (NY: Academic, Press, 1973).

J. H. Wilkinson, *The Algebraic Eigenvalue Problem*, (Oxford: Clarendon Press, 1965).

Program Listing And Test Problem Output
```
/*
```

header file to aid in conversion of FORTRAN code to C
(from "C Tools for Scientists and Engineers" by L. Baker)

PURPOSE:

performs in-line a number of useful chores including loops,
array subscripting, and finding minimum,maximum, and absolute value.

DEPENDENCIES:

USAGE:

invoke with preprocessor directive:
#include "ftoc.h"
    or
#include <ftoc.h>
 near the beginning of your program

```
*/
```

```
/* in-line functions for use with 2D arrays: */

/* row major order as in C  indices run 0..n-1 as in C*/
#define INDEX(i,j)  [j+(i)*coln]

/*various loop constructors */
#define DOFOR(i,to) for(i=0;i<to;i++)
#define DFOR(i,from,to) for(i=from-1;i<to;i++)
#define DOBY(i,from,to,by) for(i=from-1;i<to;i+=by)
#define DOBYY(i,from,to,by) for(i=from;i<t;i+=by)
#define DOBYYY(i,from,to) for(i=from;i<to;i++)
#define DOV(i,to,by) for(i=0;i<to;i+=by)
/* row major order as in C  indices run 1..n */
```

```
/*#define INDEX1(i,j)  [j-1+(i-1)*n]
*/
/* column major order, as in fortran: */
#define INDEXC(i,j) [i-1+(j-1)*rown]

/* usage: if a(20,30) is matrix, then
a(i,j) in C will be a INDEX(i,j) if n=30. */

/* to index vectors starting with 1 */
#define VECTOR(i) [i-1]

#define min(a,b) (((a)<(b))? (a): (b))
#define max(a,b) (((a)<(b))? (b): (a))
#define abs(x)  ( ((x)>0.)?(x):-(x))
```

```
/*
routines for linear systems processing via LU factorization
(from "C tools for Scientists and Engineers" by L. Baker)

PURPOSE:

perform LU factorization

CONTENTS:

lufact(a,coln,n,pivot,info)
    Factor an n by n matrix contained in type float array a
    which is dimensioned a[m][coln].  pivot is an integer array
    of size n which will contain pivoting information to be used
    by later routines.  info is pointer to an integer which returns
    0 if all is well, otherwise the row in which problems occurred.

DEPENDENCIES:

requires header file ftoc.h and lus.c routines

*/
#include "ftoc.h"

lufact (a,coln,n,pivot,info)
float *a;
int coln,n,*pivot,*info;
{
    int i,j,k,l,kp1,nm1,last;
    float t;
    *info=0;
    nm1=n-1;
    if (nm1>=1)
    {/*nontrivial pblm*/
        DOFOR(k,nm1)
        {
            kp1=k+1;
            /*partial pivoting ROW exchanges-search over column*/
```

```
/* in FORTRAN, the increment would be 1 not n in ismax call*/
pivot [k]=l=isamax((n-k),&(a INDEX(k,k)),coln)+k;
if (a INDEX(l,k)!=0.)
{/*nonsingular pivot found*/
   if(l!=k)
   {/*interchange needed*/
      t=a INDEX(l,k);
      a INDEX(l,k)=a INDEX(k,k);
      a INDEX(k,k)=t;
   }
   t=-1./a INDEX(k,k);/*scale row*/
   sscal(nm1-k,t,&(a INDEX(k+1,k)),coln);
   DOBYYY(j,kp1,n)
   {
      t=a INDEX(l,j);
      if(l!=k)
      {
         a INDEX(l,j)=a INDEX(k,j);
         a INDEX(k,j)=t;
      }
      saxpy(nm1-k,t,&(a INDEX(k+1,k)),
          coln,&(a INDEX(k+1,j)),coln);
   }
}
   else /*pivot singular*/
   { *info=k;}
}/*main loop over k*/
}
pivot [nm1]=nm1;
if (a INDEX(nm1,nm1) ==0.0)*info=nm1;
return;
}
```

```
#include "ftoc.h"
/*
```
routines for linear systems processing via LU factorization
(from "C Tools for Scientists and Engineers" by L. Baker)

PURPOSE:
support routines for LU factorization

CONTENTS:
isamax(n,sx,incx)
> Finds the location of the element of greatest absolute
> value in a vector sx of length n. Each incx-th element
> is examined (hence, if sx is a 2-D matrix, may be used
> to find largest elements in each row or column, depending
> upon whether incx is 1 or n.

saxpy(n,sa,sx,incx,sy,incy)
> Performs an elementary row operation sy= sy+sa sx where sx
> and sy are vectors and sa is a scalar. Used to subtract
> a scaled row sx from the sy row. incx,incy are as in isamax.
> Vectors of length n.

sdot(n,sx,incx,sy,incy)
> Takes the dot product of 2 vectors sx and sy, of length n.

sswap(n,sx,incx,sy,incy)
> Exchanges two vectors sx and sy. Used for row exchanges
> which occur during pivoting operation.

sscal(n,sa,sx,incx)
> Scale a vector sx= sa sx where a is a scalar and sx a vector.

sasum(n,sx,invx)
> Function type float which returns the sum of the absolute
> values of the elements of a vector.

(The above are all based upon BLAS routines.)

printm(a,coln,rown,col,row)
> Prints a 2-dimensional matrix a in readable form.

The actual data of the form a(row,col) is stored
within a matrix dimensioned a[rown][coln].

```c
*/
#include "ftoc.h"

int isamax(n,sx,incx)
int n,incx; float *sx;
{int maxi,ix,i;
    float temp,smax;
/*returns 1 less than corresponding FORTRAN version*/
    if (n<=0)return -1;
    if(n==1)return 0;
/* ix=0*/
    maxi=0;
    smax=abs(sx[0]);
    ix=incx;/*ix=ix+incx=incx*/
    DFOR(i,2,n)
    { temp=abs(sx[ix]);
        if (temp>smax)
        {smax=temp;
            maxi=i;
/* return ith element as max,NOT subscript a[ix] ix=i*incx*/
        }
        ix+=incx;
    }
    return maxi;
}


saxpy (n,sa,sx,incx,sy,incy)
int n,incx,incy;
float sa,*sx,*sy;
{/*sy=sa*sx+sy*/
    int i,iy,ix;
    if(n<=0)return;
    if(sa==0.)return;

    iy=ix=0;
```

```
    if(incx<0) ix=incx*(1-n);
    if(incy<0) iy=incy*(1-n);
    DOFOR(i,n)
    {
        sy[iy]=sy[iy]+sa*sx[ix];
        iy+=incy;
        ix+=incx;
    }
    return;
}

float sdot(n,sx,incx,sy,incy)
int n,incx,incy;
float *sx,*sy;
{float stemp;
    int i,ix,iy;
    if(n<=0)return(0.);
    ix=iy=0;
    stemp=0.0;
    if(incx<0) ix=incx*(1-n);
    if(incy<0) iy=incy*(1-n);
    DOFOR(i,n)
    {
        stemp+=sy[iy]*sx[ix];
        iy+=incy;
        ix+=incx;
    }
    return stemp;
}

sswap(n,sx,incx,sy,incy)
int n,incx,incy;
float *sx,*sy;
{
    int ix,iy,i;
    float t;
    if(n<=0)return;
    ix-iy-0;
```

```
    if(incx<0) ix=incx*(1-n);
    if(incy<0) iy=incy*(1-n);

    DOFOR(i,n)
    {
        t=sx [ix];
        sx [ix]= sy [iy];
        sy [iy]=t;
        ix+=incx;
        iy+=incy;
    }
    return;
}

sscal(n,sa,sx,incx)
int n,incx; float sa,*sx;
{/*scale vector*/
    int i,nincx;

    if (n<=0) return;
    nincx=incx*n;
    DOV(i,nincx,incx)
    sx[i]=sx[i]*sa;
    return;
}

float sasum(n,sx,incx)
float *sx;
int incx,n;
{/* ssum abs values*/
    int i,nincx;
    double stemp;
    stemp=0.0;
    nincx=n*incx;
    if (n<=0)return 0.0;
    DOV(i,n,nincx) stemp=stemp+abs(sx[i]);
    return (stemp);
}
```

```
printm(a,coln,rown,col,row) int rown,row,col,coln; float a[];
{
    int i,j,btm,top,count;
    printf("\n");
    btm=top=0;
    while(btm<col)
    {
        top=min(col,(btm+8));
        printf(" printing matrix columns %d to %d\n",btm,(top-1));
        DOFOR(j,row)
        {
            for(i=btm;i<top;i++)
            {
                printf(" %e",a INDEX(j,i));
            }
            printf("\n");
        }
        btm+=8;
    }
    return;
}
```

```
#include "ftoc.h"

/*
routines for linear systems processing via LU factorization
(from "C Tools for Scientists and Engineers" by L. Baker)

PURPOSE:

solve linear system given factorization of a matrix in a

CONTENTS:

backsub(a,coln,n,pivot,b)
    Solves system  ax = b. Assumes a contains LU factors, pivot
    pivoting information. The matrix stored as a[m][coln] with the
    system to be solved n x n. Answer vector returned in b.

backt(a,coln,n,pivot,b)
    As above, but will return the solution to a[T]x = b where a[T]
    is the transpose of matrix a.   This is useful in inverse
    iteration for eigenvalue determination if the matrix a is
    non-symmetric, and in determining matrix condition number.

DEPENDENCIES:

requires header file ftoc.h and routines in lus.c

*/


backsub(a,coln,n,pivot,b)
int coln,n,*pivot;
float *a,*b;
{
    float t;
    int k,l,nm1;
    nm1=n-1;
```

```
    {
        l=pivot[k];
        t=b[l];
        if(l!=k)
        {
            b [l]=b [k];
            b [k]= t;
        }
        saxpy( nm1-k,t, &(a INDEX(k+1,k)),coln,&(b[k+1]),1);
    }

    /* solve Ux=y*/
    DOFOR(l,n)
    {
        k=nm1-l;
        b [k]= b [k]/ a INDEX(k,k);
        t=-b [k];
        saxpy(k,t,&(a INDEX(0,k)),coln,b,1);
    }

    return;
}

backt(a,coln,n,pivot,b)
int coln,n,*pivot;
float *a,*b;
{/* like backsub, except solves A(T)x=b */
    float t,sdot();
    int k,l,nm1;
    nm1=n-1;

    /* solve u(T)y=b first*/
    DOFOR(k,n)
    {
        t=sdot(k,&(a INDEX(0,k)),coln,b,1);
printf(" k= %d t=%f\n",k,t);
        b[k]=(b[k]-t)/a INDEX(k,k);
    }
```

```
/* solve l(T)x=y*/
if(nm1<1)return;
for(k=nm1-1;k>=0;k--)
{
   b[k]+=sdot(nm1-k,&(a INDEX(k+1,k)),coln,&(b[k+1]),1);
   l=pivot[k];
   if(l!=k)
   {
      t=b[l];
      b[l]=b[k];
      b[k]=t;
   }
}

   return;
}
```

```
#include "ftoc.h"

/*
routines for linear systems processing via LU factorization
(from "C Tools for Scientists and Engineers" by L. Baker)

PURPOSE:

invert a matrix given the LU factorization of that matrix

CONTENTS:

invm(a,coln,n,pivot,work)
     a contains LU factors of a matrix. a[m][coln], n is size of
     the actual matrix to be inverted.  pivot has pivot information.
     work is a type float work array of size n.

DEPENDENCIES:

requires header ftoc.h and routines in LUS.C

*/

invm(a,coln,n,pivot,work)
int coln,n,*pivot;
float *a,*work;
{
    float t,ten;
    int i,j,k,l,kb,kp1,nm1;
    nm1=n-1;
/* no det calc.*/
/* inverse u*/
    DOFOR(k,n)
    {
        a INDEX(k,k)=t=1./ a INDEX(k,k);
        t= -t;
        sscal(k,t,&(a INDEX(0,k)),coln);
        kp1=k+1;
        if (nm1>=kp1)
```

```
      {
        DOBYYY(j,kp1,n)
        {
          t=a INDEX(k,j);
          a INDEX(k,j)=0.0;
          saxpy(k+1,t,&(a INDEX(0,k)),coln,&(a INDEX(0,j)), coln);
        }
      }

    }
/*inv(u)*inv(l)*/
   if (nm1>=1)
   {
      DOFOR(kb,nm1)
      {
        k=nm1-kb-1;
        kp1=k+1;
        DOBYYY(i,kp1,n)
        {
          work [i]=a INDEX(i,k);
          a INDEX(i,k)=0.0;
        }
        DOBYYY(j,kp1,n)
        {
          t=work [j];
          saxpy(n,t,&(a INDEX(0,j)),coln,&(a INDEX(0,k)),coln);
        }
        l=pivot [k];
        if(l!=k) sswap(n,&(a INDEX(0,k)),coln,&(a INDEX(0,l)),coln);
      }
   }
   return;
}
```

/* two routines for finding determinants
(from "C Tools for Scientists and Engineers" by L. Baker)

PURPOSE: return value of determinant of a matrix

CONTENTS:
det()
    Returns the determinant of a matrix factored in LU form.

deti()
    Returns the determinant in the form a*10**j where j
    is an integer. It is useful if the determinant might be
    very large or small, resulting in overflows or underflows.

DEPENDENCIES:
ftoc.h header file
assumes lufact() has performed the matrix factorization
*/

```c
#include <ftoc.h>

double dabs(x) double x;
{
    if(x>=0.)return x;
    return (-x);
}


double det(a,pivot,coln)
int pivot[],coln;
float *a;
{
    int i,sign;
    double d;
    sign=0;
    d=1.;
    for (i=0;i<coln;i++)
    {
```

```
        if(pivot[i]!=i)sign++;
        d*= a INDEX(i,i);
    }
    sign=sign-((sign>>1)<<1);
    if (sign) d=-d;
    return d;
}

double deti(a,pivot,coln,expon)
int pivot[],coln,*expon;
float *a;
{
    int i,sign;
    double d,dabs();
    sign=0;
    d=1.;
    *expon=0;
    for (i=0;i<coln;i++)
    {
        if(pivot[i]!=i)sign++;
        d*= a INDEX(i,i);
        if(dabs(d)>10.)
        {
            (*expon)++;
            d*=.1;
        }
        else if(dabs(d)<.1)
        {
            (*expon)--;
            d*=10.;
        }

    }
    sign=sign-((sign>>1)<<1);
    if (sign) d=-d;
    return d;
}
```

```
/*
test driver for linear system solver:
LU factorization and related routines
(from  "C Tools for Scientists and Engineers" by L. Baker)

PURPOSE:

tests LU factorization, solution of ordinary and transposed
systems, calculation of inverse matrix and determinant

*/

#include "ftoc.h"

main (argc,argv) int argc; char **argv;
{
    float a[3][3],b[3],c[3][3];
    int i,j,pivot[3],n,info,coln;float work[3];
    double det(),deti(),determ;
/* simultaneous equation test fix*/
    n=coln=3;
    b[0]=5.;
    b[1]=3.;
    b[2]=1.;
    a[0][0]=2.;a[0][1]=3.;a[0][2]=-1.;
    a[1][0]=4.;a[1][1]=4.;a[1][2]=-3.;
    a[2][0]=-2.; a[2][1]=3.; a[2][2]=-1.;
/* ans 1.,2.,3. */
    printf(" lufact coln=%d,n=%d\n",coln,n);
    lufact(a,coln,n,pivot,&info);
    printf(" lufact info=%d %d %d %d\n",info,pivot[0],pivot[1],pivot[2]);
    printm(a,3,3,3,3);
/* packed LU:  4 4 -3
        -.5 5 -2.5
```

```
.5 .2  1. */
   determ=det(a,pivot,coln);
   printf(" determinant=%f \n",determ);
   determ=deti(a,pivot,coln,&i);
   printf(" determinant= %f x 10^ %d\n",determ,i);
   backsub(a,coln,n,pivot,b);
   printf("\n solution to linear system:");
   printf(" ans= %f %f %f\n",b[0],b[1],b[2]);
/* transposed system */
   b[0]=5.;
   b[1]=3.;
   b[2]=1.;
   backt(a,coln,n,pivot,b);
   printf("\n solution to transposed system:");
   printf(" ans= %f %f %f\n",b[0],b[1],b[2]);
/*inverse*/
   printf("\n LU factors as stored in a:");
   printm(a,3,3,3,3);
/* .25 0. -.25
   .5 -.2 .1
1. -.6  -.2  is inverse*/
   invm(a,coln,n,pivot,work);
   printf("\n inverse of a:");
   printm(a,3,3,3,3);
/* check transposed system solution */
   b[0]=5.;
   b[1]=3.;
   b[2]=1.;
   a[0][0]=2.;a[1][0]=3.;a[2][0]=-1.;
   a[0][1]=4.;a[1][1]=4.;a[2][1]=-3.;
   a[0][2]=-2.; a[1][2]=3.; a[2][2]=-1.;
   lufact(a,coln,n,pivot,&info);
   backsub(a,coln,n,pivot,b);
   printf("\n check transposed system\n ans= %f %f %f\n",
                                b[0],b[1],b[2]);
   exit(0);
}
```

lufact coln=3,n=3
lufact info=0 1 2 2

printing matrix columns 0 to 2
4.000000e+000 4.000000e+000 -3.000000e+000
-5.000000e-001 5.000000e+000 -2.500000e+000
5.000000o-001 -2.000000e-001 1.000000e+000
determinant=20.000000
determinant= 2.000000 x 10^ 1

solution to linear system: ans= 1.000000 2.000000 3.000000
k= 0 t=0.000000
k= 1 t=5.000000
k= 2 t=-2.750000

solution to transposed system: ans= 3.750000 -1.200000 -1.150000

LU factors as stored in a:
printing matrix columns 0 to 2
4.000000e+000 4.000000e+000 -3.000000e+000
-5.000000e-001 5.000000e+000 -2.500000e+000
5.000000e-001 -2.000000e-001 1.000000e+000

inverse of a:
printing matrix columns 0 to 2
2.500000e-001 0.000000e+000 -2.500000e-001
5.000000e-001 -2.000000e-001 1.000000e-001
1.000000e+000 -6.000000e-001 -2.000000e-001

check transposed system
ans= 3.750000 -1.200000 -1.150000

CHAPTER 4

Eigenvalue and Discriminant Analysis

Chapter Objectives

In this chapter we will present tools to:

-determine the eigenvalues and eigenvectors of a matrix by the robust QR iteration

-determine a few of the largest or smallest eigenvalues and, associated with them by means of power iteration, inverse iteration, and the Rayleigh quotient methods

-provide a collection of tools for useful operations on matrices and vectors, e.g., for swapping rows and columns of matrices.

The method of deflating the matrix for each eigenvalue found, to simplify the problem of determining the next eigenvalue, will be presented. The problem of determining eigenvalues will be reviewed, and many of the methods in common use discussed. We will also discuss the application of eigenvalue analysis to statistical problems such as discriminant analysis. Useful techniques such as the Sherman-Morrison formula and Prony's method will also be discussed in this chapter.

Eigenvalue Analysis

In this chapter we will discuss a wide variety of methods for determining eigenvalues and eigenvectors. We will concentrate on iterative methods which are most appropriate when only a few of the eigenvalues (and their associated eigenvectors), those with either the largest or smallest magnitudes, are to be determined. We will discuss symmetric and non-symmetric matrices, determining complex eigenvalues, and the generalized eigenvalue problem.

Please note that many problems which may be handled by eigenvalue/eigenvector methods should instead be treated by the Singular Value Decomposition (SVD), which is discussed in the following chapter. This is particularly true in statistical problems involving the correlation matrix.

For such problems, the matrix is positive-definite (has only positive eigenvalues) and the singular values determined by the SVD are the squares of the eigenvalues of the matrix. The SVD determines these values more robustly than an eigenvalue analysis and is to be preferred. Many older books on numerical methods in statistics do not discuss the SVD, so please be aware that, while you may have been conditioned to think in terms of an eigenvalue analysis, this may not be the best currently available method.

How Eigenvalue Problems Arise

The term "eigenvalue" comes from the German term "eigenwert," which can be translated as "own" or "characteristic value." The sense is that of numbers which characterize invariant properties of the matrix (or the problem which gave rise to the matrix).

Mathematically, for a square matrix A of dimension n, the problem is to determine a number e and a vector x such that $Ax = ex$. There will in general be n solutions. Indeed, if we rewrite the equation as $(A - Ie)x = 0$, where I is the unit matrix, we can only have solutions (aside from the trivial solution $x = 0$) if the matrix $A - Ie$ has a zero determinant, and this condition is equivalent to an n-th degree polynomial equation in e. Such a polynomial equation, by the fundamental theorem of algebra, will have n roots for e.

In Boundary Value Problems (BVP's) involving ordinary differential equations, the term eigenvalue occurs, although in the company of eigenfunctions rather than eigenvalues. The meaning is completely analogous, with the multiplication of a vector x by a matrix A replaced by the multiplication of a function x by a linear differential operator A, the function x required to satisfy given boundary conditions. In general, nontrivial solutions for x can be found only for certain values of the parameter e, called eigenvalues, with those corresponding solutions the eigenfunctions. Arbitrary solutions of the BVP can be expanded in such eigenfunctions, which then allows us to abandon the differential equation and use matrix algebra to treat the problem! Solutions are then represented as vectors of coefficients in the expansion in terms of the eigenfunctions. This is how Schroedinger's wave equation and Heisenberg's matrix mechanics, both originally independent forms of quantum mechanics, can be shown to be consistent and equivalent.

The eigenvalues of the quantum mechanics problems are the resonant frequencies of the system, i.e., the frequencies at which the system "naturally" can find itself vibrating, without external forcing. For a bound system such as an isolated atom, these frequencies give the energy levels of the atom, i.e., those states in which the atom can remain stable (interaction with the radiation field, which is not explicitly included in the simplest forms of Schroedinger's equation, modifies the situation so that transitions between these states occur, and the atom will decay from one to another until reaching the "ground" state, from which it is energetically incapable of going anywhere else). Such frequencies or energy levels (in quantum mechanics the two are equivalent, since the energy is Planck's constant times the frequency) are clearly "characteristic" of the atom involved, which justifies the use of the "eigen" of eigenvalue in discussing them.

In a slightly different guise, the eigenvalue problem is called that of "diagonalizing" a matrix. This means finding a so-called similarity transform of the matrix A to the matrix D,

$$D = U^{-1}AU$$

where U is an orthogonal, or real unitary matrix (i.e., such that $U^{\wedge}U = U^{-1}U = 1$) and the matrix D is diagonal, i.e.

$$D = \begin{pmatrix} d(1,1) & 0 & \cdots \\ 0 & d(2,2) & \cdots \\ 0 & 0 & d(3,3) \end{pmatrix}$$

(Because U is orthogonal, the transformation is also a congruent transformation, i.e., $D = U^{\wedge}AU$.) This transformation may be shown to be possible for any symmetric matrix A. The diagonal elements of D are its eigenvalues, and are also the eigenvalues of A. The eigenvectors of D are just the unit axes, i.e., the eigenvector corresponding to $d(1,1)$ is the vector $(1,0,0,...)$, that to $d(2,2)$ is $(0,1,0,...)$, etc. The U matrix is one whose columns are the eigenvectors of A (normalized so that each has length one). The U matrix may be viewed as a rotation of the axes of the coordinate system to the principal axes of the matrix. Perhaps the most familiar orthogonal matrix is of the form

$$\begin{pmatrix} \cos\theta & \sin\theta \\ -\sin\theta & \cos\theta \end{pmatrix}$$

and corresponds to a rotation by an angle t about the z axis of the xy coordinate system. For example, if θ is 90 degrees the vector (x, y) when multiplied by this matrix, which is then

$$\begin{pmatrix} 0 & 1 \\ -1 & 0 \end{pmatrix}$$

is taken into $(y, -x)$. This should make the geometric interpretation of the diagonalization process as a rotation plausible. Such a rotation is an orthogonal transformation. A vector y is transformed in Uy, a matrix A into $U^A U$. To make this concrete, consider as our example the moment of inertia of a solid body. The (scalar) mass or inertia of a body relates its momentum p to its velocity, v, both vectors, by $p = mv$. It also determines its acceleration by applied forces through Newton's Second Law $F = ma$, where a is the acceleration vector and F the force vector. The inertia tensor M similarly relates the angular momentum vector L to the angular velocity w (both vectors) by $L = Mw$. Because m was a scalar, p and v had to be parallel, as did a and F, but as M is a tensor L need not be parallel to w. M is a matrix of order three for three dimensional objects; for simplicity we will consider two-dimensional objects. The angular momentum of a rotating body composed of N mass points m[i] is given by the vector:

$$L = \overset{N}{\underset{}{\Sigma}}\, m[i]\ r[i]\ x\ \ v[i]$$

where r is the position vector and v the velocity of the point, with x denoting the vector cross product. But $v = w\ x\ r$, where w is the angular rotation vector. Thus

$$L = \Sigma\ m[i]\ \{\ r[i]x(w\ x\ r[i])\}$$

which may be rewritten as

$$L = \Sigma\ m[i]\ \{w\,|\,r\,[i]|^2 -\ r[i](\ r[i]*w\ )\}$$

with * denoting the scalar or "dot" product. We rewrite this as

$$L = M\ w$$

where M is a "dyad" or second order tensor, i.e., a matrix. For the two-dimensional inertia tensor in the xy plane, for example,

$M(1,1)=\int \rho^2 y \quad dV$ (often written M_{xx}) and $M_{xy}=M_{yx}= -\int \rho \; xy \; dV$ where ρ is the mass density of the object. The kinetic energy of any specific rotation specified by w is the scalar

$$T = w*M*w/2$$

If we express the vector $w = (a,b)$ then we have T as the quadratic form:

$$T = a^2 M(1,1) + b2M(2,2) + ab\{M(1,2) + M(2,1)\}.$$

This polynomial in a and b is called a quadratic form (see, e.g., Mirsky). We know from the definition of the inertia tensor **M** that it is symmetric, and further as the kinetic energy can never be negative, the matrix **M** must be positive definite. Hence it can certainly be diagonalized, that is, a set of variables A and B which are related to a and b through a rotation found such that the cross product term AB disappears in the rotated quadratic form. Because the quadratic form is positive definite, the eigenvalues d are positive. We then have

$$T = \{A^2 \; d(1,1) + B^2 \; d(2,2) \}/2$$

where A and B are the components of w in the directions of the "principal axes", i.e., the eigenvectors of the matrix **M**, and the new matrix d is related to **M** through a similarity transform by the rotation matrix to the new coordinate system. We can view the vector $W = U^{\wedge}w = (A,B)$ as the w vector rotated in the direction of the principal axes. These axes are perpendicular because the eigenvectors may be shown to be orthogonal. Furthermore, the preceeding expression for T shows clearly that our quadratic form is that of an ellipse, since both coefficients are positive. The principal axes or eigenvectors are in the directions of the major and minor axes of that ellipse (called the inertia ellipsoid for the problem at hand). The eigenvalue then corresponds to the inverse square root of the corresponding axis.

Under the alias "principal component factor analysis," eigenvalues show up in statistics. They are useful in the problem of classifying objects. Discriminant analysis is closely related. If the object is a pattern, for which classification is recognition, the Karhunen-Loeve expansion is the term used for the "statistical pattern recognition" method of principal factor or eigenmode analysis. All of these topics will be discussed further in this and the following chapter.

The Karhunen-Loeve expansion may be used for data compression. Once the eigenvectors and their associated eigenvalues are determined, any data vector can be expanded as a linear sum of the eigenvectors. The coefficients in the expansion represent the projection of the vector onto the eigenvectors (the dot product of the data vector and each eigenvector). If we then discard the coefficients corresponding to the smallest eigenvalues (in absolute value), we obtain an economical representation of the data vector which still retains the principal features of interest. This method of compression is often used in image processing.

The Generalized Eigenvalue Problem

We will also consider the generalized eigenvalue problem, namely the determination of e and x for $Ax=eBx$. This problem can occur, for example, in calculating the normal modes of a system of oscillators (see, e.g., Goldstein). In this case, the matrix B corresponds to a kinetic energy term, A to a potential energy term, and the eigenvalue e to the square of the oscillation frequency. In finite-element problems, B is often written as M and called the mass matrix, while A is written as K and called the spring matrix, an analogy with the usual terminology for the simple harmonic oscillator. One could calculate the inverse of B (assuming that it is well-behaved) and multiply both sides of the equation to reduce the generalized problem to the ordinary one. This would cost us significantly, however, as it would require order n^3 operations to invert the matrix and a similar amount to multiply the two matrices, assuming that they are both full matrices (see Chapter 3). If, as often happens in such problems, B is sparse, this reduction to the ordinary problem is even more undesirable. The inverse of B will generally not be sparse, and the resulting eigenproblem will therefore not be sparse. It would be highly desirable to preserve the sparseness of the problem if possible. The iterative methods discussed here are easily adapted to treat such problems. Most often, the matrices involved are symmetric and often either or both are positive definite. Such problems often arise in the application of finite-element methods. They are well-suited to the iterative methods discussed here.

Table 4.1 summarizes the applications of eigenvalue analysis.

Table 4.1

Typical Applications of Eigenvalue Analysis

Mechanics:
    Normal modes of vibration
    Resonant frequencies
    Generalized eigenproblem from finite-element models

Quantum Mechanics:
    Stationary states and energy levels

Statistics:
    Principal component analysis
    Discriminant analysis
    Multivariate analysis of variance (MANOVA)

Pattern Recognition:
    Karhunen-Loeve expansion

Data Compression:
    Principal component or Karhunen-Loeve expansion

Basic Theory of Eigenvalues

In general, a symmetric matrix **A** will have an eigenvector that is of unique direction corresponding to each unique eigenvalue. Each eigenvector may of course be multiplied by a constant and remain an eigenvector, due to the linearity of the problem. The eigenvectors corresponding to distinct eigenvalues are orthogonal (perpendicular), that is, their dot product is zero. If the eigenvalue is degenerate, i.e., it is a repeated eigenvalue, then its eigenvectors may possibly be orthogonalized and span a space, but in some cases will not. Such pathological cases are called "rank deficient."

If the matrix is not symmetric, these results may be generalized. For symmetric matrices, if e is an eigenvalue, then

$$x^\wedge A = Ax = ex$$

for the corresponding eigenvector **x**. For non-symmetric matrices, we must consider different right eigenvectors **x** and left eigenvalues **y** corresponding to the same eigenvalue such that

$$y^\wedge A = ey^\wedge$$

and

$$Ax = ex$$

The right and left eigenvectors of different eigenvalues are now orthogonal, i.e. $y^\wedge x = 0$. The sets of right and left eigenvectors are termed "bi-orthogonal" because of this property. (The conjugacy property, namely $y^\wedge Ax = 0$ for a symmetric matrix A, is called "biconjugacy" for asymmetric matrices.) As a specific example, consider the asymmetric matrix:

$$A = \begin{pmatrix} 1 & 1 \\ 9 & 1 \end{pmatrix}$$

This matrix has eigenvalues 4 and -2. For $e = 4$, the right eigenvector is $(1 , 3)$ (actually a column vector but written transposed for convenience) and the left is $(1 , 1/3)$. For $e = -2$, the right eigenvector is $(1, -3)$ and the left is $(1 , -1/3)$. The bi-orthogonality may be checked easily. Note that the right eigenvectors are not orthogonal. An example of a rank deficient matrix would be any matrix of the form:

$$\begin{pmatrix} a & b \\ 0 & a \end{pmatrix}$$

which has the eigenvalue a repeated twice, and has as eigenvectors only (z 0), where z may be any number. This vector is both a right (column) and left (row) eigenvector.

Symmetric matrices have a number of convenient properties. Their eigenvalues must be real if the matrices are (Hermetian matrices, in which $a(i,j)$ is the complex conjugate of $a(j,i)$, have real eigenvalues and are the appropriate generalization of symmetric matrices to the domain of complex matrices). Their eigenvectors will form an orthogonal set which spans the space and hence any arbitrary vector may be expanded in the eigenvectors.

Iterative Methods

Let us consider first symmetric matrices, generalizing to non-symmetric matrices later.

Often, only a few of the largest or smallest eigenvalues, and possibly the associated eigenvectors, are required. In the determination of normal modes, for example, one generally wants the lowest or most fundamental frequencies, and these correspond to the smallest eigenvalues. In other problems, notably statistics (see below), the largest eigenvalues are the most significant. There are two types of iterative methods designed to treat these two problems.

Consider first an arbitrary vector, expanded in the set of eigenvectors of the matrix

$$\mathbf{y} = \Sigma \; c[i]x[i]$$

If we multiply $\mathbf{y}$ by the matrix $\mathbf{A}$, then we get a vector $\mathbf{y}'$

$$\mathbf{y}' = \mathbf{A}\mathbf{y} = \Sigma \; c[i]\mathbf{A}x[i] = \Sigma \; c[i] \; e[i]x[i]$$

and

$$\mathbf{y}'' = \mathbf{A}\mathbf{A}\mathbf{y} = \mathbf{A}\mathbf{y}' = \Sigma \; c[i] \; e[i]^2 x[i]$$

etc. We see that as we multiply by $\mathbf{A}$, each term is multiplied by a higher power of the corresponding eigenvalue. This gives us a method for determining the largest eigenvalues and their associated eigenvectors. Choose and arbitrary vector $\mathbf{y}$ as a starting point. Call the largest eigenvalue $e[0]$, with eigenvector $x[0]$. If we are not so unlucky that $\mathbf{y}^{\wedge}x[0] = 0$, which would cause $c[0] = 0$ in our expansion, then as we obtain $\mathbf{y}'$, $\mathbf{y}''$, etc., by successively multiplying the vector obtained by the matrix $\mathbf{A}$, the dominant term will be that corresponding to the largest eigenvalue, and soon the ratio of successive products, i.e., the Rayleigh quotient

$$\mathbf{y}^{\wedge}\mathbf{A}\mathbf{y} \; / \mathbf{y}^{\wedge}\mathbf{y}$$

will be the largest eigenvalue. Note that we never multiply matrices (that would be expensive!), only a vector by a matrix. This method is called the "power method" for finding the largest eigenvalue (its background is fully discussed in the books by Stewart, Wilkinson, Franklin, and Parlett). It is similar to Krylov iteration, as well as other methods (bi-iteration, treppen-iteration) in which, instead of starting with a single vector $\mathbf{y}$, a number of vectors are used simultaneously to better avoid problems.

One obvious problem is that if the two largest eigenvalues have equal magnitudes, the method will not converge. This problem can be overcome by a shift—the matrix $\mathbf{A}' = \mathbf{A} - \mathbf{I}s$ will have the eigenvalues $e[i] - s$, where the e[i] are the eigenvalues of A. In "canned" packages of matrix routines intended for batch use, this difficulty makes the power method unsuitable, but in circumstances where the program is running interactively, the power method can be faster than more robust methods, and when trouble occurs, the user can try again with a different shift.

If the smallest eigenvalues are desired, the method to be used is "inverse iteration." It is equivalent to iteration with the inverse of the matrix A, whose eigenvalues are the reciprocals of those of A. Consequently, the largest magnitude eigenvalue of the inverse of A is the reciprocal of the smallest eigenvalue of A. In practice, we do not invert A because it is expensive to do so. Rather, we solve the system $Ay' = y$, then the system $Ay'' = y'$, etc. This can be done more economically, particularly if A is sparse. The LU factorization of A can be done once, and costs (see Chapter 3) $n^3/3$ floating point operations if the matrix A is full. Subsequently, each iteration requires only n^2 operations. If the matrices are sparse, iterative methods are even cheaper and often much more so than other methods.

There is a trick in inverse iteration which can greatly improve convergence. If we use our ability to shift the eigenvalues as discussed above, and if we choose this shift to be the Rayleigh quotient, which is our latest and best guess as to what the eigenvalue is, then convergence can be very rapid (cubic). The sharp reader may note a potential problem in that if s is close to an eigenvalue, the matrix $A - Is$ is ill-conditioned (see Chapter 3). This turns out not to be a problem (see Wilkinson or Parlett). While the solution for y'' might be inaccurate in such a case, the error lies in the direction of the eigenvector desired, so that all is well. Rayleigh quotient iteration may be used with the power method for finding the largest eigenvalue, but it is not as dramatically effective. The obvious cost is that each time a shift is done, we have a new matrix to iterate upon and, therefore, the LU factorization of that new matrix must take place. If the matrix is full, the costs of Rayleigh quotient iteration are probably uneconomically large.

With either method, once convergence to the desired tolerance is achieved, y is the (approximate) desired eigenvector and the Rayleigh quotient gives the desired eigenvalue.

If all eigenvalues are to be found, inverse iteration is to be preferred over the power method (also called "forward iteration") in general because its convergence properties are typically better.

Deflation

Once you have found the largest (or smallest) eigenvalue and the associated eigenvector, you may wish to continue and find the next largest (or smallest) eigenvalue. There are a number of possible ways to achieve this. You could start your iteration with a vector orthogonal to the found eigenvector. This is very dangerous, as roundoff errors will cause you to loose orthogonality and the dominant eigenvalue will "take over." You can form the matrix

$$\mathbf{A'} = \mathbf{A} - e[0] \; \mathbf{x}^\wedge[0]\mathbf{x}[0]$$

where the last term is treated as a dyad, i.e., $a(i,j) = a(i,j) - e[0] \, x[0][i] \, x[0][j]$. This is somewhat better, but loss of orthogonality will still catch up with you. We will discuss below the use of Prony's method to simultaneously determine a number of the largest eigenvalues. The method we will apply is to "deflate" the matrix to a matrix of order $n - 1$, this new matrix lacking the found eigenvalue. This deflation works for any eigenvalue and so may be used with either iteration method discussed above.

Most books (e.g., Franklin or Wilkinson) discuss how to form from the matrix $\mathbf{A}$ the new matrix $\mathbf{T}^{-1}\mathbf{A}\mathbf{T}$ of the form

$$\begin{pmatrix} e[0] \; .... \; \\ 0 \\ 0 \quad R \\ 0 \end{pmatrix}$$

where the square matrix $\mathbf{R}$ of order one less than $\mathbf{A}$ has the same eigenvalues as $\mathbf{A}$ but omits the eigenvalue $e[0]$. It is more convenient computationally to form a matrix

$$\begin{pmatrix} R \quad 0 \\ \quad\quad 0 \\ .... \; e[0] \end{pmatrix}$$

since such a new matrix $\mathbf{R}$ would be addressable in storage at the same location as the matrix $\mathbf{A}$ was. This may be done by a simple modification of the methods in Franklin. Let the eigenvector $\mathbf{x}[0]$ be normalized so that its nth component is one (i.e., divide all the elements of the cigenvalue by the last). Let the matrix $\mathbf{T}$ have one's along the main diagonal and have the eigenvector as it final column

$$T = \begin{pmatrix} 1 & & & x[0][0] \\ & 1 & & x[0][1] \\ & & 1 & x[0][2] \end{pmatrix}$$

Then we may show that the inverse of **T** (see the next section of this chapter) is given by:

$$T^{-1} = \begin{pmatrix} 1 & & & -x[0][0] \\ & 1 & & -x[0][1] \\ & & \cdots & \\ & & 1 & -x[0][n] \end{pmatrix}$$

Working out the details, we find that the elements of **R** are simply related to those of **A** via $r(i,j) = a(i,j) - \Sigma x(i,n)\, a(n,j)$. The lowest row of T^{-1} **AT** is the lowest row of **A** except for the last column.

Once we find the next eigenvalue and eigenvector of **R**, we can use the above representation for determination of the eigenvector of **A**. We have found, say, eigenvalue e[1] and eigenvector y[1] of **R**, that is we have the matrix equation:

$$\begin{pmatrix} R & 0 \\ a & e[0] \end{pmatrix}\begin{pmatrix} y[1] \\ q \end{pmatrix} = e[0] \begin{pmatrix} y[1] \\ q \end{pmatrix}$$

We can solve for q: $q = a*y[1]/(e[1] - e[0])$. We now multiply by **T** the vector (y[1] q) to get the corresponding eigenvector of **A**. This may be generalized to the third eigenvalue, etc., and is implemented in the codes at the end of this chapter.

A "bonus" of this approach is that the size of the matrix in use decreases with each eigenvalue determined.

What if the last component of the eigenvector is small or zero? This can be solved by pivoting on the largest element of the eigenvector, and exchanging the rows and columns of **A** and the eigenvector, so that the element of largest magnitude in the eigenvector is the last. This ensures good numerical behavior of the deflation process. The programs listed in this chapter perform these exchanges.

The Sherman-Morrison Form of the Inverse

A very useful formula for modifying the inverse of a matrix whose inverse is already known is given on page 32 of Wilf's book. It is known as th Sherman-Morrison form of the inverse, and is:

$$(A + u^\wedge v)^{-1} \ = A^{-1} - \ A^{-1} \ u^\wedge v \ A^{-1}/(1 + v^\wedge A^{-1}u)$$

In this formula, the term $u^\wedge v$ on the right-hand side must be interpreted as a dyad, not a scalar. Our inversion of matrix **T** is a special case of this formula, with **A** the identity matrix **I**, **u** the row vector $u = (0,0,....,1)$, and **v** the column vector equal to the eigenvector (normalized so that its last component is one) except for the last component of **v** which is zero (the 1 in the (n,n) location of the transformed matrix is supplied by the **I** matrix).

This formula has many other practical applications. I once was asked to develop an enhanced approximate solution to a problem concerning a spectral line in a laser. The simplest approximation produced a system of equations of the form

$$n[j] \, d[j] \ = \ w[j] \ \ j = 1,...N$$

where $n[j]$ represented the populations at discretized points in frequency. This system was simply solved for the variables $n[j] = w[j]/d[j]$ as they were uncoupled. Now, as the next improved approximation, coupling between the $n[j]$ was permitted, and a new term of the form

$$q[j] \int n[\text{frequency}] \ C(\text{frequency})d(\text{frequency})$$

was added to the left-hand side. This integral was turned into a sum over j (see Chapter 9 on quadrature). Thus the system equation to be solved was of the form

$$n[j] \ + \ q[j]/d[j] \Sigma \, c[k]n[k] \ = \ w[j]/d[j].$$

Solving a full-blown linear system was unnecessary, thanks to the Sherman-Morrison formula.

Householder discusses both a generalization of the Sherman-Morrison formula, attributed to Woodbury, and the application of the formula as the "Method of Modification" for inverting matrices (Chapter 5, Section 5.1, pp 123ff).

Non-Symmetric Matrices

The power and inverse methods do not require the matrix to be symmetric. However, asymmetric matrices can be more problematical—for example, their eigenvalues might be complex numbers for real matrices. One can also iterate to find left eigenvectors, or, if the eigenvalue is already known, the eigenvector can be easily found (see Franklin).

Complex Eigenvalues

If a real asymmetric matrix has complex eigenvalues, these will occur in conjugate pairs. Such a pair will have equal modulus and the iteration will not converge to either. However, such non-convergence can be detected and used to determine the complex eigenvalues. The procedure is fairly simple and discussed in Franklin. Form three successive iterates of the approximate eigenvector in the power method, e.g., y, y', y''. These will be linearly dependent, to machine accuracy, if the eigenvalue corresponding to them (i.e., the largest in absolute value if the power method is in use) is complex. After testing this, you will have coefficients a and b such that $y'' + ay' + by = 0$. The corresponding quadratic equation $x^2 + ax + b = 0$ will yield the desired eigenvalues.

The Prony Method and Multiple Eigenvalues

One interesting variant of the power method to determine multiple eigenvalues is given by A. E. Siegman and H. Y. Miller in *Applied Optics,* 9,p.2729, 1970. Instead of considering only the leading term in the iterative multiplication for y, y', y'', etc., we find that the k-th iterate will have the form:

$$y^{[k]} = \Sigma c[i]\, e[i]^k\, x[i]$$

For a symmetric matrix, in which the eigenvectors are orthogonal, we can generate a set of (scalar) equations for the c[i] and the e[i] by taking the product of each successive y with the last. (If the matrix is asymmetric, we could use bi-orthogonality in a similar manner.) We then get a sequence of equations of the form

$$\Sigma\, c[i] \qquad = S[0]$$

$$\Sigma\, c[i]e[i] \qquad = S[1]$$

$$\Sigma\, c[i]e[i]^2 \qquad = S[2]$$

etc. By a technique known as "Prony's method," we could in principle at least, solve these equations for the e[i]. To determine the N largest eigenvalues, we would need 2N equations, and the assumption that the subsequent eigenvalues not included were of smaller magnitude and negligible (it would be desirable to iterate a few times on any initial y to attempt to "lose" these smaller eigenvalues in the sum). In forming these 2N equations the one for S[0] is not used. The trick is to determine the coefficients of the polynomial whose roots are the e[i]. If this polynomial is taken as

$$x^N + q[1] \, x^{N-1} + \ldots + q[N] = 0$$

then the system of equations for the vector q has the form

$$\begin{pmatrix} S[N] & S[N-1] \\ S[N+1] & S[N] \\ \ldots \end{pmatrix} \begin{pmatrix} q[1] \\ q[2] \\ \ldots \end{pmatrix} = \begin{pmatrix} -S[N+1] \\ -S[N+2] \\ \ldots \end{pmatrix}$$

which may be solved by the usual methods. In practice, the method often is used as a least-squares procedure, with more equations than unknowns. The methods of the next chapter are useful in this case. The Prony method is ill-conditioned, however, so some care should be exercised (see R. Hamming).

The Generalized Eigenvalue Problem Revisited

The power and inverse iteration methods easily generalize to the handle iterations where the right-hand side contains a matrix. Essentially all that need be added is to add the appropriate matrix multiplication. Bathe and Wilson discuss the use of iterative methods in this application rather extensively. For the problem $Ax = eBx$, we can use inverse iteration to find the smallest eigenvalues by solving the system $Ax' = Bx$, while the largest eigenvalues may be found by the power method (also called "forward iteration" by Bathe and Wilson), i.e. by solving the system $Bx' = Ax$. In each case we are solving for the newest iterate x' given x. Rayleigh quotient iteration and shifts may be used as in the ordinary eigenvalue problem.

Discriminant Analysis and the Generalized Eigenproblem

The multiple-discriminant analysis problem of statistics reduces to the generalized eigenproblem, with one of the matrices positive definite (it is a correlation matrix) and the other symmetric. There actually are a set of "discriminant analysis" methods, and they occur under a variety of names. The generalized-t statistic, Mahalanobis' D^2 statistic, Fisher's discriminant, and Hotelling's T^2 are all related (see Koch and Link, Section 10.5 of Volume II). Hotelling's statistic is in fact simply related to that of Mahalanobis.

One standard problem called discriminant analysis (there are others—see Chapter 5) is that discussed in Section 18.7 of Wilks. Suppose we have two sample populations. We wish to determine a line onto which these populations are projected (i.e., each population point is projected by a line through it and perpendicular to that line) such that the variation between the two samples is as large as possible (relative to their internal variances). The utility of this is fairly clear—we will wind up with a one-dimensional criterion, namely position along the line (after projection) which will enable us, at least in principle, to determine what is the best sample into which to assign a future individual based upon its measurements. The problem of finding that line's direction should suggest itself an eigenproblem. Fisher studied this problem in 1938. The solution is that of the generalized eigenvalue problem of the form $\mathbf{Ax} = e\mathbf{Wx}$, where $\mathbf{W}$ is a correlation matrix the "within groups cross products matrix," and $\mathbf{A} = \mathbf{T} - \mathbf{W}$, where $\mathbf{T}$ is the "total cross products matrix." We have

$$w(i,j) = \Sigma \Sigma \{x(i,k,n) - X(i,k)\}\{x(j,k,n) - X(j,k)\}$$

and $t(i,j) = \Sigma \Sigma \{X(i,n) - X(i)\} \{X(j,n) - X(j)\}$ where the $x(i,k,n)$ are individual observations and the $X(...)$ are means over suitable groups of observations. The matrix $\mathbf{A}$ can be then thought of as the "among group cross products matrix." The Rayleigh quotient for our problem is now of the form

$$x^\wedge Ax /(x^\wedge Wx)$$

and it is clear that the largest eigenvalue, i.e., the largest Rayleigh quotient, will maximize the among group variance given the within group variance. The eigenvector $\mathbf{x}$ gives the direction of the discriminant function, i.e., the coefficients. If one test, based on the largest eigenvalue, is insufficient in "discriminating power," the next largest eigenvector may be used as a subsequent discriminator. The "discriminating power" of such a test is related to the distribution of eigenvalues, and may be put in the form of Wilk's lambda criterion. Wilk's lambda is actually $|\mathbf{W}|/|\mathbf{T}|$. As $\mathbf{W}$ and $\mathbf{T}$ are both positive definite matrices, the eigenvalues are all positive, and the determinants are therefore positive (they are the products of the eigenvalues). Wilk's lambda is therefore a number between 0 and 1, with larger values indicating that the the "discriminating power" is small, i.e., that we really cannot distinguish two groups in the data (see Wilks or Cooley and Loh-nes). These books provide excellent background material and examples, but the numerical methods for eigenvalue determination, linear system solution, etc., in Cooley and Lohnes, are out-of-date and should not be used. Note how this problem is almost tailor-made for an iterative method, both in the need for a generalized eigenvalue solution and generally the need for only a few of the largest eigenvalues and corresponding eigenvectors.

Wilks contains information on the generalization to multiple samples. Note that the principal goal is to determine the effectiveness of the dis-criminant function. The proper classification of an individual (which group?) is another problem which we will encounter in the next chapter.

The Singular Value Decomposition (SVD) discussed in the next chapter may be applied to discriminant analysis.

QR Method

More robust methods that reliably find eigenvalues and eigenvectors, but with much larger codes and possibly with greater expenditures, are available. The EISPACK package is perhaps the best, and is certainly the state-of-the-art. The standard method involves factoring the matrix **A** as **QR**, where **R** is an upper triangular matrix (just like the **U** matrix in the **LU** decomposition), and **Q** is an orthogonal matrix (such as **T**). Such a fac-torization can be done robustly, without pivoting (exchanges of rows or columns). It is usually done in two stages. First, the matrix is transformed to a similar matrix which is tridiagonal in the case of symmetric matrices, or so-called upper-Hessenberg form (tri-diagonal with additional arbitrary elements above the diagonal) for general matrices. Such a transformation can be performed by Householder transformations (see references at the end of the next chapter). This reduction is done to economize later operations. Then an iterative procedure must be used, since the eigenvalue problem is equivalent to solving an nth degree polynomial equation, and those must be solved iteratively for n greater than or equal to five. In the QR method **A** is factored into the form **QR** by Householder transformations, then a new matrix **RQ** is (implicitly) formed. As **Q** is orthogonal, $Q^\wedge Q = 1$, and $R = Q^\wedge A$, this new matrix **RQ** is $Q^\wedge AQ$. This matrix is again factored into the form **QR**, etc. The iteration can be shown to converge, giving the eigenvalues as the diagonal of the product matrix (there are complications if there are multiple or complex eigenvalues, but these can be handled rather well by present day codes). In practice, a shift is introduced, as in Rayleigh quotient iteration, to speed convergence.

A number of tricks are used to speed the process. By performing a double shift as a single step, it is possible to avoid much complex arithmetic associated with a complex conjugate pair of eigenvalues, and often to find a pair of real eigenvalues. Further, when two adjacent, sufficiently small subdiagonal elements are found, or a zero subdiagonal element is found, the matrix can be decomposed to further reduce the work required.

Balancing

E. E. Osborne observed that the error in eigenvalue calculations was typically limited to the machine precision multiplied by the norm of the matrix (the square root of the sum of the squares of all of the elements). He suggested pre-conditioning matrices before eigenvalue calculations in order to reduce this norm and the associated error limit. The matrix A to be factored is replaced by $S^{-1}AS$ where S is a diagonal matrix whose elements are chosen to reduce the condition number of the matrix. The eigenvalues are of course unchanged. Programs to do this are given in EISPACK and Wilkinson and Reinsch's *Linear Algebra*, and are given here as part of the QR package. Their use is made optional, but as the cost is slight they are typically worth the effort. The eigenvectors of the balanced matrix must be transformed by the routine balbak() to give the eigenvectors of the original matrix.

Test Problems

QR Method

The routine for producing Hessenberg matrices is tested separately from the QR iteration code. The test cases are from Wilkinson and Reinsch. They normalize eigenvectors such that the largest element (real or complex) is one. We post-process our answers for ready comparison. The first test case only exercises the "two roots found" case, both real and complex, so we include the 3 x 3 matrix to test the single root entry. This case is somewhat pathological due to the repeated eigenvalue of 2. Note that the associated eigenvectors are not uniquely determined because of this degeneracy.

Power Methods

Two programs are included, for the "power method " or forward iteration (largest eigenvalues) and for Rayleigh quotient iteration (inverse iteration using the Rayleigh quotient to supply the shift for improved convergence).

The test problem is from page 38 of Bathe and Wilson, namely the matrix:

$$\mathbf{a} = \begin{pmatrix} 5 & -4 & -7 \\ -4 & 2 & -4 \\ -7 & -4 & 5 \end{pmatrix}$$

which has eigenvalues 12, 6, and − 6. Although not obviously pathological, this matrix provided me with a number of unexpected headaches. First, I used as my initial guess the vector (1,1,1). As this was in fact the exact eigenvector for the eigenvalue 6, the power method did not find 12 as the first (largest) eigenvalue as expected. Changing initial guesses (Franklin suggests using a "bizarre" guess), I next encountered trouble as the two eigenvalues 6 and − 6 have the same magnitude. This was fixed by the use of a shift.

In practice, the user may find it necessary to supply shifts if convergence has failed, or to alter the initial vector used in the iteration. I have not written this into the code, nor have I provided for complex eigenvalues which might occur for asymmetric matrices. That is my way of encouraging users to get their hands dirty with these codes. If you do not feel capable of changing pieces of this code, you should be using a more cumbersome but robust eigenvalue.

A shift is included between eigenvalue determinations in the inverse iteration method in an attempt to ensure that the successive smallest eigenvalues are found. Otherwise, if, say, 6 is found, and we have shifted the matrix to this new origin, the "smallest" eigenvalue of the new matrix is 12 (it is 6 away from the origin, while − 6 is now 12 away from the origin).

The C Tools

Two programs are included for determining eigenvalues either by inverse iteration with a Rayleigh-quotient shift, or by forward iteration.

The programs include a Gram-Schmidt orthogonalization procedure at the end to ensure the orthogonality of the eigenvectors. See, for example, the books by Strang or by Franklin for a description of the Gram-Schmidt process. It involves subtracting from a vector its projection on another vector to achieve a resultant vector whose projection on the other vector is zero. Starting with a given vector, one orthogonalizes the next vector with it, then the next with the first two, and so on as each eigenvector is orthogonalized with its predecessors. It can produce different answers depending upon the sequence of the vectors. Ideally, the Gram-Schmidt procedure should have no effect on the eigenvectors, as they should be orthogonal without it. This of course assumes that the matrix is symmetric and the eigenvectors should be orthogonal—it should be omitted for asymmetric matrices. The procedure might be more effective if each eigenvector were orthogonalized immediately after it was found. Due to the deflation procedure, this would be extremely cumbersome.

In the program to find the smallest eigenvalues,Rayleigh-quotient iteration is used although the matrix is full (but small). In practice, inverse iteration might be more efficient for a large, full matrix than Rayleigh quotient iteration. In that case, the call of the routine lufact() to replace the matrix **A** with its LU factors should be removed from within the iteration and placed before it. Of course, the shift of the eigenvalues by subtracting the Rayleigh quotient from the diagonal of **A** should be deleted from the program. Each iteration for the full matrix will then require time of order n^2 rather than order n^3, which is obviously significant.

The program listing includes some general purpose routines for vector and matrix algebra not included in the previous chapters. This includes the routine vdif() to find the difference of two vectors, routines swaprow() and swapcol() to swap the rows and columns of a matrix (used in the pivoting when we move the element of largest magnitude in the eigenvector to adjust the matrix accordingly), dot() to form the dot product (a streamlined cousin of the BLAS routine used in Chapter 3, dot as used here assumes that adjacent elements from each matrix are used), pv() to print a vector, mvc() to multiply a vector by a matrix, normv() to normalize a vector by determining its length (norm) and then multiplying each element by that norm, mvtc() to multiply a vector by the transpose of a matrix (this would be of use in some problems in which the matrix is not symmetric), resid() to determine the residual vector **r** = **Ax** − **y**, vs() to multiply a vector by a scalar, vset() to set a vector to a constant value, vcopy() to copy a vector to another, vv() to perform an elementary row operation of the form **a** = **b** + s* **c** where s is a scalar and **a,b,c** are vectors (another simplified cousin of a BLAS routine used in Chapter 3), and mcopy() to copy a matrix to another similarly dimensioned matrix.

Table 4.2

Programs of Chapter 4

QR Method

eigenvv Finds eigenvalues and eigenvectors
hqr2   Does QR iteration on Hessenberg matrix
elmhes   Converts matrix to upper Hessenberg form
eltran   Transforms eigevectors to those of original matrix
balance Balances matrix
balbak   Inverse of balance transform
pnormwr Print normalized eigenvectors

Power and Inverse Iteration

esmall() Rayleigh quotient iteration to determine smallest
         eigenvalues (generally preferable to the use of elarge()—see text).
elarge() Determines largest eigenvalues and associated eigenvectors
         (optionally)
vdiff   Difference vector of two vectors
swaprow Swaps a matrices' rows
swapcol Swaps its columns
mvc   Multiply vector by matrix-like mv but generalized to allow the matrix
         to be dimensioned for coln columns while only operating on n of these
mvtc   Similar to mvc but multiplies by the transpose of the matrix.

References

K.-J. Bathe and E. L. Wilson, *Numerical Methods in Finite Element Analysis,* (Englewood Cliffs, NJ: Prentice-Hall, 1976).

W. R. Cooley and P. R. Lohnes, *Multivariate Procedures for the Behavioral Sciences*, (NY: John Wiley, 1962).

J. N. Franklin, *Matrix Theory*, (Englewood Cliffs, NJ: Prentice-Hall, 1968).

R. W. Hamming, *Numerical Methods for Scientists and Engineers*, (NY: McGraw-Hill, 1973).

A. S. Householder, *The Theory of Matrices in Numerical Analysis*, [NY: Dover, 1975 (reprint)].

G. S. Koch and R. F. Link, *Statistical Analysis of Geological Data*, (NY: Dover, 1970).

L. Mirsky, *Introduction to Linear Algebra*, (NY: Dover, 1982).

B. N. Parlett, *The Symmetric Eigenvalue Problem* (Englewood Cliffs, NJ: Prentice-Hall, 1980).

G. W. Stewart, *An Introduction to Matrix Computations*, (NY: Academic Press, 1973).

G. Strang, *Linear Algebra and its Applications*, (NY: Academic Press, 1980).

H. Wilf, *Mathematics for the Physical Sciences*, (NY: Dover, 1972).

S. S. Wilks, *Mathematical Statistics* (NY: John Wiley, 1962).

J. H. Wilkinson, *The Algebraic Eigenvalue Problem*, (Oxford: Clarendon Press, 1965).

J. H. Willinson and C. Reinsch, *Linear Algebra,* (Berlin: Springer, 1971).

Program Listings and Test Problem Output

(listings begin next page).

```
/*
matrix eigenvalues/eigenvectors via QR decomposition
(from  "C Tools for Scientists and Engineers" by L. Baker)

CONTENTS:

eigenvv()
   computes eigenvalues and eigenvectors of a matrix
hqr2()
   applies QR method to Hessenberg matrix
elmhes()
   converts general matrix to Hessenberg form
eltran()
   creates transform. matrix from elmhes output
balance()
   balances a matrix
balbak()
   inverse transform of balance(used on eigenvectors)
pnormwr()
   normalize and print eigenvectors. largest element=1.
printmd()
   prints type double 2D matrix

DEPENDENCIES:
NONE
*/


/* defines below are from ftoc.h except for IU,DFFOR,DFFR,DFFRR */
#define INDEX(i,j) [j+(i)*coln]
#define IU(i,j) [j+(i)*colu]
#define DOFOR(i,j) for(i=0;i<j;i++)
#define DFFOR(i,from,to) for(i=from;i<to;i++)
#define DFFR(i,from,to) for(i=from;i<=to;i++)
#define DFFRR(i,from,to) for(i=from;i>=to;i--)
#define min(a,b) (((a)<(b))? (a): (b))
#define max(a,b) (((a)<(b))? (b): (a))
/*#define abs(x)  ( ((x)>0.)?(x):-(x)) using fabs */
```

```
#define itmax 30


printmd(a,coln,rown,col,row) int rown,row,col,coln; double a[];
{
   int i,j,btm,top,count;
   printf("\n");
   btm=top=0;
   while(btm<col)
   {
     top=min(col,(btm+8));
     printf(" printing matrix columns %d to %d\n",btm,(top-1));
     DOFOR(j,row)
     {
       for(i=btm;i<top;i++)
       {
         printf(" %e",a INDEX(j,i));
       }
       printf("\n");
     }
     btm+=8;
   }
   return;
}


double macheps;

eigenvv(coln,n,a,iwork,scale,z,wr,wi,bal,cnt)
int coln,n,iwork[],bal,cnt[];
double *a,*scale,*z,wr[],wi[];
{
int i,low,high,m,ierr;
if (bal)
   {
   balance(coln,n,a,&low,&high,scale);
   printmd(a,coln,n,n,n);
/*   DOFOR(i,n)printf(" scale=%e\n",scale[i]);
   printf (" balance low=%d high=%d\n",low,high);*/
```

```
        }
    else
        {
        low=0;
        high=n-1;
        }
    elmhes(coln,n,low,high,a,iwork);
    printmd(a,coln,n,n,n);
    printf(" low=%d high=%d\n",low,high);
    /*DOFOR(i,n)printf(" intar=%d\n",iwork[i]);*/
    eltran(coln,n,low,high,a,iwork,z);
    printmd(z,coln,n,n,n);
      hqr2(coln,n,low,high,a,wr,wi,z,&ierr,cnt);
      if(ierr) printf(" ierr=%d\n",ierr);
      m=n;/*unless fewer returned?*/
    /*hqr2 uses z to transform eigenvectors which are returned in z */
    if(ierr)return;
    if(bal)
        {
        balbak(coln,n,low,high,scale,m,z);
        }
}


hqr2(coln,n,low,igh,h,wr,wi,vecs,ierr,cnt)
int coln,n,low,igh,*ierr,cnt[];
double *vecs,*h,wr[],wi[];
{
/* coln, n have "FORTRAN" values
low,igh  have    "FORTRAN-1" values */

    int i,j,k,l,m,ii,jj,kk,mm,na,nm,nn,its, mpr,enm2,en;
    int it1=10,it2=20,itlim=30,notlast;
    double p,q,r,s,t,w,x,y,z,ra,sa,vi,vr,zz,norm;
    double xr,yr,xi,yi,zr,zi,sqrt();
    *ierr=0;
/* balance must have been called first! */
/* calculation of norm here as in EISPACK FORTRAN code*/
    norm=0.;
```

```
   k=0;

   DOFOR(i,n)
   {
      if(i<low || i>igh)
      {
         wr[i]= h INDEX(i,i);
         wi[i]=0.0;
      }
      for(j=k;j<n;j++) norm+=fabs(h INDEX(i,j));
      k=i;
      cnt[i]=0;
   }
   en=igh;
   t=0.;
nextw:
   if(en>=low)
   {
      its=0;
      na=en-1;
      enm2=na-1;
nextit:
      DFFRR(l,en,low)/*algol code had one less iteration than ftn*/
      {/* as in EISPACK*/
      s=fabs(h INDEX(l-1,l-1) )+ fabs(h INDEX(l,l) );
      if(s==0.)s=norm;
         if( fabs(h INDEX(l,l-1) ) <= s*macheps )goto break1;
      }
      l=low;
      break1:
      x= h INDEX(en,en);
      if(l==en)
      {/*found a root*/
/*printf(" single root its=%d\n",its);*/
         wr[en]= x+t;
         wi[en]=0.;
         h INDEX(en,en)=x+t;
         en=na;
```

```
          cnt[en]=its;
          goto nextw;
      }
      y= h INDEX(na,na);
      w= h INDEX(en,na) * h INDEX(na,en);
      if(l!=na)
      {
        if(its==itlim)
        {
           cnt[en]=31;
          *ierr=en;
          return;
        }
        if(its==it1 || its==it2)
        {
          t+=x;
          DFFR(i,low,en) h INDEX(i,i) -=x;
          s= fabs( h INDEX(en,na) ) +fabs( h INDEX(na,en-2));
          x=.75*s;
          y=x;
          w=-0.4375*s*s;
        }
        its++;
/*printf(" its=%d\n",its);*/
        for(m=en-2;m>=l;m--)
        {
          mm=m+1;
          z= h INDEX(m,m);
          r=x-z;
          s=y-z;
          p=(r*s-w)/(h INDEX(mm,m)) + h INDEX(m,mm);
          q= h INDEX(mm,mm)-z-r-s;
          r= h INDEX(m+2,mm);
          s= fabs(p)+fabs(q)+fabs(r);
          p/=s;
          q/=s;
          r/=s;
          if(m==l)break;
```

```
    if( fabs( h INDEX(m,m-1)) * (fabs(q)+fabs(r)) <=
    macheps*fabs(p)*
    (fabs(h INDEX(m-1,m-1))+fabs(z)+fabs(h INDEX(mm,mm)))
    )break;
}

for(i=m+2;i<=en;i++) h INDEX(i,i-2)=0.;
for(i=m+3;i<=en;i++) h INDEX(i,i-3)=0.;
for(k=m;k<=na;k++)
{
  notlast= (k!=na);
  if(k!=m)
  {
    p= h INDEX(k,k-1);
    q= h INDEX(k+1,k-1);
    r= notlast ? h INDEX(k+2,k-1) : 0.;
    x=fabs(r)+fabs(q)+fabs(p);
    if (x==0.)break;/*exit for loop*/
    p/=x;q/=x;r/=x;
  }
  s= sqrt(p*p+q*q+r*r);
  if (p<0.) s=-s;
  if (k!=m)
    h INDEX(k,k-1)=-s*x;
  else
    if(l!=m)
    h INDEX(k,k-1)=-h INDEX(k,k-1);
  p+=s;
  x=p/s;y=q/s;z=r/s;q/=p;r/=p;
  /*row modification*/
  for(j=k;j<n;j++)
  {
    p= h INDEX(k,j)+q*h INDEX(k+1,j);
    if (notlast)
    {
      p+=r*h INDEX(k+2,j);
      h INDEX(k+2,j) -=p*z;
    }
```

```
            h INDEX(k+1,j) -=p*y;
            h INDEX(k,j) -=p*x;
          }
          j= (k+3)<en ? k+3 : en ;
          /*column mods*/
          DFFR(i,0,j)
          {
            p=x*h INDEX(i,k)+y*h INDEX(i,k+1);
            if (notlast)
            {
              p+=z*h INDEX(i,k+2);
              h INDEX(i,k+2) -=p*r;
            }
            h INDEX(i,k+1) -=p*q;
            h INDEX(i,k)-=p;
          }
          /*accumulate*/
          for(i=low;i<=igh;i++)
          {
            p=x* vecs INDEX(i,k)+y*vecs INDEX(i,k+1);
            if(notlast)
            {
              p+=z*vecs INDEX(i,k+2);
              vecs INDEX(i,k+2)-=p*r;
            }
            vecs INDEX(i,k+1) -=p*q;
            vecs INDEX(i,k) -=p;
          }
        }/*end of for k loop*/
        goto nextit;
      }/* l!=na block*/
/* else, l=na, two roots found*/
/*printf(" double its=%d\n",its);*/
    p=.5*(y-x);
    q=p*p+w;
    z=sqrt(fabs(q));
    x+= t;
    h INDEX(en,en)=x;
```

```
  h INDEX(na,na)=y+t;
cnt[en]=-its;cnt[na]=its;
 if (q>=0.) /*q>0 in algol */
 {/*real pair*/
   z= p<0. ? p-z : p+z ;
   wr[na]=x+z;
   wr[en]=wr[na]; /*EISPACK version */
   if (z !=0.)
         {
         s=x-w/z;
         wr[en]=s;
         }
   wi[en]=0.;
   wi[na]=0.;
   x=h INDEX(en,na);
   /* r=sqrt(x*x+z*z);
   p=x/r;
   q=z/r;
   algol version */
   s= fabs(x)+fabs(z);
   p=x/s;
   q=z/s;
r= sqrt(p*p+q*q);
   p/=r;
   q/=r;
   for(j=na;j<n;j++)
   {
     z=h INDEX(na,j);
     h INDEX(na,j) = q*z+p*h INDEX(en,j);
     h INDEX(en,j) = q*h INDEX(en,j)-p*z;
   }
   DFFR(i,0,en)
   {
     z=h INDEX(i,na);
     h INDEX(i,na)=q*z+p*h INDEX(i,en);
     h INDEX(i,en)=q*h INDEX(i,en)-p*z;
   }
   for(i=low;i<=igh;i++)
```

```
        {
          z=vecs INDEX(i,na);
          vecs INDEX(i,na)=q*z+p*vecs INDEX(i,en);
          vecs INDEX(i,en)=q*vecs INDEX(i,en)-p*z;
        }
      } /* end if real pair */
      else /*complex pair*/
      {
        wr[en]=x+p;
        wr[na]=x+p;
        wi[na]=z;
        wi[en]=-z;
      }
      en--;en--;
      goto nextw;
  }

/* all eigenvalues found*/

  for(en=n-1;en>=0;en--)
  {
    p=wr[en];
    q=wi[en];
    na=en-1;
    if(q==0.)
    {
      /*real vector*/
      m=en;
      h INDEX(en,en)=1.;
      for(i=na;i>=0;i--)
      {
        w=h INDEX(i,i)-p;
        r=h INDEX(i,en);
        DFFR(j,m,na)
        {
          r+=h INDEX(i,j)*h INDEX(j,en);
        }
        if(wi[i]<0.0)
```

```
        {
          z=w;
          s=r;
        }
        else
        {
          m=i;
          if (wi[i]==0.)
          {
            h INDEX(i,en)= -r/( (w!=0.)? w : macheps*norm);
          }
          else
          {
            x=h INDEX(i,i+1);
            y=h INDEX(i+1,i);
            q=(wr[i]-p);
            yr=wi[i];
            q=q*q+ yr*yr;
            t=(x*s-z*r)/q;
            h INDEX(i,en)=t;
            h INDEX(i+1,en)= (fabs(x)>fabs(z))?
              (-r-w*t)/x :(-s-y*t)/z ;
          }/*wi!=0*/
        } /*wi>=0*/
      }/*for i loop*/
    }/*real vector,q=0*/
    else
    {   if(q<0.)
      {
        m=na;
        /* in algol, was -q, with xi=0 .
        EISPACK commment says this alternate choice
        was to make last eigenvector component imag.
        so that eigenvector matrix triangular*/
        if(fabs(h INDEX(en,na))>fabs(h INDEX(na,en)))
        {
          h INDEX(na,en)=-(h INDEX(en,en) -p)/h INDEX(en,na);
          h INDEX(na,na)= q/h INDEX(en,na);
```

```
    }
    else
    {
      xr=0.;
      xi=- h INDEX(na,en);
      yr= h INDEX(na,na)-p;
      yi=q;
      if(fabs(yr)>fabs(yi))
      {
        t=yi/yr;
        yr+=t*yi;
        zr=(xr+t*xi)/yr;
        zi=(xi-t*xr)/yr;
      }
      else
      {
        t=yr/yi;
        yi+=t*yr;
        zr=(t*xr+xi)/yi;
        zi=(t*xi-xr)/yi;
      }
      h INDEX(na,na)=zr;
      h INDEX(na,en)=zi;
    }
    h  INDEX(en,na)=0.;
    h INDEX(en,en) =1.;
    for(i=na-1;i>=0;i--)
    {
      w= h INDEX(i,i)-p;
      /* caveat- in algol, the assignments to ra,sa
      below were switched. This code is as
      in EISPACK */
      sa= h INDEX(i,en);
      ra=0.;
      for (j=m;j<=na;j++)
      {
        ra+= h INDEX(i,j)*h INDEX(j,na);
        sa+= h INDEX(i,j)*h INDEX(j,en);
```

```
            }
            if(wi[i]<0.)
            {
              z=w;
              r=ra;
              s=sa;
            }
            else
            {
              m=i;
              if(wi[i]==0.)
              {
                /*cdiv complex division*/
                /* more expensive but more robust
                than version in COMPLEX.H*/
                xr=-ra;
                xi=-sa;
                yr=w;
                yi=q;
                if(fabs(yr)>fabs(yi) )
                {
                  t=yi/yr;
                  yr+=t*yi;
                  zr=(xr+t*xi)/yr;
                  zi=(xi-t*xr)/yr;
                }
                else
                {
                  t=yr/yi;
                  yi+=t*yr;
                  zr=(t*xr+xi)/yi;
                  zi=(t*xi-xr)/yi;
                }
                h INDEX(i,na)=zr;
                h INDEX(i,en)=zi;
              }
              else
              {
```

```
x=h INDEX(i,i+1);
y=h INDEX(i+1,i);
vi=wi[i];
t=(wr[i]-p);
vr=t*t+vi*vi-q*q;
vi=2.0*q*t;
if(vr==0. && vi==0.)
{
  vr=macheps*norm*
    (fabs(w)+fabs(q)+fabs(x)+fabs(y)+fabs(z) );
}/*zero vr and vi*/
  /*cdiv*/
  xr= x*r-z*ra+q*sa;
  xi=s*x-z*sa-q*ra;
  yr=vr;
  yi=vi;
  if(fabs(yr)>fabs(yi) )
  {
    t=yi/yr;
    yr+=t*yi;
    zr=(xr+t*xi)/yr;
    zi=(xi-t*xr)/yr;
  }
  else
  {
    t=yr/yi;
    yi+=t*yr;
    zr=(t*xr+xi)/yi;
    zi=(t*xi-xr)/yi;
  }
  h INDEX(i,na)=zr;
  h INDEX(i,en)=zi;
if(fabs(x)>(fabs(z)+fabs(q)))
{
  h INDEX(i+1,na)=
    (-ra-w*h INDEX(i,na)+q*
    h INDEX(i,en))/x;
  h INDEX(i+1,en)=
```

```
                        (-sa-w*h INDEX(i,en)-q*
                        h INDEX(i,na) )/x;
                }
                else
                {
                  /*cdiv*/
                  xr=-r-y* h INDEX(l,na);
                  xi=-s-y*h INDEX(i,en) ;
                  yr=z;
                  yi=q;
                  if(fabs(yr)>fabs(yi))
                  {
                    t=yi/yr;
                    yr+=t*yi;
                    zr=(xr+t*xi)/yr;
                    zi=(xi-t*xr)/yr;
                  }
                  else
                  {
                    t=yr/yi;
                    yi+=t*yr;
                    zr=(t*xr+xi)/yi;
                    zi=(t*xi-xr)/yi;
                  }
                  h INDEX(i+1,na)=zr;
                  h INDEX(i+1,en)=zi;
                }
            }/* wi!=0*/
          }
        }/*for i*/

      }/*q<0. complex vector*/
    }/*end else*/
  }/*end for*/
/* vector of roots*/
  DOFOR(i,n)
  {
    if(i<low || i>igh)
```

```
        {
          for(j=i;j<n;j++)
          {
            vecs INDEX(i,j)= h INDEX(i,j);
          }
        }

    }
    for(j=n-1;j>=low;j--)
    {
      m= min( j , igh) ;
      DFFR(i,low,igh)
        {
        z=0.;DFFR(k,low,m) z += vecs INDEX(i,k) * h INDEX(k,j);
        vecs INDEX(i,j)=z;
        }
    }/*end for j loop*/
    return;
}


elmhes(colm,n,low,igh,a,intar)
int colm,n,low,igh, intar[];
double *a;
{
    int i,j,m,la,kp1,mm1,mp1;
    double x,y;
    int coln;
    coln=n;
    la= igh-1;
    kp1=low+1;
    if(la<kp1)return;
    DFFR(m,kp1,la)
    {
      mm1=m-1;
      x=0.;
      i=m;
      DFFR(j,m,igh)
```

```
    {
      if( fabs( a INDEX(j,mm1) ) > fabs(x ) )
      {
        x= a INDEX(j,mm1);
        i=j;
      }
    }
    intar[m]=i;
  if(i!=m)
  {
    DFFOR(j,mm1,n)
    {
      y= a INDEX(i,j);
      a INDEX(i,j) = a INDEX(m,j);
      a INDEX(m,j) = y;
    }
    DFFR( j,0,igh)
    {
      y= a INDEX(j,i);
      a INDEX(j,i) = a INDEX(j,m);
      a INDEX(j,m) = y;
    }
  }
  if(x!=0.)
  {
    mp1=m+1;
    DFFR(i,mp1,igh)
    {
      y= a INDEX(i,mm1);
      if (y!=0.)
      {
        y/=x;
        a INDEX(i,mm1) =y;
        DFFOR(j,m,n) a INDEX(i,j) -= y* a INDEX(m,j);
        DFFR(j,0,igh) a INDEX(j,m) += y* a INDEX(j,i);
      }
    }
  }
}
```

```
}
}

eltran(coln,n,low,igh,a,intar,z)
int coln,low,igh,n,intar[];
double *a,*z;
{/*form matrix of accumulated transforms z*/
  int colu,i,j,k,l,kl,mn,mp,mp1;
/* set z(n x n) to identity matrix; */
  colu=n;
  DOFOR(i,n)
  {
    DOFOR(j,n) z IU(i,j) =0.;
    z IU(i,i) = 1.;
  }
  kl=igh-low-1;
  if(kl<1)return;
  DFFRR(i,(igh-1),(low+1))
  {
    j= intar[i];
    DFFR(k,i+1,igh) z IU(k,i) =a INDEX(k,i-1);
    if(i!=j)
    {
      DFFR(k,i,igh)
      {
        z IU(i,k) = z IU(j,k);
        z IU(j,k)  =0.;
      }
      z IU(j,i)=1.;
    }
  }

}

/* not used as hqr2 does it
elmbak(colu,n,m,low,igh,a,intar,z)
int colu,n,low,igh,m,intar[];
double *z,*a;
```

```
{
    int coln,i,j,la,l,mm,mp,kp1,mp1;
    double x;
    if(m<0)return;
    la=igh-1;
    kp1=low+1;
    coln=n;
    if(la<kp1)return;
    DFFRR(mp,l-1,kp1)
    {
        mp1=mp+1;
        for (i=mp1;i<=igh;i++)
        {
            x= a IU(i,mp-1);
            if(x!=0.0)
            {
                DOFOR(j,m)
                z INDEX(i,j)+=x*z INDEX(mp,j);
            }
        }
        i=intar[mp];
        if(i!=mp)
        {
            DOFOR(j,m)
            {
                x= z INDEX(i,j);
                z INDEX(i,j) = z INDEX(mp,j);
                z INDEX(mp,j) = x;
            }
        }
    }
}
*/
    balbak(coln,n,low,igh,scale,m,z)
    int coln,n,low,igh; double scale[],*z;
    {/* m is number of eigenvectors to transform*/
        int i,j,k,l;
        double s;
```

```
   if(m==0)return;
   if(igh!=low)
   {
      DFFR(i,low,igh)
      {
         s=scale[i];
         DOFOR(j,m) z INDEX(i,j) *=s;
      }
   }
   DOFOR(l,n)
   {
      i=l;
      if(i<low || i>igh)
      { /* l=0 i=low-1 l=low-1 i=0*/
         if(i<low)i=low-l-1;
         k=scale[i];
         if(k!=i)
            {
            DOFOR(j,m)
               {
                  s= z INDEX(i,j);
                  z INDEX(i,j)=z INDEX(k,j);
                  z INDEX(k,j)=s;
               }
            }
         }
      }
   }
   return;
}



int k,l,j,m,nn;

exch(m,d,a)
int m;
double d[],*a;
{
```

```
        double f;
        int i,coln;
        coln=nn;
        d[m]=j;
/* note an integer is being stored in scale, d type double array*/
        if (j!=m)
        {
          DFFR(i,0,k)
          {
            f= a INDEX(i,j);
            a INDEX(i,j)= a INDEX(i,m);
            a INDEX(i,m)=f;
          }
DFFOR(i,l,nn)
          {
            f= a INDEX(j,i);
            a INDEX(j,i)= a INDEX(m,i);
            a INDEX(m,i)=f;
          }
        }
      }


    balance(coln,n,a,low,igh,scale)
    double scale[],*a;
    int coln,n,*low,*igh;
    {/* assumed matrix a has coln columns, working on n x n portion */
      double radix=2.,b2,bi,b2i,r,c,b,s,f,g;
      int i,kt,noconv,lim;
      l=0;
      k=n-1;
      nn=n;
      lim= max(20,n*2);
      b=radix;
      b2=radix*radix;
      bi=1./b;
      b2i=1./b2;
      kt=0;
l1:
```

```
DFFRR(j,k,0)
{
  r=0.;
  DFFR(i,0,k)
  {
    if(i!=j)
    {
      r+=fabs( a INDEX(j,i) );
    }
  }
  if(r==0.)
  {
    exch(k,scale,a);
    k--;
    kt++;
    if(kt<lim)goto l1;
    else
       {
       exit(0);
       }
  }
}
kt=0;
```

l2:
```
DFFR(j,l,k)
{
  c=0.;
  DFFR(i,l,k)
  {
    if(i!=j) c+=fabs(a INDEX(i,j) );
  }
  if (c==0.)
  {
    exch(l);
    l++;
    kt++;
    if(kt<lim)goto l2;
    else
```

```
            {
            exit(0);
            }
        }
    }
    *low=l;
    *igh=k;
    DFFR(i,l,k) scale[i]=1.;
    kt=0;
iteration:
    noconv=0;
    DFFR(i,l,k)
    {
       r=0.;
       c=0.;
       DFFR(j,l,k)
       {
         if (i!=j)
         {
            c+=fabs( a INDEX(j,i) );
          r+=fabs( a INDEX(i,j) );
      }
    }
        g=r/b;
        f=1.;
      s=c+r;
      if(c==0. || r==0.) continue;
      /* above if added in FORTRAN avoids infinite loops*/
        l3: if(c<g)
    {
          f*=b;c*=b2;goto l3;
        }
        g=r*b;
        l4: if(c>=g)
    {
       f*=bi;c*=b2i;goto l4;
        }
        if( (c+r)/f < .95*s)
```

```
              {
                 g=1./f;
                 scale[i]*=f;
                 noconv=1;
                 DFFOR(j,l,n) a INDEX(i,j) *= g;
                 DFFR(j,0,k)  a INDEX(j,i) *= f;
              }
           }/* do i */
           kt++;
           if(noconv && kt>lim)
                 {
                 printf(" balance iteration limit\n");
                 exit(0);
                 }
       if (noconv)goto iteration;
    }


pnormwr(coln,n,z,wr,wi)
double *z,wr[],wi[];
int coln,n;
{/* normalize as in Wilkinson & Reinsch with largest element=1*/
int i,j,k;
double  t,xr,xi,yi,yr,zr,zi,emax,ei;
printf(" un normalized matrix:\n");
printmd(z,coln,n,n,n);

DOFOR(i,n)
   {
   if(wi[i]==0.)
     {
     emax=0.;
     DOFOR(j,n)
        {
        if ( fabs(z INDEX(j,i))>fabs(emax) )
                   emax=z INDEX(j,i);
        }
     if(emax!=0.)
        {
```

```
      emax=1./emax;
      DOFOR(j,n)
          {
          z INDEX(j,i) *=emax;
          }
      }
  }
else /*complex eigenvector*/
  {
  emax=0.;
  k=0;
  DOFOR(j,n)
      {
      xr= z INDEX(j,i)    ; yr=z INDEX(j,i+1);
      xr= sqrt(xr*xr+yr*yr);
      if(xr>emax)
          {
          emax=xr;
          k=j;
          }
      }
  emax=z INDEX(k,i);
  ei=z INDEX(k,i+1);

  DOFOR(j,n)
      {
      yr=emax;
      yi=ei;
      xr=z INDEX(j,i);
      xi=z INDEX(j,i+1);
              if(fabs(yr)>fabs(yi) )
              {
                 t=yi/yr;
                 yr+=t*yi;
                 zr=(xr+t*xi)/yr;
                 zl=(xi-t*xr)/yr;
              }
              else
```

```
                        {
                            t=yr/yi;
                            yi+=t*yr;
                            zr=(t*xr+xi)/yi;
                            zi=(t*xi-xr)/yi;
                        }
                z INDEX(j,i)=zr;
                z INDEX(j,i+1)=zi;
                }
            i++;
            }
    }   /* DOFOR i loop*/
printf(" normalized matrix of eigenvectors:\n");
printmd(z,coln,n,n,n);

}
/* specify matrices by row*/
double et[4][4]={1.,2.,3.,5.,2.,4.,1.,6.,1.,2.,-1.,3.,2.,0.,1.,3.};
double ev[4][4]={3.,1.,2.,5.,2.,1.,3.,-1.,0.,4.,1.,1.,0.,0.,2.,1.};
double ex[3][3]={2.,4.,4.,0.,3.,1.,0.,1.,3.};
double ey[3][3]={5.,-4.,-7.,-4.,2.,-4.,-7.,-4.,5.};

main(argc,argv)
int argc;
char **argv;
{/*test driver*/
double wr[4],wi[4],z[16],d[4];
float mach;
int i,j,iwork[4],cnt[4],bal;
elmhes(4,4,0,3,et,iwork);
printf(" elmhes test\n");
printmd(et,4,4,4,4);
printf(" enter macheps ");scanf("%e",&mach);
macheps=mach;
printf(" macheps=%e\n",macheps);
printf(" eigenv test\n");
bal=1;
eigenvv(4,4,ev,iwork,d,z,wr,wi,bal,cnt);
```

```
DOFOR(i,4)
    printf(" eigenvalue real= %e imag=%e it=%d\n",wr[i],wi[i],cnt[i]);
printmd(z,4,4,4,4);
pnormwr(4,4,z,wr,wi);
printf(" eigenv test 2\n");
bal=0;
eigenvv(3,3,ex,iwork,d,z,wr,wi,bal,cnt);
DOFOR(i,3)
    printf(" eigenvalue real= %e imag=%e it=%d\n",wr[i],wi[i],cnt[i]);
printmd(z,3,3,3,3);
pnormwr(3,3,z,wr,wi);
printf(" eign test 3\n");
bal=1;
eigenvv(3,3,ey,iwork,d,z,wr,wi,bal,cnt);
DOFOR(i,3)
    printf(" eigenvalue real= %e imag=%e it=%d\n",wr[i],wi[i],cnt[i]);
printmd(z,3,3,3,3);
pnormwr(3,3,z,wr,wi);
}
```

elmhes test

printing matrix columns 0 to 3
1.000000e+000 8.500000e+000 5.321429e+000 3.000000e+000
2.000000e+000 1.050000e+001 6.107143e+000 1.000000e+000
5.000000e-001 -7.000000e+000 -3.000000e+000 0.000000e+000
1.000000e+000 1.071429e-001 1.607143e-001 -1.500000e+000
enter macheps macheps=1.000000e-007
eigenv test

printing matrix columns 0 to 3
3.000000e+000 5.000000e-001 1.000000e+000 2.500000e+000
4.000000e+000 1.000000e+000 3.000000e+000 -1.000000e+000
0.000000e+000 4.000000e+000 1.000000e+000 1.000000e+000
0.000000e+000 0.000000e+000 2.000000e+000 1.000000e+000

printing matrix columns 0 to 3
3.000000e+000 5.000000e-001 1.000000e+000 2.500000e+000
4.000000e+000 1.000000e+000 3.000000e+000 -1.000000e+000
0.000000e+000 4.000000e+000 1.000000e+000 1.000000e+000
0.000000e+000 0.000000e+000 2.000000e+000 1.000000e+000
low=0 high=3

printing matrix columns 0 to 3
1.000000e+000 0.000000e+000 0.000000e+000 0.000000e+000
0.000000e+000 1.000000e+000 0.000000e+000 0.000000e+000
0.000000e+000 0.000000e+000 1.000000e+000 0.000000e+000
0.000000e+000 0.000000e+000 0.000000e+000 1.000000e+000
eigenvalue real= 6.077906e+000 imag=0.000000e+000 it=0
eigenvalue real= -3.195529e+000 imag=0.000000e+000 it=0
eigenvalue real= 1.558812e+000 imag=2.001516e+000 it=4
eigenvalue real= 1.558812e+000 imag=-2.001516e+000 it=-4

printing matrix columns 0 to 3
9.301637e-001 -1.465495e-001 5.554721e-001 -1.429410e+000
6.522062e-001 6.428047e-001 -5.311325e-001 -9.691423e-002
5.569601e-001 -6.914051e-001 -2.045459e-001 7.045126e-001
2.193660e-001 3.295914e-001 6.001342e-001 3.719449e-001

un normalized matrix:

printing matrix columns 0 to 3
9.301637e-001 -1.465495e-001 5.554721e-001 -1.429410e+000
6.522062e-001 6.428047e-001 -5.311325e-001 -9.691423e-002
5.569601e-001 -6.914051e-001 -2.045459e-001 7.045126e-001
2.193660e-001 3.295914e-001 6.001342e-001 3.719449e-001
normalized matrix of eigenvectors:

printing matrix columns 0 to 3
1.000000e+000 2.119589e-001 1.000000e+000 1.581557e-017
7.011735e-001 -9.297077e-001 -6.654547e-002 -3.457149e-001
5.987764e-001 1.000000e+000 -4.765180e-001 4.207790e-002
2.358359e-001 -4.766979e-001 -8.432142e-002 4.526150e-001
eigenv test 2

printing matrix columns 0 to 2
2.000000e+000 4.000000e+000 4.000000e+000
0.000000e+000 3.000000e+000 1.000000e+000
0.000000e+000 1.000000e+000 3.000000e+000
low=0 high=2

printing matrix columns 0 to 2
1.000000e+000 0.000000e+000 0.000000e+000
0.000000e+000 1.000000e+000 0.000000e+000
0.000000e+000 0.000000e+000 1.000000e+000
eigenvalue real= 2.000000e+000 imag=0.000000e+000 it=0
eigenvalue real= 4.000000e+000 imag=0.000000e+000 it=0
eigenvalue real= 2.000000e+000 imag=0.000000e+000 it=0

printing matrix columns 0 to 2
1.000000e+000 2.828427e+000 0.000000e+000
0.000000e+000 7.071068e-001 -7.071068e-001
0.000000e+000 7.071068e-001 7.071068e-001
un normalized matrix:

printing matrix columns 0 to 2
1.000000e+000 2.828427e+000 0.000000e+000

```
0.000000e+000 7.071068e-001 -7.071068e-001
0.000000e+000 7.071068e-001 7.071068e-001
```
normalized matrix of eigenvectors:

printing matrix columns 0 to 2
```
1.000000e+000 1.000000e+000 -0.000000e+000
0.000000e+000 2.500000e-001 1.000000e+000
0.000000e+000 2.500000e-001 -1.000000e+000
```
eign test 3

printing matrix columns 0 to 2
```
5.000000e+000 -4.000000e+000 -7.000000e+000
-4.000000e+000 2.000000e+000 -4.000000e+000
-7.000000e+000 -4.000000e+000 5.000000e+000
```

printing matrix columns 0 to 2
```
5.000000e+000 -9.285714e+000 -4.000000e+000
-7.000000e+000 2.714286e+000 -4.000000e+000
5.714286e-001 -4.408163e+000 4.285714e+000
```
low=0 high=2

printing matrix columns 0 to 2
```
1.000000e+000 0.000000e+000 0.000000e+000
0.000000e+000 5.714286e-001 1.000000e+000
0.000000e+000 1.000000e+000 0.000000e+000
```
eigenvalue real= -6.000000e+000 imag=0.000000e+000 it=0
eigenvalue real= 1.200000e+001 imag=0.000000e+000 it=0
eigenvalue real= 6.000000e+000 imag=0.000000e+000 it=0

printing matrix columns 0 to 2
```
-6.767155e-001 6.595145e-001 -3.734378e-001
-6.767155e-001 2.452205e-014 7.468756e-001
-6.767155e-001 -6.595145e-001 -3.734378e-001
```
un normalized matrix:

printing matrix columns 0 to 2
```
-6.767155e-001 6.595145e-001 -3.734378e-001
-6.767155e-001 2.452205e-014 7.468756e-001
```

-6.767155e-001 -6.595145e-001 -3.734378e-001
normalized matrix of eigenvectors:

printing matrix columns 0 to 2
1.000000e+000 -1.000000e+000 -5.000000e-001
1.000000e+000 -3.718198e-014 1.000000e+000
1.000000e+000 1.000000e+000 -5.000000e-001

```
/*
find smallest eigenvalues of a symmetric square matrix
uses Rayleigh quotient iteration (easily changed to inverse iteration)

(from "C Tools for Scientists and Engineers" by L. Baker)

CONTENTS:

int esmall(a,value,vector,work,worka,pivot,workp,n,m,eigvect)
    matrix a(n,n). Find the m eigenvalues of smallest(see text)
    absolute value. If eigvect nonzero, return eigenvalues
    as well in vector[].  Eigenvalues returned in value.
    Returns count of eigenvalues found.  Other arguments work space.

DEPENDENCIES:

ftoc.h header file required
vector.c routines
linear algebra routines in luf.c,lus.c,luback.c
*/

#include <ftoc.h>

#define wait 6
#define waitrs 3
#define maxit 100
#define tola 1.e-9
#define tolr .00000
#define tola2 .000000
#define tolr2 .000000

int esmall(a,value,vector,work,worka,pivot,workp,n,m,eigvect)
int n,m,pivot[],workp[],eigvect;
float a[],value[],vector[],work[],worka[];
/* find m smallest eigenvalues of symmetric matrix a(n,n)
 by inverse iteration  Rayleigh quotient iteration*/
/* pivot,work must be at least n long*/
/* the i-th eigenvalue is returned in value[i-1]
```

```
    "        vector is in the i-th ROW of vectors
note that the rows may have been swapped. This info is in pivot.
eigvect=0 if we only want eigenvalues.

*/
{
double sqrt();
double enew,eold;
double alpha,resid,deltrq,rnew,dot(),sqnor(),rq,rqold,shift,shifto;
int iflag,info,i,j,it,ke,nn,nn1,coln,index,k;
float *v1,sdot();
nn=n;
coln=n;
index=0;
rqold=1.e10;
rnew=resid=1.e6;
DOFOR(i,m*n) vector[i]=0.;
DOFOR(ke,m)
    {
    nn1=nn-1;
    shift=0.;
    /* will it still work midway between two eigenvalues? YES*/
    if(ke>0)shift=value[ke-1];
        /*above is attempt to ensure the smallest m eigenvalues
            are found */
    shifto=shift;
    v1=&(vector[coln*ke]);
    if(nn==1)
        {value[ke]= a[0];
        v1[0]=1.00;
/* set single known component of eigenvector to 1. (arb.)
 this will work except in the rare case its identically zero.
*/
        iflag=1;
        pivot[ke]=0;
printf(" going to loner\n");
        goto loner;
        }
```

```
      vset(work,1.,n);work[0]=-.5;
      DOFOR(it,maxit)
        {
        vcopy(work,v1,nn);
        /*shift*/
/*printm(a,coln,nn,nn,nn);*/
        mcopy(a,worka,coln,nn,nn);
        DOFOR(index,nn) worka INDEX(index,index)-= (shift);
/*printm(worka,coln,nn,nn,nn);*/
        lufact(worka,coln,nn,workp,&info);
/*printf(" info=%d\n",info);pv(v1,nn);*/
        if (info!=0)
               {/* we are there v1 is eigenvector*/
               rq= 0.;/*eigenvalue=shift */
               goto convg;
               }
        backsub(worka,coln,nn,workp,v1);
/*pv(v1,nn);*/
        /* Rayleigh quotient*/
        rq= dot(v1,work,nn)/dot(v1,v1,nn);
/*printf(" shift=%f,rq=%f\n",shift,rq);*/
        alpha=1./ sqrt(sqnor(v1,nn));
        vs(v1,alpha,nn);/*renormalize v1*/
        alpha=1./ sqrt(sqnor(work,nn));
        vs(work,alpha,nn);
        if(it>wait)
           {/* check for termination*/
/*pv(v1,nn);pv(work,nn);*/
           if( v1[0]*work[0]<0.)
               vs(work,-1.,nn);
           /* don't need work any more*/
           vdif(v1,work,work,nn);
           rnew= sqnor(work,nn);
           deltrq=abs(rq-rqold);
/*printf("dif=");pv(work,nn);
printf(" rnew=%f,resid=%f\n",rnew,resid);*/
           if ( rnew*(alpha*alpha)<tolr ||rnew<tola
               || deltrq<tola2
```

```
          || deltrq<tolr2*rq)
          {/*converged*/
          convg:
          value[ke]=shift+rq;
/*printf(" eigenvalue=%f ke=%d\n",value[ke],ke);
printf(" eigenvector:");pv(v1,nn);*/
          /*deflate*/
/*printf(" before deflation");printm(a,coln,coln,nn,nn);*/
          alpha=0.;/*find max element*/
          DOFOR(i,nn)
             {resid=abs(v1[i]);
              if(resid>alpha)
                 {
                 j=i;
                 alpha=resid;
                 }
             }
          pivot[ke]=j;
        /*swap eigenv elements, a row and col j<->nn*/
          index=nn-1;
          vcopy(v1,work,nn);
          if(j!=index)
             {
             resid=work[j];
             work[j]=work[index];
             work[index]=resid;
             swaprow(a,index,j,coln);
             swapcol(a,index,j,coln);
             alpha=1./resid;
             }
          else
             alpha=1./work[j];

          work[index]=1.;
          DOFOR(i,index) work[i]*=alpha;
          /* work[nn-1]=1.. all other work<1*/
/*printf(" work vector=\n");   pv(work,nn);*/
          DOFOR(i,index)
```

```
                {
printf(" deflating row %d\n",i);
                DOFOR(j,index)
                    {
                    a INDEX(i,j)-=
                    work[i]* a INDEX(index,j);
                    /* stmt ok DeSmet, error Aztec*/
printf("work=%f,a=%f,i=%d j=%d index=%d\n"
        ,work[i],a INDEX(index,j),i,j,index);

                    }
                }
                nn--;
printf(" after deflation ");printm(a,coln,coln,coln,coln);
                iflag=0;
loner:          if( eigvect && ke>0)
                {
                enew=value[ke];
                index=ke;
                for(j=coln-ke;j<coln;j++)
                {
                index--;
                eold=value[index];
                if(enew==eold)
                    {
                    printf(" degenerate eigenvalues\n");
                    goto giveup;
                    }
                alpha= dot(&(a INDEX(j,0) ),v1,j)/(enew-eold);
printf(" eold %f enew %f j %d ke %d\n",eold,enew,j,ke);
printf(" alpha=%f\n",alpha);
                v1[j]=alpha;
                /* multiply by all previous t matrices, latest first;
                this is the permuted vector,not just vector!
                Don't unpermute until done */
pv(v1,j+1);

                /* modify alpha to account for fact eigenvectors
                are not stored with last component (biggest)=1.
```

```
                We do not use this last component of the prev
                eigvector in vv() below.
                */
                vcopy(&(vector[coln*(index)]),work,n);
                i=pivot[index];
                If(I!=0)
                    {
                    resid=work[i];
                    work[i]=work[j];
                    work[j]=resid;
                    }
                alpha/=work[j];
printf(" norm alpha by %f,new alpha%f\n",vector[coln*index+j],alpha);
                vv(v1,v1,work,alpha,j);
pv(v1,j+1);
pv(&(vector[coln*index]),j);
                normv(v1,j+1);
printf(" renorm v now\n");pv(v1,j+1);


                }

                if(iflag)goto fini;

                }/*if */
            giveup: break;
            }/* if converged*/
/*          if(rnew>resid*1.1)
                {
printf(" diverging %f %f eigenvalues permuted\n",rnew,resid);
                return(ke);
                }
*/
        }/* it> wait*/
    /*update iteration*/
    resid=rnew;
    rqold=rq,
    vcopy(v1,work,nn);
    shifto=shift;
```

```
        if(it>waitrs)shift+=rq;/*Rayleigh quotient iteration*/
        }/* do it*/
    if(it>=(maxit-1)){/* iteration count exceeded,no conv*/
        printf(" no converg, eigevalues permuted\n");
         return(ke);
         }
    if(nn==0)break;
    }/* loop over eignvalues*/
fini:
DOFOR(i,m)printf(" pivot[%d]=%d\n",i,pivot[i]);

for(i=1;i<m;i++)
    {/* which element to pivot*/
    /*permute eigenvalues*/
    k=pivot[i-1];
    if(k)
       {
       for(j=i;j<m;j++)/*loop over eigenvectors to be affected*/
          {
          index= j*coln+k;
          ke= j*coln+ (coln-i) ;/*coln-i was nn for ith eigenv.*/
          alpha= vector[index];
          vector[index]=vector[ke];
          vector[ke]=alpha;
          }
       }
    }
/*Gram-Schmidt improvement orthog. with respect to previous
eigenv. Cannot do sooner easily due to permutations*/
if(eigvect)
{
DOFOR(i,m)
   {
   DOFOR(j,i)
      {
      alpha= dot(&(vector[i*coln]),&(vector[j*coln]),n);
      DOFOR(k,n) vector[i*coln+k]-=alpha*vector[j*coln+k];
      }
```

```
    normv(&(vector[i*coln]),n);
    }
}
return(m);
}
```

```
/*
Driver for small eigenvalue solver
(from "C Tools for Scientists and Engineers" by L. Baker)

DEPENDENCIES:
    ftoc.h  header file
    pv() in vector.c
    esmall(),etc. in esmall.c
*/

#include <ftoc.h>

main(argc,argv) int argc; char **argv;
{
static float a[9]={5.,-4.,-7.,-4.,2.,-4.,-7.,-4.,5.};
/* ex 2.24 of Bathe & Wilson, eigenvalues 6,-6,12 */
float value[3],vector[9],work[9],aa[9],worka[9];
int i,n,m,iter,pivot[3],workp[3];
/* must preserve a, as deflation modifies it*/
DOFOR(i,9)aa[i]=a[i];
m=esmall(aa,value,vector,work,worka,pivot,workp,3,3,1);
printf(" %d eigenvalues found\n",m);
DOFOR(i,3)
    {
    printf(" eigenvalue=%f\n",value[i]);
    }
DOFOR(i,3)
    {
    pv(&(vector[3*i]),3);
    }
exit(0);
}
```

deflating row 0
work=0.999806,a=-4.000000,i=0 j=0 index=2
work=0.999806,a=-4.000000,i=0 j=1 index=2
deflating row 1
work=0.999809,a=-4.000000,i=1 j=0 index=2
work=0.999809,a= 4.000000,i=1 j=1 index=2
after deflation
printing matrix columns 0 to 2
8.999224e+000 -3.000777e+000 -4.000000e+000
-3.000765e+000 8.999235e+000 -4.000000e+000
-4.000000e+000 -4.000000e+000 2.000000e+000
deflating row 0
work=0.999996,a=-3.000777,i=0 j=0 index=1
after deflation
printing matrix columns 0 to 2
1.200000e+001 -3.000765e+000 -4.000000e+000
-3.000777e+000 8.999224e+000 -4.000000e+000
-4.000000e+000 -4.000000e+000 2.000000e+000
eold -6.000000 enew 5.998459 j 2 ke 1
alpha=-0.471465
printing vector from 0 to 2
7.071082e-001 7.071054e-001 -4.714651e-001
norm alpha by 0.577314,new alpha-0.816497
printing vector from 0 to 2
2.357347e-001 2.357305e-001 -4.714651e-001
printing vector from 0 to 1
5.773123e-001 5.774244e-001
renorm v now
printing vector from 0 to 2
4.082520e-001 4.082447e-001 -8.164966e-001
going to loner
eold 5.998459 enew 12.000000 j 1 ke 2
alpha=-0.500001
printing vector from 0 to 1
1.000000e+000 -5.000010e-001
norm alpha by 0.408245,new alpha-1.224758
printing vector from 0 to 1
4.999900e-001 -5.000010e-001

printing vector from 0 to 0
4.082520e-001
renorm v now
printing vector from 0 to 1
7.070990e-001 -7.071146e-001
eold -6.000000 enew 12.000000 j 2 ke 2
alpha=0.000003
printing vector from 0 to 2
7.070990e-001 -7.071146e-001 3.457069e-006
norm alpha by 0.577314,new alpha0.000006
printing vector from 0 to 2
7.071025e-001 -7.071111e-001 3.457069e-006
printing vector from 0 to 1
5.773123e-001 5.774244e-001
renorm v now
printing vector from 0 to 2
7.071025e-001 -7.071111e-001 3.457069e-006
pivot[0]=1
pivot[1]=0
pivot[2]=0
3 eigenvalues found
eigenvalue=-6.000000
eigenvalue=5.998459
eigenvalue=12.000000
printing vector from 0 to 2
5.773123e-001 5.774244e-001 5.773140e-001
printing vector from 0 to 2
4.083044e-001 -8.164442e-001 4.082971e-001
printing vector from 0 to 2
7.071054e-001 4.927770e-006 -7.071082e-001

```
/*
```
find largest eigenvalues of a symmetric square matrix
uses vector iteration

(from "C Tools for Scientists and Engineers" by L. Baker)

CONTENTS:

int elarge(a,value,vector,work,worka,pivot,workp,n,m,eigvect)
    matrix a(n,n). find the m eigenvalues of smallest(see text)
    absolute value. If eigvect nonzero, return eigenvalues
    as well in vector[]. Eigenvalues returned in value.
    Function itself returns count of eigenvalues found.
    Other arguments work space.

DEPENDENCIES:

ftoc.h   header file required
vector.c routines
```
*/
```

```
#include <ftoc.h>
/*#include "libc.h"
#include "math.h"
*/
#define INDEX(i,j)  [j+(i)*coln]
#define INDEK(i,j)  [j+(i)*k]
#define DOFOR(i,to) for(i=0;i<to;i++)
#define min(a,b)  ((a)<(b)?(a):(b))
#define max(a,b)  ((a)>(b)?(a):(b))
#define abs(a)   ((a)>0?(a):-(a))

#define wait 6
#define waitrs 3
#define maxit 100
#define tola 1.e-9
#define tolr .00000
#define tola2 .000000
```

```
#define tolr2 .000000

int elarge(a,value,vector,work,worka,pivot,workp,n,m,eigvect)
int n,m,pivot[],workp[],eigvect;
float a[],value[],vector[],work[],worka[];
/* find m largest eigenvalues of symmetric matrix a(n,n)
 by iteration */
/* pivot,work must be at least n long*/
/* the ith eigenvalue is returned in value[i-1]
    "       vector is in the i-th ROW of vectors
note that the rows may have been swapped. This info is in pivot.
eigvect=0 if we only want eigenvalues

*/
{
double sqrt();
double enew,eold;
double alpha,resid,deltrq,rnew,dot(),sqnor(),rq,
      rqold,shift,shifto;
int iflag,info,i,j,it,ke,nn,nn1,coln,index,k;
float *v1,sdot();
nn=n;
coln=n;
index=0;
rqold=1.e10;
rnew=resid=1.e6;
DOFOR(i,m*n) vector[i]=0.;
DOFOR(ke,m)
   {
   nn1=nn-1;
   shift=0.;
   /* will it still work midway between two eigenvalues? YES*/
   if(ke>0)shift=value[ke-1];
      /*above is attempt to insure the largest m eigenvalues
        are found */
   shifto=shift;
   v1=&(vector[coln*ke]);
   if(nn==1)
```

```
        {value[ke]= a[0];
        v1[0]=1.00;
/* set single known component of eigenvector to 1. (arb.)
 this will work except in the rare case it's identically zero-
*/
        iflag=1;
        pivot[ke]=0;
printf(" going to loner\n");
        goto loner;
        }
    vset(work,1.,n);work[0]=-1.;
    DOFOR(it,maxit)
        {
        vcopy(work,v1,nn);
        /*shift*/
/*printm(a,coln,nn,nn,nn);*/
        mcopy(a,worka,coln,nn,nn);
        DOFOR(index,nn) worka INDEX(index,index)-= (shift);
/*printm(worka,coln,nn,nn,nn);*/
        mvc(worka,work,v1 ,nn ,nn ,coln);
        /* Rayleigh quotient*/
        rq= dot(v1,work,nn)/dot(work,work,nn);
/*printf(" shift=%f,rq=%f\n",shift,rq);*/
        alpha=1./ sqrt(sqnor(v1,nn));
        vs(v1,alpha,nn);/*renormalize v1*/
        alpha=1./ sqrt(sqnor(work,nn));
        vs(work,alpha,nn);
        if(it>wait)
          {/* check for termination*/
/*pv(v1,nn);pv(work,nn);*/
          if( v1[0]*work[0]<0.)
              vs(work,-1.,nn);
          /* don't need work any more*/
          vdif(v1,work,work,nn);
          rnew= sqnor(work,nn);
          deltrq=abs(rq-rqold);
/*printf("dif=");pv(work,nn);
printf(" rnew=%f,resid=%f\n",rnew,resid);*/
```

```
            if ( rnew*(alpha*alpha)<tolr ||rnew<tola
                || deltrq<tola2
                || deltrq<tolr2*rq)
                {/*converged*/
                convg:
                value[ke]=shift+rq;
/*printf(" eigenvalue=%f ke=%d\n",value[ke],ke);
printf(" eigenvector:");pv(v1,nn);*/
                /*deflate*/
/*printf(" before deflation");printm(a,coln,coln,nn,nn);*/
                alpha=0.;/*find max element*/
                DOFOR(i,nn)
                    {resid=abs(v1[i]);
                     if(resid>alpha)
                        {
                        j=i;
                        alpha=resid;
                        }
                    }
                pivot[ke]=j;
            /*swap eigenv elements, a row and col j<->nn*/
                index=nn-1;
                vcopy(v1,work,nn);
                if(j!=index)
                    {
                    resid=work[j];
                    work[j]=work[index];
                    work[index]=resid;
                    swaprow(a,index,j,coln);
                    swapcol(a,index,j,coln);
                    alpha=1./resid;
                    }
                else
                    alpha=1./work[j];

                work[index]=1.;
                DOFOR(i,index) work[i]*=alpha;
                /* work[nn-1]=1., all other work<1*/
```

```
/*printf(" work vector=\n");    pv(work,nn);*/
            DOFOR(i,index)
                {
printf(" deflating row %d\n",i);
            DOFOR(j,index)
                {
                a INDEX(i,j)-=
                work[i]* a INDEX(index,j);
printf("work=%f,a=%f,i=%d j=%d index=%d\n"
        ,work[i],a INDEX(index,j),i,j,index);


                }
            }
            nn--;
printf(" after deflation ");printm(a,coln,coln,coln,coln);
            iflag=0;
loner:          if( eigvect && ke>0)
            {
            enew=value[ke];
            index=ke;
            for(j=coln-ke;j<coln;j++)
            {
            index--;
            eold=value[index];
            if(enew==eold)
                {
                printf(" degenerate eigenvalues\n");
                goto giveup;
                }
            alpha= dot(&(a INDEX(j,0) ),v1,j)/(enew-eold);
printf(" eold %f enew %f j %d ke %d\n",eold,enew,j,ke);
printf(" alpha=%f\n",alpha);
            v1[j]=alpha;
            /* multiply by all previous t matrices, latest first
            this is the permuted vector,not just vector!
            don't unpermute until done */
pv(v1,j+1);
            /* modify alpha to account for fact eigenvectors
```

```
                    are not stored with last component (biggest)=1.
                    we do not use this last component of the previous
                    eigvector in vv() below.
                    */
                    vcopy(&(vector[coln*(index)]),work,n);
                    i=pivot[index];
                    if(i!=0)
                        {
                        resid=work[i];
                        work[i]=work[j];
                        work[j]=resid;
                        }
                    alpha/=work[j];
printf(" norm alpha by %f,new alpha%f\n",vector[coln*index+j],alpha);
                    vv(v1,v1,work,alpha,j);
pv(v1,j+1);
pv(&(vector[coln*index]),j);
                    normv(v1,j+1);
printf(" renorm v now\n");pv(v1,j+1);

                    }

                if(iflag)goto fini;

                }/*if */
            giveup: break;
            }/* if converged*/
/*          if(rnew>resid*1.1)
            {
printf(" diverging %f %f eigenvalues permuted\n",rnew,resid);
            return(ke);
            }
*/
        }/* it> wait*/
      /*update iteration*/
      resid=rnew;
      rqold=rq;
      vcopy(v1,work,nn);
```

```
          shifto=shift;
          }/* do it*/
    if(it>=(maxit-1)){/* iteration count exceeded,no conv*/
          printf(" no converg, eigevalues permuted\n");
           return(ke);
          }
    if(nn==0)break;
    }/* loop over eignvalues*/
fini:
DOFOR(i,m)printf(" pivot[%d]=%d\n",i,pivot[i]);

for(i=1;i<m;i++)
   {/* which element to pivot*/
   /*permute eigenvalues*/
   k=pivot[i-1];
   if(k)
      {
      for(j=i;j<m;j++)/*loop over eigenvectors to be affected*/
         {
         index= j*coln+k;
         ke= j*coln+ (coln-i) ;/*coln-i was nn for ith eigenv.*/
         alpha= vector[index];
         vector[index]=vector[ke];
         vector[ke]=alpha;
         }
      }
   }
/*Gram-Schmidt improvement orthog. with respect to
previous eigenv. cannot do sooner easily due to permutations*/
if(eigvect)
{
DOFOR(i,m)
   {
   DOFOR(j,i)
      {
      alpha= dot(&(vector[i*coln]),&(vector[j*coln]),n);
      DOFOR(k,n) vector[i*coln+k]-=alpha*vector[j*coln+k];
      }
```

```
    normv(&(vector[i*coln]),n);
    }
}
return(m);
}
```

```
/*
Driver for large eigenvalue solver
(from "C Tools for Scientists and Engineers" by L. Baker)


DEPENDENCIES:
    ftoc.h
    pv() in vector.c
    elarge() in elarge.c
*/

#include <ftoc.h>

/*#include "libc.h"
#include "math.h"
*/

main(argc,argv) int argc; char **argv;
{
static float a[9]={5.,-4.,-7.,-4.,2.,-4.,-7.,-4.,5.};
/* ex 2.24 of Bathe & Wilson, eigenvalues 6,-6,12 */
float value[3],vector[9],work[9],aa[9],worka[9];
int i,n,m,iter,pivot[3],workp[3];
/* must preserve a, as deflation modifies it*/
DOFOR(i,9)aa[i]=a[i];
m=elarge(aa,value,vector,work,worka,pivot,workp,3,3,1);
printf(" %d eigenvalues found\n",m);
DOFOR(i,3)
    {
    printf(" eigenvalue=%f\n",value[i]);
    }
DOFOR(i,3)
    {
    pv(&(vector[3*i]),3);
    }
exit(0);
}
```

deflating row 0
work=-1.000000,a=-7.000000,i=0 j=0 index=2
work=-1.000000,a=-4.000000,i=0 j=1 index=2
deflating row 1
work=0.000015,a=-7.000000,i=1 j=0 index=2
work=0.000015,a=-4.000000,i=1 j=1 index=2
after deflation
printing matrix columns 0 to 2
-2.000000e+000 -8.000000e+000 -7.000000e+000
-3.999893e+000 2.000061e+000 -4.000000e+000
-7.000000e+000 -4.000000e+000 5.000000e+000
deflating row 0
work=0.500007,a=-8.000000,i=0 j=0 index=1
after deflation
printing matrix columns 0 to 2
6.000120e+000 -3.999893e+000 -4.000000e+000
-8.000000e+000 -2.000000e+000 -7.000000e+000
-4.000000e+000 -7.000000e+000 5.000000e+000
eold 12.000000 enew -6.000089 j 2 ke 1
alpha=0.372678
printing vector from 0 to 2
8.944246e-001 4.472189e-001 3.726776e-001
norm alpha by 0.707107,new alpha0.527046
printing vector from 0 to 2
5.217469e-001 4.472245e-001 3.726776e-001
printing vector from 0 to 1
-7.071068e-001 1.076857e-005
renorm v now
printing vector from 0 to 2
6.674170e-001 5.720882e-001 4.767281e-001
going to loner
eold -6.000089 enew 6.000120 j 1 ke 2
alpha=-0.666655
printing vector from 0 to 1
1.000000e+000 -6.666551e-001
norm alpha by 0.572088,new alpha-1.165301
printing vector from 0 to 1
2.222581e-001 -6.666551e-001

printing vector from 0 to 0
6.674170e-001
renorm v now
printing vector from 0 to 1
3.162787e-001 -9.486663e-001
eold 12.000000 enew 6.000120 j 2 ke 2
alpha=-0.895943
printing vector from 0 to 2
3.162787e-001 -9.486663e-001 -8.959429e-001
norm alpha by 0.707107,new alpha-1.267054
printing vector from 0 to 2
1.212222e+000 -9.486800e-001 -8.959429e-001
printing vector from 0 to 1
-7.071068e-001 1.076857e-005
renorm v now
printing vector from 0 to 2
6.806166e-001 -5.326480e-001 -5.030380e-001
pivot[0]=2
pivot[1]=0
pivot[2]=0
3 eigenvalues found
eigenvalue=12.000000
eigenvalue=-6.000089
eigenvalue=6.000120
printing vector from 0 to 2
-7.071068e-001 1.076857e-005 7.071068e-001
printing vector from 0 to 2
5.773489e-001 5.773618e-001 5.773401e-001
printing vector from 0 to 2
4.082502e-001 -8.164884e-001 4.082627e-001

```
/* vector processing routines
often simplified versions of BLAS routines for vectors
with contiguous storage

(from "C Tools for  Scientists and Engineers" by L. Baker)

CONTENTS:

dot(a,b,n)
      returns double value of dot product of two vectors a,b
      of n elements
pv(v,n)
      prints vector of n elements
mv(a,x,y,m,n)
      y=ax where a is m x n matrix
normv(v,n)
      normalize a vector (scale its length to one)
sqnor(v,n)
      square of the length of vector v of n elements
mvt(a,x,y,m,n)
      like mv except y=a^x a^ =transpose of a
resid(r,a,x,n)
      r=ax-x, a matrix all other vectors
vs(v,s,n)
      scale vector by multiplying each element by s
vset(v,s,n)
      set vector v to scalar value s for each element
vcopy(x,y,n)
      y=x, vectors
vv(a,b,c,s,n)
      a=b+c*s, s scalar, a,b,c,vectors


DEPENDENCIES:
NONE
*/


#include "ftoc.h"
```

```
double dot(a,b,n) int n; float a[],b[];
{
int i;
double sum;
if(n<=0)return(0.);
sum=0.;
DOFOR(i,n)sum+=a[i]*b[i];
return(sum);
}


pv(v,n) int n;float v[];
{
int btm,top,i;
btm=0;
top=0;
while (btm<n)
    {
    top=min(btm+6,n);
    printf(" printing vector from %d to %d\n",btm,(top-1));
    for(i=btm;i<top;i++)printf(" %e",v[i]);
    printf("\n");
    btm+=6;
    }
return;
}


mv(a,x,y,m,coln) int coln,m;
float x[],y[],a[];
/* y=ax a(m,n) m rows n columns [row of length n]*/
{
int i,j,k;
float sum;
DOFOR(i,m)
    {
    sum=0.;
    DOFOR(j,coln) sum+= x[j]*a INDEX(i,j);
    y[i]=sum;
    }
```

```
return;
}

normv(v,n) int n; float v[];
{
double x,sqrt(),sqnor();
x=sqnor(v,n);
if(x!=0.)x=1./sqrt(x);
vs(v,x,n);
return;
}

double sqnor(x,n) float x[]; int n;
{
int i;
double ans;
ans=0.;
if(n<=0)return(ans);
DOFOR(i,n)ans+= x[i]*x[i];
return(ans);
}

mvt(a,x,y,m,coln) int coln,m;
float a[],x[],y[];
{
/* y= a^x  a(m,n) a m rows n columns [n elements/row]
a^ n rows m columns*/
float sum;
int i,j;
DOFOR(i,coln)
    {
    sum=0.;
    DOFOR(j,m)sum+= x[j]*a INDEX(j,i);
    y[i]=sum;
    }
return;
}
```

```
resid(a,x,y,r,n) int n;
float a[],x[],y[],r[];
{
int i;
mv(a,x,r,n,n);
DOFOR(i,n)r[i]-=y[i];
return;
}


vs(v,s,n) int n; float v[],s;
{
int i;
DOFOR(i,n)v[i]*=s;
return;
}


vset(x,s,n) int n; float s,x[];
{
int i;
DOFOR(i,n)x[i]=s;
return;
}



vcopy(x,y,n) int n; float x[],y[];
{
int i;
DOFOR(i,n)y[i]=x[i];
return;
}


vv(a,b,c,s,n) int n; float a[],b[],c[],s;
{
int i;
DOFOR(i,n) a[i]=b[i]+s*c[i];
return;
}
```

/* matrix & vector processing routines

(from "C Tools for Scientists and Engineers" by L. Baker)

CONTENTS:

vdif(a,b,dif,n)
      vector difference of two vectors a and b
swaprow(a,from,to,coln)
      swap rows from and to of matrix a
swapcol(a,from,to,coln)
      swap columns coln=# of columns

The following two routines are similar to mv()and mvt()
in VECTOR.C Here, we process the first n columns of a
matrix of coln columns. Previously, it was assumed n=coln. Note
that there is one additional argument, the last.

mvc
      multiply vector by matrix
mvct
      multipy vector by transpose of matrix
mcopy(a,aa,coln,nrow,ncol)
      Copy the upper left-hand portion of one 2D matrix, a, to
      matrix aa. nrow rows and ncol columns are copied. It is
      assumed that both a and aa are dimensioned to have coln columns.

DEPENDENCIES:
NONE
*/

#include <ftoc.h>

vdif(a,b,dif,n) int n; float a[],b[],dif[];
{
int i;
DOFOR(i,n) dif[i]=a[i]-b[i];
return;

```
}

swaprow(a,from,to,coln) int from,to,coln; float a[];
{
int i;
float x;
DOFOR(i,coln)
    {
    x= a INDEX(from,i);
    a INDEX(from,i)= a INDEX(to,i);
    a INDEX(to,i)=x;
    }
return;
}

swapcol(a,from,to,coln) int from,to,coln; float a[];
{/*matrix assumed to be square=>number of rows=coln*/
int i;
float x;
DOFOR(i,coln)
    {
    x= a INDEX(i,from);
    a INDEX(i,from)= a INDEX(i,to);
    a INDEX(i,to)=x;
    }
return;
}

mvc(a,x,y,n,m,coln) int n,coln,m;
float x[],y[],a[];
/* y=ax a(m,n) */
{
int i,j,k;
float sum;
DOFOR(i,m)
    {
    sum=0.;
    DOFOR(j,n) sum+= x[j]*a INDEX(i,j);
```

```
        y[i]=sum;
        }
return;
}


mvtc(a,x,y,n,m,coln) int coln,n,m;
float a[],x[],y[];
{
/* y= a(T)x  a(n,m)*/
float sum;
int i,j;
DOFOR(i,m)
    {
    sum=0.;
    DOFOR(j,n)sum+= x[j]*a INDEX(j,i);
    y[i]=sum;
    }
return;
}


mcopy(a,aa,coln,nrow,ncol) float a[],aa[];
int coln,nrow,ncol;
/* copy upper left part of one matrix to another.
assumed matrices are float, and have same number of columns*/
{
int i,j;
DOFOR(i,nrow)
    {
    DOFOR(j,ncol) aa INDEX(i,j)=a INDEX(i,j);
    }
return;
}
```

CHAPTER 5

Singular Value Decomposition:Robust Least-Squares Estimation, Factor Analysis

Chapter Objectives

In this chapter tools will be presented which:

-obtain the Singular Value Decomposition (SVD) of a matrix

-use the SVD to perform least-squares fits robustly

We will present the theory behind the SVD. We will continue the discussion begun in the previous chapter (on eigenvalues) concerning statistical applications of the SVD, concentrating on factor analysis in this chapter.

The Singular Value Decomposition

It might be tempting to christen the Singular Value Decomposition the "Swiss Army knife of numerical analysis" because of its versatility, but this would be unfair to the SVD. The SVD is the method of choice for many problems, whereas the Swiss Army knife is handy but rarely the optimal tool for the job. In this chapter, we will discuss the method and apply it to least-squares fits of data, as well as factor analysis (principal component, R- and Q-mode). The SVD has applications to such problems as canonical correlation, generalized least-squares multivariate analysis of variance (MANOVA) and covariance, and constrained least squares, but space limitations preclude a full discussion of all its uses.

The SVD

For any matrix A of dimension m x n, the matrix $A^{\wedge}A$ is a square (n x n), positive definite (see Chapters 2 and 3) matrix. Its eigenvalues (see Chapter 4) must be non-negative, so that they may each be written in the form s^2. These numbers s are called the "singular values of the matrix A." We will see that wherever the product $A^{\wedge}A$ crops up, the SVD is likely to be of value. We have already discussed a variety of methods involving factoring a matrix A into the product of a number of other matrices with useful properties: the LU decomposition in Chapter 2, and the QR decomposition in Chapter 4. In the SVD, we factor a matrix **A**, which in general need not be a square matrix but may have dimensions m x n, as

USV^

where **S** is a diagonal matrix of dimensions m x n, and **U** and **V** are orthogonal matrices of dimensions m x m and n x n, respectively. The diagonal elements of **S** are the singular values of **A**, as may be shown by forming **A^A**, using **A^** = **VSU^** and **U^U** = **I**. The singular values are required to be non-negative, and if any are zero, these must follow (have higher indices than) all the non-zero (positive) singular values. There is a tendency in the algorithms used to produce the singular values in declining size, but this must not be counted upon, for we will give an example where this is not the case. In general, if the matrix **A** is ill-conditioned (see Chapter 2), then the singular values will very likely not be so ordered.

We will present a program which permits the full **U** matrix to be found. Usually, only the leading n x n part of **U** is of interest, and most of the programs available only provide this part of **U** as output.

The SVD has considerable non-uniqueness in the **U** matrix in the elements beyond the n x n submatrix, as well as in the elements associated with zero singular values. Thus, if your implementation does not agree with the results presented here for those components, do not worry too much. However, if your singular values or significant results (such as those of the least-squares tests) disagree—worry. If you encounter negative singular values, then you should REALLY worry.

The Numerical Method

If you read the brief outline of the QR method contained in the previous chapter, nothing about the SVD method should surprise you. You will recall that in the QR factorization of a general matrix **A**, the matrix was typically reduced first to upper Hessenberg form (or tridiagonal form if symmetric). This is accomplished by a similarity transformation which leaves the eigenvalues unaltered. This is typically done by Householder transformations, which zero-out all of the elements below the main diagonal except for the element immediately below that diagonal. Among the EISPACK routines, ELMHES and TREDN (N = 1,2, or 3 depending upon options desired) accomplish this transformation. Then the QR or QL iteration is used (the latter merely differs in using a lower triangular matrix instead of an upper triangular matrix—see Parlett's book in particular on the relationship between the two iteration methods). With the additional flexibility of another orthogonal matrix on the right-hand side of the matrix, we can zero-out the matrix above the diagonal, leaving a bi-diagonal matrix. As discussed in Chapter 4, there is no procedure guaranteed to reduce a matrix to a diagonal form exactly, in finite time, because that would be equivalent to solving for the roots of an n-th order problem. So an iterative method is used to diagonalize the remaining S matrix, the iteration terminating when sufficient accuracy has been achieved. By first doing the reduction to bi-diagonal form, the economy of the method is much improved. The cost is (roughly) $2mn^2 + 4n^3$ for the implementation presented here. If m > n, somewhat more economical methods exist (see below).

Orthogonal Similarity Transformations

There are two basic types of similarity transformations used to introduce zeros in desired places of the matrix. These are reflections and rotations.

The reflection method was developed by Householder and utilizes multiplication by a matrix $P = I - 2w^\wedge w$, where (as in the Sherman-Morrison formula discussed in Chapter 4) the second term must be considered a dyad (and not a scalar product), with the scalar product $w^\wedge w = 1$. When a vector v is multiplied by this matrix, the resultant vector has its component in the direction of the w vector reversed in sign, while the component of the vector perpendicular to the vector w is unchanged. It is as if the vector v were reflected in a mirror for which w is the unit normal vector; hence the term "reflection." We can successively multiply a matrix by suitable P matrices to null out suitable portions of each column. The orthogonal matrix of the similarity transformation is then this product of P matrices. The details of the appropriate choice of the w vector to accmplish this magic are left to Wlkinson or Stewart (see previous chapter for references), but in general, to zero-out the lowest n − r elements (of the r + 1 st column of a matrix of order n), write $P = I - u^\wedge u/q$, then the first r elements of u are zero ($u[i] = 0$, $i = 0,1,...r - 1$), $u[r] = a[r - 1][r] + S$, $u[i] = a[r -1][i]$, ($i = r + 1, n - 1$)

$$S = A \{ \sum_{i=r}^{n} (a[r - 1][i])^2 \}^{1/2}, q = S u[r]$$

and where A is chosen as + 1 or − 1 so as to give S the same sign as $a[r - 1][r]$ (and thus avoid cancellation and the possible attendant numerical difficulties). We have used the C subscripting convention so that all subscripts are based at zero, the r + 1 st column has column index r, etc.

A more selective method of zeroing-out elements is by rotations. In Chapter 4 we encountered the basic rotation matrix, which generalizes to the form

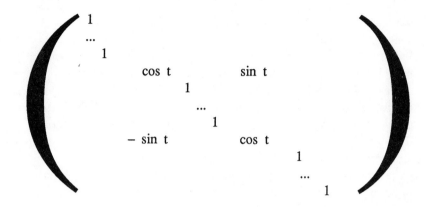

This type of orthogonal transformation is associated with the name Givens. (See Golub and van Loan, or Parlett or Stewart (referenced in Chapter 4) for discussions, the first two in particular for a discussion of "Fast Givens Transformations.") The second half of the SVD algorithm, i.e., after the bidiagonalization, uses these transforms to reduce the S matrix to diagonal form. In zeroing the off-diagonal elements, additional non-zero elements are introduced, and these must be eliminated, resulting in an iterative method. One starts at the upper left of the matrix, and "chases" these elements (in the terminology of Golub and van Loan) along the diagonal (they alternate above and below the diagonal when this is done). After a few iterations, the matrix is generally reduced quite accurately to diagonal form.

The Least-Squares Problem

If we have n linear equations in n unknowns, we can generally obtain a unique solution. But if we are attempting to determine n variables by fitting empirical (experimental) data, we often wish to take many more than the minimal n observations. Due to random errors, etc., we cannot expect to get a solution which satisfies all of the m observation points. We want then a "best fit." One of the most convenient best fits is the least-squares fit, which minimizes the sum of the squares of the residuals, i.e., the differences between the fit and the data points being fit.

This is the "multiple regression" problem. We will also see that the standard analysis of variance (ANOVA) problem is much more similar to this problem than might be expected on the basis of the rather different terminology and approach used in ANOVA.

Application of the SVD to Least-Squares Problems

In the least squares problem, we want to minimize the value of $|Ax - b|$, where **b** is the vector of the m observed values, **x** a vector of n parameters which are to be determined, and **A** is an m x n matrix of coefficients. We are considering here only linear, unconstrained least-squares problems. That is, we do not allow constraints, e.g. $x[1] < 0$ or $x[1] + x[2] = 5$, to be imposed in addition to the regression equations. We also assume that our model for the observation is linear, i.e. that the observations b[i] are assumed to be modeled as the sum of terms, each of which is proportional to the parameters x[i]. We can look upon the x[i] as the coefficients of these terms. For example, suppose we were trying to model the electrical resistivity of a plasma as the sum of two terms: one due to collisions of the current carriers with neutral particles, and one due to collisions with charged particles. We could make a number of measurements at different temperatures and densities, with a model

$$R(temp,density) = x[0] \ Rneut(temp,density)$$

$$+ \ x[1] \ Rionic(temp,density)$$

where our models for Rneut and Rionic would have dependencies upon temperature and density based upon our knowledge of the physics of the relevant temperature and density regime being studied. Even if these models were perfect, however, there would be the assumption that the total resistance was representable as the sum of these two terms.

Suppose we wish to minimize $|Ax - b|$. Using the SVD, this becomes a problem to minimize $|USV^\wedge x - b|$. Define $z = V^\wedge x$ and multiply through by $U^\wedge$, defining $d = U^\wedge b$. We now need to minimize $|Sz - d|$. It is permissible to multiply through by $U^\wedge$ because it is an orthogonal matrix, with $|U| = 1$, so multiplication by **U** will not change the minimum. We have of course used the fact that $U^\wedge U = 1$. Because **S** is diagonal, this problem is now trivial to solve for z: $z[i] = d[i]/s[i][i]$ for s[i][i] nonzero. If s[i][i] is zero, the value of z[i] is immaterial to the problem—it could be assigned any value. Typically, z[i] is set equal to zero in such cases, giving the minimum norm (length) **z** vector in the process. Once **z** is known, $x = Vz$ is the desired solution to the (unconstrained) linear least squares problem.

Note that one could simply factor **A** as **QR** instead of using the SVD. Then minimize $|QRx - b|$ by setting $c = Q^\wedge b$ and solving the system $Rx = c$ (as **R** is upper triangular, this is easily done as it is in the second half of the procedure in the backsub() program of Chapter 2). Why go to the additional trouble of the full-blown SVD, i.e., further factoring **R** into

$SV^\wedge$? In this case, because the SVD tells us more about the character of the solution. The singular values that are zero (or very small) tell us the rank of the problem, i.e., if the least squares fit is unique ("full rank" problem with n nonzero singular values), of if there is non-uniqueness in the least squares solution. The relative values of the singular values tell us the relative importance of the components of z in determining the fit (see the discussion of factor analysis below). If the singular values do not monotonically decrease (we will encounter this in our second test problem), we have an indication of a possible ill-conditioning of the matrix being treated.

The solution of the least squares problem for a matrix A may also be written as $x = (A^\wedge A)^{-1} A^\wedge b$. The matrix product on the right-hand side is called the "generalized inverse," or "Moore-Penrose inverse," of the matrix A and is sometimes written as A^+. As will be shown below, actually doing the multiplications and inversions required in this representation should be avoided if at all possible, and the SVD provides an alternative:

$$A^+ = VS^+ U^\wedge$$

where S^+ is defined to be the diagonal matrix whose elements are the reciprocals of those of S, i.e. the reciprocals of the singular values, unless the singular value is 0, in which case the corresponding element of S^+ is also zero. See Forsythe, Malcolm and Moler for a discussion of some of the computational caveats associated with small singular values when dealing with the pseudoinverse matrix, and Stewart for more information about the theory.

Note that the QR factorization can be used as the LU factorization was, to solve linear systems. If $QRy = b$, obtain $d = Q^\wedge b$ and solve $Ry = d$ This costs more operations than the LU factorization, but is numerically stable without pivoting. It is, therefore, of interest for parallel processing architectures for which pivoting strategies may cause communication nightmares between processors.

Factor Analysis

In this section we will discuss principal component factor analysis, and touch upon R- and Q- mode factor analysis. Other types of factor analysis—the "rotations" such as Varimax, Equimax, Quartimax, Quartimin, Promax, Covarmin, etc., will not be discussed in this book. The rotational methods are subjective in their interpretation, as might be guessed from the large number of alternative rotations to choose from. Given any rotation, another can be obtained by an orthogonal transformation (rotation). Even the number of factors obtained from such an analysis can vary.

In older books especially, the principal component method is discussed as an eigenvalue problem. While it can indeed by treated in such a manner, the SVD is a more robust way of dealing with the problem.

A correlation coefficient matrix is actually of the form $X^{\wedge}X$ (see below). Such a matrix product must be symmetric positive definite. The condition number of such a matrix is the square of that of the matrix X. Thus, if the condition number of X is large, that of $X^{\wedge}X$ is much larger. This can easily cause numerical difficulties.

As an example (due to J. C. Nash), specific to a Data General computer, consider the matrix A

$$\begin{pmatrix} 1 & 1 & 1 \\ e & 0 & 1 \\ 0 & e & 1 \\ 0 & 0 & 1 \end{pmatrix}$$

where $|e|<1$. The product $A^{\wedge}A$ is

$$\begin{pmatrix} 1+e^2 & 1 & 1+e \\ 1 & 1+e^2 & 1+e \\ 1+e & 1+e & 4 \end{pmatrix}$$

The matrix A would have the first two columns or the second and third row singular if $|e|$ were smaller than machine precision. The product matrix will be singular (either the first two rows or the first two columns will be identical) if e^2 is smaller than machine precision. If $|e|$ is small, its square is much smaller, so it is easy to turn an almost singular matrix into a singular one by the process of forming $A^{\wedge}A$. This is why one should not do so if there is an alternative (aside from the fact that it costs order n-cubed floating point operations!).

Even more pathological examples can be constructed from asymmetric matrices. The matrix A:

$$\begin{pmatrix} 1 & L \\ 0 & 1 \end{pmatrix}$$

has the degenerate eigenvalue 1 repeated twice. Furthermore, it has only one eigenvector in the direction (1,0). The spectral radius or condition number of this matrix, i.e. the range of its eigenvalues, is one. The matrix $A^\wedge A$

$$\left(\begin{array}{cc} 1 & L \\ L & 1 + L^2 \end{array} \right)$$

has eigenvalues $2 + L^2$ and $1/(2 + L^2)$, resulting in a spectral radius or condition number of order L^4 if L is large. While this is a particularly pathological case, the moral that one should not attempt to form $A^\wedge A$, if at all possible, is reinforced.

The bi-conjugate gradient algorithm attempts to apply the conjugate gradient method to an asymmetric A while avoiding the process of forming $A^\wedge A$ by instead forming the symmetric matrix

$$\left(\begin{array}{cc} 0 & A \\ A^\wedge & 0 \end{array} \right)$$

This noble effort is not always satisfctory, however.

Suppose we are given the correlation matrix R. The diagonal elements are all 1, as any variable is perfectly correlated with itself. The other elements represent the correlation of one variable with another. The matrix is clearly symmetric, as the correlation of variable i with j must be the same as variable j with i. In principal component analysis we are attempting to determine those linear combinations of the variables which are least correlated, i.e., orthogonal (no correlation). This is seen to be the eigenvalue problem, as eigenvectors (if they correspond to different eigenvalues) are orthogonal. But it may be treated with greater robustness by the SVD, as the correlation matrix of the form $A^\wedge A$ need never be formed.

Instead of dealing with the possibly ill-conditioned correlation matrix R, we deal with the data matrix. This is an m x n matrix X where n is the number of variables and m the number of observations, as in the least squares problem. It is desirable for numerical reasons to form the "zero-mean" data matrix (see Nash's book or S. Hammarling, "The SVD in Multivariate Statistics," *SIGNUM* vol. 20, no.3, July 1985, p.2), which is of the form $Y = X - u\,x^\wedge$, where $x^\wedge$ is a vector of the means of the variables, and u is a vector of ones: $(1,1,...,1)$, and the vector product shown is a dyad. Further, given the standard deviations for each variable i as $s[i]$, we form a diagonal matrix D as we formed the S^+ matrix using the singular values. Then the matrix $Z = YD$ is the "standardized" data matrix, the matrix $Y^\wedge Y/(n-1)$ is the covariance matrix, and $Z^\wedge Z/(n-1)$ is the correlation matrix. Rather than form the correlation matrix, perform the SVD on the zero means matrix **Y**. The **V** matrix then contains the orthogonal singular vectors. The variance associated with the i-th column is $s[i]^2/(n-1)$. As s[0] should be the largest singular value, the first column of **V** will most often be principal component—but as noted before this is not always true, particularly if the matrix is ill-conditioned, so be sure to check which singular value is the largest and use the associated column as the first principal component. The remaining components, if desired, should be ordered in declining singular value. The transformed data matrix is given by the matrix **US**. Its columns should have as large a variance as possible, with the variance of the first column the largest and the subsequent variances not increasing (again, take care if the singular values are not ordered). See J. M. Chambers for further discussion of principal component analysis via the SVD, and Chapter 10 of Menke's book on R- and Q-mode analysis.

Table 5.1

Matrices Formed from the Data Matrix X

Zero-mean data matrix	**Y**	**X** $-u^\wedge x$
standardized data matrix	**Z**	**YD**
covariance matrix	**C**	**Y**^**Y**/(n − 1)
correlation matrix	**R**	**Z**^**Z**/(n − 1)

where:

n = number of variables

u = (1,1,1,...)

x = vector of means of the variables over the observations data matrix (mean of each row)

D = diagonal matrix of standard deviations of each variable

Table 5.1 lists the various matrices which have come into play. This accomplishes the principal component analysis. For R- and Q-mode analysis, fictitious correlation matrices (or datamatrices) are formed. In R-mode, the self-variances are set equal to 1, while in Q-mode, the roles of the variables and observations are interchanged. In each of these methods, the principal component analysis is then applied to these matrices. See Koch and Link (reference in Chapter 4) for examples. Typically, only a few of the eigenvalues are of interest, so there may be an incentive for the use of eigenvalue analysis instead of the SVD.

Program Listing and Test Problems

This program is based upon the FORTRAN code in Forsythe, Malcolm, and Moler, which in turn is a modification of that in the EISPACK 2 package, which in turn is based upon the ALGOL program in Wilkinson and Reinsch. The section of the code designed to compute the full U matrix is based upon the last reference and is not present in the first two references. The alterations in the algorithm introduced by Forsythe, Malcolm, and Moler to prevent underflows is particularly important in the DeSmet C environment. In addition, they introduced a change for greater machine independence which is retained here. We have broken the SVD routine into two programs as the program, when written as one subroutine, was too large for the DeSmet C compiler.

We use two test problems. In the first, we determine the SVD of a matrix given in Forsythe, Malcolm, and Moler. This matrix is degenerate, that is, has a zero singular value. We do the decomposition twice, once requesting only the m x n portion of the U matrix, and later requesting the full m x m U matrix. Please note that in general the full U matrix will not be unique. Indeed, because of the zero singular value in this case only that 3 x 2 portion of the matrix corresponding to the nonzero singular values will be unique. Our results do not agree with Forsythe, Malcolm, and Moler (see Chapter 3 for references) for the full matrix, although they agree for the 3 x 2 submatrix of U as well as for the full V and S matrices. In a FORTRAN implementation of the SVD we have written to run on an IBM PC with 8087 and using Microsoft FORTRAN, we have obtained still other values for the U matrix.

In the same program listing, program main() obtains a least-squares solution to exercise 11.16 on page 428 of Mendenhall and Sincich. This problem involved the least square fit of a quadratic polynomial to a set of data (see the main program for the data). The results obtained by the SVD agree with the results presented in the book, which were obtained there not by means of the SVD but through the formation of the X^X matrix.

Table 5.2

Programs of Chapter 5

svd	SVD
diagon	Used by SVD for second part of SVD determination
lstsq	Call SVD to perform least-squares fit.
printmd	Type double version of printm
vdifd	" " " " vdif
mvd	" " " " mv
mvtd	" " " " mvt
pvd	" " " " pv
dsign	Transfer of sign (as FORTRAN)
setrow	Used for test problem setup

References

In addition to the references listed in the preceding chapter, we have cited:

J. M. Chambers, *Computational Methods of Data Analysis*, (NY: J. Wiley, 1977).

G. H. Golub and C. F. van Loan, *Matrix Computations,* (Baltimore: Johns Hopkins Press,1983).

G. S. Koch, Jr. and R. F. Link, *Statistical Analysis of Geologicial Data,* (NY: Dover, 1971).

W. Mendhall and T. Sincich, *Statistics for the Engineering and Computer Sciences*, (San Francisco: Dellen Publishing Co., 1984).

W. Menke, *Geophysical Data Analysis: Discrete Inverse Theory, (NY: Academic Press, 1984).*

J. C. Nash, *Compact Numerical Methods for Small Computers: Linear Algebra and Function Minimization, (Bristol: Adam Hilger Ltd., 1979).*

J. H. Wilkinson and C. Reinsch, *Linear Algebra,* (Berlin: Springer, 1971).

Program Listing and Test Problem Output

(listing begins next page.)

```
/* perform robust least-squares regession using SVD
note- uses double-precision storage- DO NOT mix with routines
from vector.c or matrix.c, as these assume vectors to be of
type float.
```

(from "C Tools for Scientists and Engineers" by L. Baker)

```
CONTENTS:
lstsq() perform lst-sq. solution Az=y
         A dimensioned for coln columns
             neq equations (rows)
             col columns in use (variables)
             other variables working storage

type double routines similar to those in vector.c and matrix.c:
pvd()
setrow()
vdifd()
mvd()
mvtd()

DEPENDENCIES:
svd() in svd.c required
*/
/*
#include "libc.h"
#include "math.h"
*/
#define INDEX(i,j) [j+(i)*coln]
#define DOFOR(i,to) for(i=0;i<to;i++)
#define min(a,b) ((a)<(b)?(a):(b))

lstsq(a,y,coln,neq,col,u,s,v,z,resid,work)
int neq,col,coln;
double a[],y[];
double u[],v[],work[],s[],z[],resid[];
{
int matu,matv,ierr,i;
```

```
matu=1;
matv=1;

svd(coln,neq,col,a,s,matu,u,matv,v,&ierr,work);
printf(" ierr=%d\n singular values=\n",ierr);
pvd(s,col);
printmd(u,coln,neq,col,neq);
printmd(v,coln,neq,col,col);

/* work d=U[t]*y*/
mvtd(u,y,work,col,neq,coln);

DOFOR(i,col)
    {
    if( s[i]>0.) work[i]/=s[i];
    }
mvd(v,work,z,col,col,coln);
printf(" answer is:\n");
pvd(z,col);
printf(" residual errors for each eqn:\n");
mvd(a,z,work,col,neq,coln);
vdifd(work,y,work,neq);
pvd(work,neq);return;
}


setrow(a,coln,row,x) int row,coln; double x,a[];
{
a INDEX(row,0)= 1.;
a INDEX(row,1)= x;
a INDEX(row,2)= x*x;
return;
}


main(argc,argv) int argc; char **argv;
{
/* test pblm lst sq.*/
static double y[10]={1.1,1.3,2.0,2.1,2.7,2.8,3.4,3.6,4.1,4.0};
int i,j,k,coln,rown,ierr;
```

```
double x,a[30],z[3],s[10],resid[10],work[30],u[30],v[30];

static double aa[5][3]={1.,6.,11.,2.,7.,
    12.,3.,8.,13.,4.,9.,14.,5.,10.,15.};
svd(3,5,3,aa,s,1,u,1,v,&ierr,resid);
printf(" ierr=%d\n" ,ierr);
DOFOR(ierr,3)printf(" sing value=%f\n",s[ierr]);
printf("u matrix:");
printmd(u,3,5,3,5);
printf("v matrix:");
printmd(v,3,3,3,3);
svd(3,5,3,aa,s,-1,u,1,v,&ierr,resid);
printf(" ierr=%d\n" ,ierr);
DOFOR(ierr,3)printf(" sing value=%f:\n",s[ierr]);
printf("u matrix:");
printmd(u,5,5,5,5);
printf("v matrix:");
printmd(v,3,3,3,3);


coln=3;
rown=10;
DOFOR(i,5)
    {
    x= (i-2);
    DOFOR(j,2)
        {
        k= j+2*i;
        setrow(a,coln,k,x);
        }
    }
printf("coef. matrix is :\n");
printmd(a,coln,rown,coln,rown);
printf(" rhs is\n");
pvd(y,rown);
lstsq(a,y,coln,rown, coln,u,s,v,z,resid,work );
exit(0);
}
```

```
pvd(v,n) int n;double v[];
{
int btm,top,i;
btm=0;
top=0;
while (btm<n)
    {
    top=min(btm+6,n);
    printf(" printing vector from %d to %d\n",btm,(top-1));
    for(i=btm;i<top;i++)printf(" %e",v[i]);
    printf("\n");
    btm+=6;
    }
return;
}

mvd(a,x,y,n,m,coln) int n,coln,m;
double x[],y[],a[];
/* y=ax a(m,n) */
{
int i,j;
double sum;
DOFOR(i,m)
    {
    sum=0.;
    DOFOR(j,n) sum+= x[j]*a INDEX(i,j);
    y[i]=sum;
    }
return;
}
mvtd(a,x,y,n,m,coln) int n,coln,m;
double x[],y[],a[];
/* y=a[t]x a(m,n) */
{
int i,j;
double sum;
DOFOR(i,n)
```

```
    {
    sum=0.;
    DOFOR(j,m) sum+= x[j]*a INDEX(j,i);
    y[i]=sum;
    }
return;
}


vdifd(x,y,z,n) int n; double x[],y[],z[];
/*z=x-y*/
{
int i;
DOFOR(i,n)z[i]=x[i]-y[i];
return;
}
```

```
/*
Singular Value Decomposition (SVD) of a matrix
(from "C Tools for Scientists and Engineers" by L. Baker)

CONTENTS:
svd()    calculates SVD
diag()    second half of SVD calculation
dsign() type double function. equivalent to FORTRAN sign
   transfer function
printmd() print double precision matrix    (as in qrn package)

DEPENDENCIES:
   NONE
*/
/*
  #include "libc.h"
  #include "math.h"
 */
/* defines below are from ftoc.h except for IU,DFFOR */
#define INDEX(i,j) [j+(i)*coln]
#define IU(i,j) [j+(i)*colu]
#define DOFOR(i,j) for(i=0;i<j;i++)
#define DFFOR(i,from,to) for(i=from;i<to;i++)
#define min(a,b) (((a)<(b))? (a): (b))
#define max(a,b) (((a)<(b))? (b): (a))
#define abs(x)  ( ((x)>0.)?(x):-(x))


#define itmax 30


printmd(a,coln,rown,col,row) int rown,row,col,coln; double a[];
{
int i,j,btm,top,count,ncol=4;/*4 col max*/
printf("\n");
btm=top=0;
while(btm<col)
   {
```

```
    top=min(col,(btm+ncol));
    printf(" printing matrix columns %d to %d\n",btm,(top-1));
    DOFOR(j,row)
        {
        for(i=btm;i<top;i++)
            {
            printf(" %e",a INDEX(j,i));
            }
        printf("\n");
        }
    btm+=ncol;
    }
return;
}
svd(coln,m,n,a,w,matu,u,matv,v,ierr,rv1)
int coln,m,n,matu,matv,*ierr;
double a[],w[],u[],v[],rv1[];
/*
    all matrices a,u,v have coln>=n columns

    a(m,n)  v(n,n) u(m,n or m )

typically, m>n.

matu = 0 do not compute u
       1 compute  u(m,n)
       -1 compute u(m,m)
NB: U MUST BE DIMENSIONED (M,N) IF MATU =1 AND (M,M) IF MATU
matv = 0 do not compute v
       1 compute v
ierr= error return integer
rv1    working storage (see text)
*/
{
int i,j,k,mn,i1,l,l1,its,m1,n1,k1,top,colu;
double sqrt(),dsign(),dum,c,f,g,h,s,x,y,z,eps,scale,anorm;
*ierr=0;
colu=n;
```

```
if (matu<0)colu=m;
/*printmd(a,coln,m,n,m);*/


m1=m-1;
n1=n-1;
DOFOR(i.m)
    {
    DOFOR(j,n) u IU(i,j)= a INDEX(i,j);
    }
/* reduction to bidiagonal form via Householder xfms*/
g=0.;
scale=0.;
anorm=0.;
DOFOR(i,n)
    {
    l=i+1;
    rv1[i]=g*scale;
    g=0.;
    s=0.;
    scale=0.;
    if(i<=m1)/* in fortran, <= but c i runs 0-m1*/
        {
        DFFOR(k,i,m)scale+= abs(u IU(k,i));
        if(scale!=0.)
            {
            DFFOR(k,i,m)
                {
                dum=u IU(k,i)/scale;
                s+=dum*dum;
                u IU(k,i)=dum;
                }
            f= u IU(i,i);
            g= -dsign(sqrt(s),f);
            h=1./(f*g-s);/* 1/h of others- * faster than / */
            u IU(i,i)=f-g;
            if (i!=n1)
                {
                DFFOR(j,l,n)
```

```
                        {
                        s=0.;
                        DFFOR(k,i,m)s+=
                         u IU(k,i)*u IU(k,j);
                        f=s*h;
                        DFFOR(k,i,m)
                           u IU(k,j)+=f*u IU(k,i);
                        }
                  }/*i!=n*/
              DFFOR(k,i,m)u IU(k,i)*=scale;
              }/*scale!=0*/
          }/* i<=m*/
w[i]=scale*g;
g=0.;
s=0.;
scale=0.;
if(i<=m1 && i!=n1)
    {
    DFFOR(k,l,n)scale+= abs(u IU(i,k));
    if(scale!=0.)
        {
        DFFOR(k,l,n)
            {
            dum= u IU(i,k)/scale;
            s+=dum*dum;
            u IU(i,k)=dum;
            }
        f=u IU(i,l);
        g=-dsign(sqrt(s),f);
        h=1./(f*g-s);
        u IU(i,l)=f-g;
        DFFOR(k,l,n)rv1[k]=u IU(i,k)*h;
        if(i!=m1)
            {
            DFFOR(j,l,m)
                {
                s=0.;
                DFFOR(k,l,n)
```

```
                        s+=u IU(j,k)*u IU(i,k);
                        DFFOR(k,l,n)u IU(j,k)+=s*rv1[k];


                    }


                }
        DFFOR(k,l,n)u IU(i,k)*=scale;
        }
    }
y=abs(w[i])+abs(rv1[i]) ;
anorm= max( anorm , y);
    }
/*accum. rhs*/
/*printf(" acc rhs\n");*/
if(matv)
    {
    for(i=n-1;i>=0;i--)
        {
        if(i!=n1)
            {
            if (g!=0.)
                {/*here FMM do division by g,u indiv*/
                /*h=1./(g*u IU(i,l));*/
                DFFOR(j,l,n)v INDEX(j,i)
                    =(u IU(i,j)/u IU(i,l) )/g;
                DFFOR(j,l,n)
                    {s=0.;
                    DFFOR(k,l,n)s+=
                        u IU(i,k)*v INDEX(k,j);
                    DFFOR(k,l,n)v INDEX(k,j)+=
                        s* v INDEX(k,i);
                    }
                }
            DFFOR(j,l,n)
                {
                v INDEX(i,j)=0.;
                v INDEX(j,i)=0.;
                }
```

```
         }
      v INDEX(i,i)=1.;
      g=rv1[i];
      l=i;
      }
   }
/*accum. lhs*/
/*printf(" accum lhs\n");*/
if(matu)
   {
   if(matu==-1)
      {
      DFFOR(i,n,m)
         {
         DFFOR(j,n,m) u IU(i,j)=0.;
         u IU(i,i)=1.;
         }
      }
   mn=n;
   if(m<n) mn=m;
   top=n;
   if(matu==-1)top=m;
   for(i=mn-1;i>=0;i--)
      {
      l=i+1;
      g=w[i];
      if (i!=n1)
         {
         DFFOR(j,l,top)u IU(i,j)=0.;
         }
      if(g!=0.)
         {
         /*h= 1./(g* u IU(i,i));*/
         if(i!=(mn-1))
         {
         DFFOR(j,l,top)
            {
            s=0.;
```

```
            DFFOR(k,l,m)
               s += u IU(k,i) * u IU(k,j);
            f=(s/u IU(i,i))/g;
            DFFOR(k,i,m)u IU(k,j)+=f*u IU(k,i);
            }/* DFFOR j */
         }/* il-mn-1*/
            DFFOR(j,i,m)u IU(j,i)/=g;


         }
      else/*g=0*/
         {
         DFFOR(j,i,m)u IU(j,i)=0.;
         }
      u IU(i,i)+=1.;
         }
      }
diagon(u,v,rv1,w,anorm,coln,colu,n,m,ierr);
return;
}
diagon(u,v,rv1,w,anorm,coln,colu,n,m,ierr)
double anorm,u[],v[],rv1[],w[];
int coln,colu,n,m,*ierr;
{
int i,j,k,l,l1,nm1,k1,i1,matu,matv,its;
double c,s,h,f,g,x,z,y;
matu=1;matv=1;
/*
printf(" diagonalizing,anorm=%f\n",anorm);
pvd(w,n);pvd(rv1,n);
printmd(u,coln,m,n,m);
printmd(v,coln,n,n,n);
*/
/* diagonalize binary form*/
for(k=n-1;k>=0;k--)
   {
   k1=k-1;
   its=0;
testsplit:
```

```
   for(l=k;l>=0;l--)
      {
      l1=l-1;
/*    if ( abs(rv1[l])<=eps)goto conv;
      if(abs(w[l1])<=eps)break;
*/
      if ( abs(rv1[l])+anorm==anorm)goto conv;
      if(abs(w[l1])+anorm==anorm)break;
      }
   c=0.;
   s=1.;
   DFFOR(i,l,k+1) /* want i to range from l to k inclusive */
      {
      f=s*rv1[i];
      rv1[i]*=c;
/*    if(abs(f)>eps)
*/
      if(abs(f)+anorm!= anorm )
          {
          g=w[i];
          h=sqrt(f*f+g*g);
          w[i]=h;
          c=g/h;
          s=-f/h;
          if(matu)
             {
             DOFOR(j,m)
                {
                y=u IU(j,l1) ;
                z=u IU(j,i) ;
                u IU(j,l1)=y*c+z*s;
                u IU(j,i)=-y*s+z*c;
                }
             }/*matu*/
          }/* if */
      }/* DFFOR i,l,k*/
   conv:;
   z=w[k];
```

```
if(l!=k)
  {
  if (its>=itmax)
    {
    *ierr=k;
    return;
    }
  its++;
  x=w[l];
  y=w[k1];
  g=rv1[k1];
  h=rv1[k];
  f=((y-z)*(y+z)+(g-h)*(g+h))/(2.*h*y);
  g=sqrt(f*f+1.);
  f=((x-z)*(x+z) +h*(y/(f+dsign(g,f))-h))/x;
  /* do another QR xfm*/
  c=1.;
  s=1.;
  DFFOR(i1,l,k1+1)/* i1 ranges l to k1 inclusive*/
    {
    i=i1+1;
    g=rv1[i];
    y=w[i];
    h=s*g;
    g=c*g;
    z=sqrt(f*f+h*h);
    rv1[i1]=z;
    c=f/z;
    s=h/z;
    f=x*c+g*s;
    g=-x*s+g*c;
    h=y*s;
    y=y*c;
    if(matv)
      {
      DOFOR(j,n)
        {
        x= v INDEX(j,i1);
```

```
                      z= v INDEX(j,i);
                      v INDEX(j,i1)=
                        x*c+z*s;
                      v INDEX(j,i)=
                        -x*s+z*c;
                      }
                 }
             z=sqrt(h*h+f*f);
             w[i1]=z;
             if(z!=0.)
                 {
                 c=f/z;
                 s=h/z;
                 }
             f=c*g+s*y;
             x=-s*g+c*y;
             if(matu)
                 {
                 DOFOR(j,m)
                     {
                     y= u IU(j,i1);
                     z= u IU(j,i);
                     u IU(j,i1)=
                        y*c+z*s;
                     u IU(j,i)=
                        -y*s+z*c;
                     }
                 }
             }
         rv1[l]=0.;
         rv1[k]=f;
         w[k]=x;
         goto testsplit;
         }/*l!=k*/
/*convergence*/
if(z<0.)
    {/* make w[k] non-neg*/
    w[k]=-z;
```

```
        if(matv)
        {
        DOFOR(j,n) v INDEX(j,k)=-v INDEX(j,k);
        }
        }
    }
return;
}

double dsign(to,from) double to,from;
{
double x;
x=0.;
if(from>0.)x=1.;
if(from<0.)x=-1.;
return( x*abs(to));
}
```

ierr=0
sing value=35.127223
sing value=2.465397
sing value=0.000000
u matrix:
 printing matrix columns 0 to 2
 -3.545570E-1 -6.886866E-1 6.055520E-1
 -3.986963E-1 -3.755545E-1 -5.059518E-1
 -4.428356E-1 -6.242241E-2 -3.441072E-1
 -4.869750E-1 2.507097E-1 -2.161381E-1
 -5.311143E-1 5.638418E-1 4.606451E-1
v matrix:
 printing matrix columns 0 to 2
 -2.016649E-1 8.903171E-1 -4.082482E-1
 -5.168305E-1 2.573316E-1 8.164965E-1
 -8.319960E-1 -3.756538E-1 -4.082482E-1
ierr=0
sing value=35.127223:
sing value=2.465397:
sing value=0.000000:
u matrix:
 printing matrix columns 0 to 3
 -3.545570E-1 -6.886866E-1 6.055520E-1 -5.757403E-1
 -3.986963E-1 -3.755545E-1 -5.059518E-1 3.668383E-1
 -4.428356E-1 -6.242241E-2 -3.441072E-1 3.270464E-1
 -4.869750E-1 2.507097E-1 -2.161381E-1 5.483533E-1
 -5.311143E-1 5.638418E-1 4.606451E-1 -6.664978E-1
 printing matrix columns 4 to 4
 -5.286540E-1
 7.463180E-1
 2.175492E-1
 -5.594363E-1
 1.242231E-1
v matrix:
 printing matrix columns 0 to 2
 -2.016649E-1 8.903171E-1 -4.082482E-1
 -5.168305E-1 2.573316E-1 8.164965E-1
 -8.319960E-1 -3.756538E-1 -4.082482E-1

coef. matrix is :

printing matrix columns 0 to 2
1.000000E0 -2.000000E0 4.000000E0
1.000000E0 -2.000000E0 4.000000E0
1.000000E0 -1.000000E0 1.000000E0
1.000000E0 -1.000000E0 1.000000E0
1.000000E0 0.000000E0 0.000000E0
1.000000E0 0.000000E0 0.000000E0
1.000000E0 1.000000E0 1.000000E0
1.000000E0 1.000000E0 1.000000E0
1.000000E0 2.000000E0 4.000000E0
1.000000E0 2.000000E0 4.000000E0
rhs is
printing vector from 0 to 3
1.100000E0 1.300000E0 2.000000E0 2.100000E0
printing vector from 4 to 7
2.700000E0 2.800000E0 3.400000E0 3.600000E0
printing vector from 8 to 9
4.100000E0 4.000000E0
ierr=0
singular values=
printing vector from 0 to 2
8.615557E0 1.942207E0 4.472136E0

printing matrix columns 0 to 2
-4.777907E-1 1.207191E-1 4.472136E-1
-4.777907E-1 1.207191E-1 4.472136E-1
-1.453291E-1 -3.385169E-1 2.236068E-1
-1.453291E-1 -3.385169E-1 2.236068E-1
-3.450857E-2 -4.915956E-1 1.495917E-16
-3.450857E-2 -4.915956E-1 1.495917E-16
-1.453291E-1 -3.385169E-1 -2.236068E-1
-1.453291E-1 -3.385169E-1 -2.236068E-1
-4.777907E-1 1.207191E-1 -4.472136E-1
-4.777907E-1 1.207191E-1 -4.472136E-1

printing matrix columns 0 to 2

-2.973106E-1 -9.547808E-1 8.657743E-17
4.814340E-17 -1.056692E-16 -1.000000E0
-9.547808E-1 2.973106E-1 -9.321233E-17
answer is:
printing vector from 0 to 2
2.788571E0 7.150000E-1 -3.928571E-2
residual errors for each eqn:
printing vector from 0 to 3
1.014285E-1 -9.857142E-2 3.428571E-2 -6.571428E-2
printing vector from 4 to 7
8.857142E-2 -1.142857E-2 6.428571E-2 -1.357142E-1
printing vector from 8 to 9
-3.857142E-2 6.142857E-2

CHAPTER 6

Newton-Raphson and Related Methods

Chapter Objectives

In this chapter you will find C tools to:

-solve systems of nonlinear equations using a modified form of the Newton-Raphson (NR) iteration. The modification is intended to increase the robustness of the method, i.e., its ability to find the solution even with a poor initial guess.

- treat a multi-species ionization equilibrium, a model for similar chemical equilibrium problems.

The Newton-Raphson iteration developed here will be encountered again in Chapter 13 where it will serve as the basis for a number of routines to determine the inverse of a function given the function itself.

Nonlinear System Solvers

In this chapter and the next, we consider the solution of nonlinear equations. We discuss here the most commonly used method for solving such problems, the Newton-Raphson method. All methods for solving nonlinear problems (except for special cases, such as polynomial equations of degree less than 5) require iteration from an initial guess. Generally, convergence of the iteration to a solution for an arbitrary initial guess cannot be assured. Indeed, the Newton-Raphson method in its most primitive form can easily go astray because of problems which are not obviously pathological. With a simple enhancement or two, it can be made much more robust, however, and we will discuss such tricks.

In Chapter 13 we apply the Newton-Raphson method to invert a known function, i.e., a system of one equation, $y - f(x) = 0$ with y known and x to be found. This is used to determine the inverse of the error function, and a general routine, invr(), is provided which is used to give the inverse of the Student's t and other distribution functions.

The Newton-Raphson Method

Let us first discuss the problem of finding a simple variable x to satisfy the equation f(x) = 0. The function f(x) is assumed to be real but otherwise general. Let us start with an initial "guess" as to the appropriate x, say x[0]. If f(x) were a simple linear function, i.e. f(x) = ax + b, we could solve for the appropriate root as x = − b/a. Let us locally (in the neighborhood of our guess for x) approximate f as such a function. The function f will be approximated by the straight line which passes through x[0],f(x[0]) and is tangent to the function at that point, i.e. has slope f′(x[0]). We wish to determine the adjustment to x[0], i.e. the point x[1] = x[0] + dx, such that at x[1] this tangent line intersects the x axis. As the function f will not exactly equal zero here—unless it is a linear function or we are very lucky—we will have to iterate to achieve the desired accuracy. So let us write more generally x[n + 1] = x[n] + dx. We find as above that dx = − f(x[n])/f′(x[n]). Thus, if we can evaluate f and its derivative, we can perform the basic Newton-Raphson iteration. Often, the derivative is evaluated numerically, i.e., something like

$$f'(x[n]) = \{f(x[n] + ds) - f(x[n] - ds)\}/2ds$$

(it would be more economical but somewhat less accurate to use uncentered differencing, so that one of the function evaluations would be f(x[n]), and thus we could re-use this value). Such a method is then very similar to the "secant method" and the "rule of false position" or regula falsi methods for the same problem. Such an iteration is carried out until either: 1) the residual value of f(x[n]) is within the desired tolerance of zero, or 2) the change in x, i.e., dx, is either so small that the root has been found to the necessary accuracy, or the precision limits of the calculation, or 3) something has gone wrong, and dx is oscillating wildly or shows some other pathological behavior. This could mean, for example, that x represents some physical variable, e.g., a density or temperature, which should be positive but which has been extrapolated along the tangent line to a negative value. We will discuss what to do in such cases below.

In many cases of importance, such problems don't arise, and the Newton-Raphson iteration can be a stellar performer. It can converge to the desired root quadratically, which means that if the error in x is small, it squares itself on each iteration. An error of .1 becomes an error of .01, then .0001, then .00000001, etc. For example, suppose we want to find the square root of a number. The square root of A solves the equation x − A = 0. Thus we set f(x) to the left-hand side of this equation, and f′ = 2x. Thus x[n + 1] = {x[n] + A/x[n]}/2 is the Newton-Raphson iteration for finding square roots. This method is well-behaved and is often used in library square root routines.

The CRAY-1 computer does its floating point long division by computing an approximate quotient, and then using a Newton- Raphson iteration to refine the answer. Suppose we were determining the reciprocal of A, $x = 1/A$. The iteration would be $x[n + 1] = x[n]\{2 - Ax[n]\}$. As an example, take $A = 3, x[0] = .5$. Then $x[1] = .25, x[2] = .3125, x[3] = .332,...$, etc.

Multi-Dimensional Form

The Newton-Raphson iteration described above may readily be extended to handle multi-variable problems. The single-variable problem may be called the "one-dimensional" search as we move from iteration to iteration along the x axis. Hence the term "multi-dimensional search" when there are a number of variables, as we will be searching in a number of directions for a number of variables. Just let **x** be a vector of values. The entire discussion carries through with f being a vector of function values **f** (n values for n variables), **dx** a vector of corrections to **x**. The operation of dividing by f′ is replaced by multiplying the **f** vector by the inverse of a matrix of derivatives, called the Jacobian matrix, $J[i][j] = df[i]/dx[j]$ (here $x[j]$ refers to the j-th variable, not the j-th iteration). That is, we solve the linear system of equations **J dx = −f** Note, as discussed in Chapter 3, it is more economical to solve this system than to form the matrix **J**, invert it, and do the matrix multiplication of the vector.

Pitfalls and Fixes

Sadly, the Newton-Raphson iteration can go wrong if the initial guess is too far from the desired zero, even if the function is not obviously pathological. An obviously pathological function would have a minimum or valley between the initial guess and the desired zero. If the valley were above the axis, we could get trapped within—without ever getting near the axis.

A more insidious case involves a point of inflection, i.e. $f''(x) = 0$, of the function. Consider, for example, $f(x) = \arctan(x)$. This function has a zero and a point of inflection at $x = 0$. If the initial guess is sufficiently close to zero, there will be no problem, and the root $x = 0$ will be found quickly. However, if the initial guess is too large, figure 6.1 illustrates what will happen. Starting at the point labeled 1, we follow the tangent to the point $x[2]$. But because there is an inflection point between 1 and 2, and because of the relatively small value of the slope of f at 2, we get sent to point x[3]. Note that the sign of dx is correct, but its magnitude is too large. The iteration diverges, as the slopes continually decrease as we get further away from the origin. For the function arctan(x), $x[n + 1] = x[n] - \arctan(x[n])(1 + x^2)$. We can show that divergence will occur if the initial guess is larger in magnitude than approximately 1.4 . Another troublesome case would be a multiple zero, i.e., $f(x) = x^2$ where the tangent to f(x) as we approach the desired root tends toward the horizontal. Thanks to finite precision arithmetic, we could easily find ourselves with a large dx due to

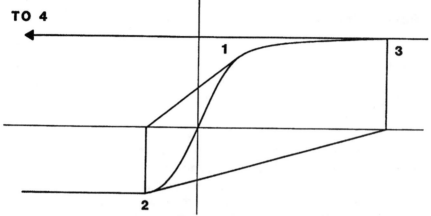

Fig. 6.1: Failure near Inflection Point.

the small divisor $f'(x)$.

In the pathological case with intermediate minima, little can be done. In the case of a multiple zero or a point of inflection, however, there is a relatively simple fix. Notice that the sign of the correction dx is correct, but that the size is too large. This in turn results in the error |f(x)| increasing instead of decreasing from the n-th step to the n +1 st step. A fix would be to remember the value of f(x[n]), and if f(x[n + 1]) were larger in magnitude, to reject the iteration, and to go into a loop in which dx was successively halved until a smaller value for f(x[n] + dx) was achieved. This new value for x would be accepted as x[n + 1]. If it were indistinguishable numerically from x[n], we would terminate the program with the knowledge that the Newton-Raphson iteration did the best it could.

This fix is not perfect of course. It won't improve a situation in which the sign of dx is wrong, or dx is too small. Either may occur if there is a valley or local minimum between the guess and the desired root. But it will work to make any "reasonable" function treatable by the NR method.

The fix clearly generalizes to the multi-dimensional problem. Some appropriate measure of error should be found, the obvious one being the length $|f(x)|$ of the vector $\mathbf{f}$, or, perhaps, the magnitude of the largest component of the vector. In the absence of any special knowledge, it would be safest to halve each component of the vector $\mathbf{dx}$.

R. W. Hamming (see reference in Chapter 4) recommends for the one-dimensional form of the NR iteration that, if it is found necessary to cut the step dx in this manner, it be limited in subsequent timesteps, e.g., not be allowed to more than double in magnitude per timestep. This gets to be cumbersome in multi-dimensional problems.

Related Methods

The simpler search methods mentioned above tend to be more robust than NR, but slower to converge to the root when near to it. Consequently, a hybrid method, which combines the best features of both, is of interest. Such methods are called "variable metric" methods, for they "evolve" from some simpler, more robust method when the error measure or metric is large, to the rapidly converging NR method when the error appears relatively small and the use of the NR iteration is probably both safe and fast. In addition, the evaluation of the Jacobian matrix can be a major computational expense, depending upon the cost of the function evaluation, and depending upon whether there is an analytic form available for computing the derivatives or whether these must be calculated numerically. This leads to so-called "updating" methods, in which the exact Jacobian is not re-computed each iteration, but merely approximately updated, and re-computed only periodically. As a result, there are a number of "quasi-Newton" methods which address one or both of the problems discussed.

Obviously, the problem of minimizing the function $F(x) = |f(x)|$ is the same as finding the root of $f(x)$, as here $F(x)$ will achieve its smallest possible value, zero. Thus, the more general problem of minimizing a function $F(x)$ provides a root-finding method. Note that the "valleys" that troubled us in the problem of finding zeros are a successful determination of a local minimum in this new context, not a failure to find a smaller minimum further away.

Program and Test Case

The test problem is a typical physics problem, to determine the ionization equilibrium of vaporized sand. Such a plasma would have silicon and oxygen atoms, in a ratio of 2:1, in equilibrium with a common sea of electrons. The total number of bound and free electrons would have to be conserved, and since the material may be assumed to have been initially uncharged, it should have no net charge. Thus, the number of electrons should equal the total charge on the ions. In addition, the number of nuclei should be conserved, both for oxygen and silicon.

In addition to these three conservation equations (electrons, oxygen, and silicon), we have the Saha equations for ionization equilibrium between the species. These may be viewed as the result of applying the law of detailed balance to the situation. Let, for example, O[0] denote the density of un-ionized oxygen, in, say, atoms per cubic centimeter, O[1] singly ionized oxygen, etc. The rate of formation of O[0] by the recombination of an electron with a singly ionized oxygen ion will be proportional to O[1]ne2, where ne is the electron number density. This assumes that the recombination is by the three-body collision mechanism. In deriving equilibrium formulae, we must assume collisional processes. Three bodies are needed to participate in the collision process if momentum and energy are both to be conserved during recombination. We will not treat radiative recombination—in local thermodynamic equilibrium, the plasma must be optically thick, and such radiation would have no net effct, as it would form a "bath" of radiation that would ionize atoms. This neutral formation rate, or loss of O[1] to O[0], must balance the rate of formation of O[1] from O[0], in equilibrium, by the principle of detailed balance. This proceeds by the inverse process, collisional ionization, in which an electron collides with a neutral oxygen atom, producing two electrons and one O[1] ion. Such a process occurs with a rate proportional to O[0]ne. Therefore, we must have a balance between rates of the form

O[0]ne/O[1] = A

where A is independent of the number densities O[i] and ne, but depends upon the physics of the collisional processes involved. Thus A depends upon the temperature, as this controls how fast things are moving in the plasma and hence how often things collide, as well as how much energy they have to transfer in such collisions to ionize atoms. As written, A will be of the general form B exp(− I/kT) $T^{3/2}$ u{O[1]}/u{O[0]} where u{ } is the statistical weight of the species involved (which is (2J+1) for atomic states, typically, where J is the spin of the state), and the factor of 2 for the statistical weight has been absorbed into the constant B, and I is the ionization potential, k is Boltzmann's constant, and T the temperature. For temperature T and I measured in electron volts, B = 6.e21, approximately. Some books will give a similar form with the exponent 5/2 replacing 3/2— they are using the partial pressures of the species rather than their densities, and this gives an extra factor of T to the expression (as well as altering B).

The program generates an initial approximation, most suitable for low temperatures, assuming that the oxygen and silicon atoms interact with separate electron seas (they do not), and that only singly-ionized atoms are present. Then ne = O[1] = x O[total] and O[0] = (1 − x)O[total], x being the fractional ionization. This permits a closed-form solution of the Saha equation with the conservation equations. An interesting numerical pitfall must be sidestepped here. In solving the quadratic equation for the electron density, we have an expression of the general form

$$\{\sqrt{(1 + 2a)} - 1\}/a$$

The proper behavior is that for small a, the square root should approximate 1 + a, and the expression should evaluate to 1, i.e., full ionization. (For large a, the expression tends to zero.) However, in finite-precision arithmetic, the square root will approach 1 for sufficiently small a, and the expression will become zero for such small values of a. The function, instead of monotonically going from 1 for small a to zero for large a, will have a maximum at fairly small a, but zeros at both large and small a. This pitfall illustrates a number of dangers, most especially the loss of precision upon subtracting two numbers of the same sign and similar magnitudes, as well as the dangers of using "exact" formulae without care.

The Jacobian matrix is obtained by numerical differentiation. I STRONGLY ADVISE you to obtain the Jacobian numerically in this manner, at least in preliminary debugging. The reason is that this will tend to ensure that the Jacobian is consistent with the system of equations you wish to solve. Once you have debugged the code in this manner, you can save computation costs by finding analytic expressions for part or all of the Jacobian matrix.

The main routine is the test problem driver, and it accepts as input the density in grams/cc. It then solves the system of equations for a variety of temperatures, iterating to desired convergence criteria which are input (see the sample program run for appropriate values to use). For the temperature regime of interest, only the un-ionized and singly and doubly ionized states of each atom are considered. The particular form of the Saha equations, as implemented in function sahac(), puts all of the fractional number densities in the numerator and the large number in the denominator to reduce numerical difficulties. This form was achieved after experimentation with other, less suitable representations. Function dr() performs the numerical differentiation required to form the Jacobian matrix. It returns the partial derivatives df[i]/dx[j]. The difference dx[j] is formed as the sum of a constant term plus a term proportional to x[j], so as to provide a significant interval in x whether x[j] is zero or x[j] is very large. Subroutine saha() does the work, namely, generating the initial guess (as we step in temperature we use as our guess the solution for the previous lower temperature, except of course for the first case). The bulk of this subroutine does the NR iteration, including the fix when the residual error vector magnitude increases.

We did not in this case write a general routine, say, nr(), which sahac() would call. To do so would have deterred the user from modifying the "guts" of such a routine, which is often desirable. For example, in the ionization equilibrium problem discussed here, it is useful to prevent the populations from becoming negative or larger than the total species population available. To modify this routine for other problems would not be difficult in general.

Table 6.1

Functions and Subroutines of Chapter 6

sahac	Type double function: returns right-hand side of Saha equation
eqn	Type double function: returns the residual of each equation to be solved (zero if the equation is exactly satisfied)
dr	Type double function: performs numerical differentiation to form Jacobian matrix
saha	Terforms NR iteration to solve the system of nonlinear ionization equilibrium equations

---

It will be seen from the sample case that our initial approximation is none too good; the low-temperature approximation is poor at our starting temperature. Indeed, the modification to the NR method for inflection points does not help, and the residuals initially increase. But once we get near the answer, the convergence is very rapid. And the subsequent higher-temperature cases rapidly converge with the superior guess provided by the previous (lower-temperature) solution.

Table 6.1 lists the routines used in this chapter's tools.

Program Listing and Test Problem Output

```
/* Newton-Raphson iteration solution of system of nonlinear
equations. Modified for greater robustness
near points of inflection.

TEST PROBLEM:
solve the Saha equations for the ionization equilibrium of
SiO2

(from "C Tools for  Scientists and Engineers" by L. Baker)

DEPENDENCIES:
uses linear system solver from Chapter 3
uses pv() function in vector.c
*/

#define abs(x)  ((x)>=0? (x): -(x))

/* in-line functions for use with 2D arrays: */

/* row major order as in C  indices run 0..n-1 as in C*/
#define INDEX(i,j)  [j+(i)*coln]

/*various loop constructors */
#define DOFOR(i,to) for(i=0;i<to;i++)
#define DFOR(i,from,to) for(i=from-1;i<to;i++)
#define DOBY(i,from,to,by) for(i=from-1;i<to;i+=by)
#define DOBYY(i,from,to,by) for(i=from;i<t;i+=by)
#define DOBYYY(i,from,to) for(i=from;i<to;i++)
#define DOV(i,to,by) for(i=0;i<to;i+=by)
/* row major order as in C  indices run 1..n */
/*#define INDEX1(i,j)  [j-1+(i-1)*n]
*/
/* column major order, as in FORTRAN: */
#define INDEXC(i,j) [i-1+(j-1)*rown]

/* usage: if a(20,30) is matrix, then
a(i,j) in C will be a INDEX(i,j) if n=30 */
```

```
#define min(a,b) (((a)<(b))? (a): (b))
#define max(a,b) (((a)>(b))? (a): (b))

float pop[10],fns,fno,fscale,dmult,dadd,tf,conv,conv2,rcon;

#define ne 8
#define neq 9

main(argc,argv) int argc;char **argv;
{
float rho,t,fne;
int i,j;
printf(" enter density (g/cc) ");
scanf(" %f",&rho);
printf(" rho=%f\n enter conv,conv2,rcon",rho);
scanf("%e %e %e",&conv,&conv2,&rcon);
printf("echo %e %e %e\n",conv,conv2,rcon);
pop[8]=0.;
fno=rho/(1.6e-24*(16.+.5*28.));
fns=.5*fno;
for(i=1;i<9;i++)
{t=i;
fne=saha(fns,fno,t);
printf(" t=%f rho=%f\n",t,rho);
pv(pop,neq);
}
exit(0);
}

/* u[]i[] i=1 silicon 2=oxygen are the statistical weights
of the ionic ground states
    pi are the ionization potentials in eV
    */
float u[12][2]={1.,5.,2.,4.,1.,1.,2.,3.,1.,1.,4.,
2.,5.,1.,4.,2.,1.,0.,3.,0.,1.,0.,3.,0.};
float pi[12][2]={8.149,13.614,16.34,35.146,33.46,54.934,
45.13,77.394,166.7,113.873,205.11,138.080,
```

```
246.41,739.114,303.87,871.12,351.83,0.,401.3,0.,476.0,0.,523.2,0.};

double sahac(iatom,istate,t)
float t;
int iatom,istate;
{
double sa; double exp();

sa= 6.e21*u[istate+1][iatom]/u[istate][iatom]
   *exp(-pi[istate][iatom]/t);
return (fscale/sa);
}
double eqn(i,f) float f[]; int i;
{
double x;
/* the equations to be solved-Saha unless noted*/
switch (i)
    {
    case 0: x=f[ne]*f[1]-f[0]/sahac(0,0,tf);
       break;
    case 1: x=f[ne]*f[2]-f[1]/sahac(0,1,tf);
       break;
    case 2: x=f[ne]*f[3]-f[2]/sahac(0,2,tf);
       break;
/* conservation of silicon nuclei: */
    case 3: x=f[0]+f[1]+f[2]+f[3]-fns/fscale;
       break;
    case 4: x=f[ne]*f[5]-f[4]/sahac(1,0,tf);
       break;
    case 5: x=f[ne]*f[6]-f[5]/sahac(1,1,tf);
       break;
    case 6: x=f[ne]*f[7]-f[6]/sahac(1,2,tf);
       break;
/* conservation of oxygen nuclei:*/
    case 7: x=f[4]+f[5]+f[6]+f[7]-fno/fscale;
       break;
/* charge neutrality:*/
    case 8: x=f[1]+2.*f[2]+3.*f[3]
```

```
            +f[5]+2.*f[6]+3.*f[7] -f[ne];
            break;

    }
return (x);
}


/* numerical differentiation for forming Jacobian matrix:*/
double dr(ieq,j,f) int ieq,j;
float f[];
{
double hold,dx,dn;
hold=eqn(ieq,f);
dx=f[j]*dmult+dadd;
f[j]+=dx;
dn=eqn(ieq,f);
f[j]-=dx;
return( (dn-hold)/dx);
}


#define itmax 20
#define ihmax 10
#define fignore 1.e-5

float b[9],a[9][9];



saha(fns,fno,t) float fns,fno,t;
{
int iter,coln,info,pivot[9],i,j,ic,ih;
double sqrt(),eqn(),dr();
float resid,newresid,fm,arg,abarg,relarg,rworst,aworst,fnsi,fnoi;
float popmin,popmax;
tf=t;
fscale=1.e20;
fnsi=fns/fscale;
fnoi=fno/fscale;
```

```
popmin=0.;
popmax=10.*(fnsi+fnoi);

printf("f=%e %e scaled %e %e\n ",fno,fns,fnoi,fnsi);
dmult=.001;
dadd=.01*fnoi;
/* initial guess*/
if (pop[neq-1]==0.)
   {
   arg=sahac(0,0,t);
   if (arg>1.e-4)
      fm=(sqrt(1.+2.*arg)-1.)/arg;
   else
      fm=1.;

   pop[0]=fns*(1.-fm);
   pop[1]=fns*fm;
   pop[ne]=pop[1];
   pop[3]=.0001*pop[1];
   pop[2]=0.;
   arg=sahac(1,0,t);
   if (arg>1.e-4)
      fm=(sqrt(1.+2.*arg)-1.)/arg;
   else
      fm=1.;

   pop[4]=fno*(1.-fm);
   pop[5]=fno*fm;
   pop[neq-1]+=pop[5];/*electron number density*/
   pop[6]=.0001*pop[5];
   pop[7]=0.;
   };
DOFOR(i,neq)printf(" guess pop=%e\n",pop[i]);

coln=neq;/* number of equations*/
/*scaling*/
DOFOR(i,neq) pop[i]=pop[i]/fscale;
```

```
/* Newton-Raphson iteration*/
DOFOR(iter,itmax)
{

/*rhs residual vector-
also calculate sq. error */
resid=0.;
DOFOR(i,neq)
    {
    arg=-eqn(i,pop);
    resid+=arg*arg;
    b[i]=arg;
    DOFOR(j,neq)
       {/* JACOBIAN*/
       a[i][j]=dr(i,j,pop);
       };
    };
printf(" square residual sum=%e\n",resid);
if (resid<rcon)
       {
       ic=-1;
       goto converged;
       }
lufact(a,coln,neq,pivot,&info);

DOFOR(i,j)printf("resid=%e\n",b[i]);
if( info!=0)
    {
    printf(" bad Jacobian, index=%d\n",info);
    goto salvage;
    }
backsub(a,coln,neq,pivot,b);
ic=-1;
rworst=0.;
aworst=0.;
DOFOR(i,neq)
    {
    arg=abs(b[i]);
```

```
    abarg=abs(pop[i]);
    relarg= (arg/(abarg+fignore));
    if(relarg<conv || arg<conv2)continue;
    ic=i;
    rworst= max(rworst,relarg);
    aworst= max(aworst,arg);
    };
converged:
if(ic<0)
    {/*converged*/
    DOFOR(i,neq)pop[i]*=fscale;
    return;
    };

printf(" no converge i %d,f[i]=%e,b[i]=%e\n rworst=%e,aworst=%e\n"
,ic,pop[ic],b[ic],rworst,aworst);
/* no good*/
salvage:
DOFOR(j,neq)printf(" f=%e,df=%e\n",pop[j],b[j]);
    /*tentatively update solution */
    DOFOR(i,neq)
        {
        pop[i]+=b[i];
        pop[i]=max(pop[i],popmin);
        pop[i]=min(pop[i],popmax);
        }
DOFOR(ih,ihmax)
    {
    /* have things gotten better? */
    newresid=0.;
    DOFOR(i,neq)
        {
        arg=-eqn(i,pop);
        newresid+=arg*arg;
        };
    if(newresid<resid)break;/* exit ih loop*/
    /*things got worse*/
    printf(" new residual=%e worse\n",newresid);
```

```
    /* cancel  half of the previous update*/
    /* this will ensure convergence near inflection points
    -it assumes we are going in the right direction with b[]
    corrections, merely too far*/
    /* example- if pop were initially 0, b 1, then
          first update(above) pop=1
          after loop below(once) b=.5 pop=1-.5=.5
                          twice b=.25 pop=.25
                          thrice b=.125 pop=.125
                          etc.
      */
    DOFOR(i,neq)
       {
       b[i]*=.5;
       pop[i]-=b[i];
       }
    }/* ih loop*/;
/*continue NR iteration*/
}/* iter loop*/
    printf(" no convergence NR\n");
exit(0);
}
```

```
nr
 enter density (g/cc) .01
 rho=0.010000
 enter conv,conv2,rcon .01 .001 1.e-10
echo 9.999999E-3 1.000000E-3 1.000000E-10
f=2.083333E20 1.041666E20 scaled 2.083333E0 1.041666E0
 guess pop=8.010783E19
 guess pop=2.405883E19
 guess pop=0.000000E0
 guess pop=2.405883E15
 guess pop=2.060879E20
 guess pop=2.245425E18
 guess pop=2.245425E14
 guess pop=0.000000E0
 guess pop=2.630425E19
 square residual sum=1.293816E-3
resid=-3.550125E-2
resid=5.781278E-7
resid=-6.328299E-6
resid=-2.404790E-5
resid=-5.785418E-3
resid=-5.907848E-7
resid=5.612334E-28
resid=-2.190226E-6
resid=-7.667548E-5
 no converge i 8,f[i]=2.630425E-1,b[i]=-7.457716E-2
 rworst=6.955301E-1,aworst=7.457716E-2
 f=8.010783E-1,df=5.896924E-2
 f=2.405883E-1,df=-5.897768E-2
 f=0.000000E0,df=1.663697E-6
 f=2.405808E-5,df=-1.723843E-5
 f=2.060879E0,df=1.562403E-2
 f=2.245425E-2,df=-1.562456E-2
 f=2.245966E-6,df=-1.609195E-6
 f=0.000000E0,df=1.966248E-9
 f=2.630425E-1,df=-7.457716E-2
 square residual sum=2.070351E-5
resid=-4.398379E-3
```

resid=1.228859E-7
resid=-1.285291E-6
resid=-5.398462E-8
resid=-1.165236E-3
resid=-1.199371E-7
resid=-3.506935E-10
resid=-6.143359E-8
resid=1.901140E-8
 no converge i 8,f[i]=1.884654E-1,b[i]=-1.400441E-2
 rworst=8.294959E-1,aworst=1.400441E-2
 f=8.600475E-1,df=8.317695E-3
 f=1.816106E-1,df=-8.312116E-3
 f=1.663541E-6,df=6.691557E-7
 f=6.819774E-6,df=-6.312907E-6
 f=2.076503E0,df=5.674012E-3
 f=6.829688E-3,df=-5.673494E-3
 f=6.363882E-7,df=-5.890997E-7
 f=1.860784E-9,df=-1.806582E-9
 f=1.884654E-1,df=-1.400441E-2
 square residual sum=1.986340E-8
resid=-1.164064E-4
resid=9.340538E-9
resid=-8.830053E-8
resid=1.838912E-9
resid=-7.945388E-5
resid=-8.115858E-9
resid=1.162455E-29
resid=-9.927820E-8
resid=1.140078E-8
 t=1.000000 rho=0.010000
 printing vector from 0 to 3
 8.683653E19 1.732985E19 2.333423E14 5.061333E13
 printing vector from 4 to 7
 2.082177E20 1.156194E17 4.651961E12 0.000000E0
 printing vector from 8 to 8
 1.744610E19
f=2.083333E20 1.041666E20 scaled 2.083333E0 1.041666E0
 guess pop=8.683653E19

```
guess pop=1.732985E19
guess pop=2.333423E14
guess pop=5.061333E13
guess pop=2.082177E20
guess pop=1.156194E17
guess pop=4.651961E12
guess pop=0.000000E0
guess pop=1.744610E19
square residual sum=3.044321E0
resid=1.741305E0
resid=1.470990E-3
resid=-8.828534E-8
resid=-5.776573E-8
resid=1.103374E-1
resid=-7.711034E-9
resid=9.866029E-18
resid=-9.927820E-8
resid=1.140078E-8
no converge i 8,f[i]=1.744610E-1,b[i]=1.213494E0
rworst=3.264007E3,aworst=1.213494E0
f=8.683653E-1,df=-6.945132E-1
f=1.732985E-1,df=6.542592E-1
f=2.333423E-6,df=4.025638E-2
f=5.061333E-7,df=-2.582452E-6
f=2.082177E0,df=-4.787276E-1
f=1.156194E-3,df=4.787288E-1
f=4.651960E-8,df=5.930091E-7
f=0.000000E0,df=-6.109744E-9
f=1.744610E-1,df=1.213494E0
square residual sum=9.702127E-1
resid=-7.939402E-1
resid=-4.885090E-2
resid=2.619960E-7
resid=-2.016382E-6
resid=-5.809347E-1
resid=-7.204198E-7
resid=1.357565E-16
resid=-1.990666E-6
```

resid=-6.048591E-6
 no converge i 8,f[i]=1.387955E0,b[i]=-4.242075E-1
 rworst=7.980300E-1,aworst=4.242075E-1
 f=1.738521E-1,df=1.387472E-1
 f=8.275578E-1,df=-1.151531E-1
 f=4.025872E-2,df=-2.359625E-2
 f=0.000000E0,df=6.960353E-8
 f=1.603449E0,df=2.618671E-1
 f=4.798850E-1,df=-2.618682E-1
 f=6.401098E-7,df=-3.894713E-7
 f=0.000000E0,df=7.641646E-9
 f=1.387955E0,df=-4.242075E-1
 square residual sum=1.482673E-2
resid=-4.884917E-2
resid=-1.000972E-2
resid=4.208303E-8
resid=1.462170E-7
resid=-1.110868E-1
resid=-1.657640E-7
resid=-7.173309E-9
resid=-5.661243E-7
resid=9.003889E-7
 no converge i 8,f[i]=9.637480E-1,b[i]=-9.433630E-2
 rworst=5.187979E-1,aworst=9.433630E-2
 f=3.125993E-1,df=-3.335788E-3
 f=7.124046E-1,df=1.198560E-2
 f=1.666246E-2,df=-8.649642E-3
 f=6.884901E-8,df=-8.143664E-9
 f=1.865316E0,df=8.902086E-2
 f=2.180168E-1,df=-8.902122E-2
 f=2.512058E-7,df=-1.797519E-7
 f=7.443137E-9,df=-5.402530E-9
 f=9.637480E-1,df=-9.433630E-2
 square residual sum=7.246934E-5
resid=1.130781E-3
resid=-8.159789E-4
resid=-1.241073E-9
resid=-2.887902E-8

resid=-8.397907E-3
resid=-1.631016E-8
resid=-1.617787E-9
resid=-7.516875E-9
resid=-1.226033E-7
 no converge i 5,f[i]=1.289956E-1,b[i]=-8.115259E-3
 rworst=6.290624E-2,aworst=8.115259E-3
 f=3.092635E-1,df=-1.895107E-3
 f=7.243902E-1,df=2.741719E-3
 f=8.012823E-3,df=-8.466367E-4
 f=6.140588E-8,df=-6.454815E-9
 f=1.954337E0,df=8.115268E-3
 f=1.289956E-1,df=-8.115259E-3
 f=7.070980E-8,df=-2.145347E-8
 f=1.860784E-9,df=-1.634508E-9
 f=8.694117E-1,df=-7.066746E-3
 square residual sum=3.700210E-9
resid=1.939694E-5
resid=-5.983755E-6
resid=-1.502965E-9
resid=1.814718E-8
resid=-5.734247E-5
resid=6.037447E-10
resid=1.026067E-17
resid=-5.678423E-9
resid=6.452549E-8
 t=2.000000 rho=0.010000
 printing vector from 0 to 3
 3.073685E19 7.271319E19 7.166188E17 5.582353E12
 printing vector from 4 to 7
 1.962452E20 1.208803E19 4.838039E12 0.000000E0
 printing vector from 8 to 8
 8.623450E19
f=2.083333E20 1.041666E20 scaled 2.083333E0 1.041666E0
 guess pop=3.073685E19
 guess pop=7.271319E19
 guess pop=7.166188E17
 guess pop=5.582353E12

CHAPTER 7

Complex Arithmetic. Muller & Jenkins-Traub Methods

Chapter Objectives

In this chapter we will develop tools to:

-perform complex arithmetic in C; this includes common complex functions such as polar to rectangular conversion, exponentiation, etc.

-find the (possibly complex) zeros of arbitrary functions

-find the zeros of polynomials with a particularly robust method for such problems, the Jenkins-Traub algorithm.

The complex arithmetic package presented here will be used below in the computation of the plasma dispersion function and the fast fourier transform.

Zeros of Nonlinear Equations; Roots of Polynomials

In this chapter we discuss the solution of a single nonlinear equation for one or more roots. The method to be used, Muller's method, has proved to be quite robust and useful in the many years I have used it. It may be used for determining complex roots of complex or real functions.

This chapter also introduces a package of declarations and functions to work with complex numbers in C. Alas, we cannot make this quite as easy as it is in FORTRAN, where complex operations are a natural part of the language. However, we can ease the burden considerably by judicious use of #define statements. Note that, as a result of using these techniques, the code to handle complex operations such as division is inserted in-line in the C code, avoiding the overhead of subroutine calls. If the C compiler optimizes and does a good job, the resulting code should be as efficient as its FORTRAN counterpart.

As noted in Chapter 6, iterative methods must be used for determining the roots of polynomials, and these may not generally converge. Press et al.

(*Numerical Recipes*) claim that Laguerre's method "is guaranteed to converge to a root from an starting point." (p. 263). This claim, is, sadly, inaccurate—as Dahlquist et. al. (*Numerical Methods*) state (p. 244), "For algebraic equations with complex roots, it is no longer true that Laguerre's method converges for every choice of initial estimate." The only "sure-fire" (to use the term of Press et al.) or globally convergent root finder for polynomials I'm familiar with is that of Jenkins and Traub. It is presented in this chapter for polynomial problems. Use Muller when the function is not a polynomial.

Determining the roots of polynomials can be a pathological problem. Wilkinson (*The Algebraic Eigenvalue Problem*—see Chapter 3) gives a much-quoted example of a polynomial whose roots give a very ill-conditioned problem. It is the polynomial $(x - 1)(x - 2)(x - 3)...(x - 20)$, whose roots are obvious. The coefficient of the term x^{20} is 1, that of x^{19} is 210, and the succeeding coefficients increase in magnitude until the constant term has a value of 20! or roughly 2.43×10^{18}. Now imagine that the value 2×10^{-23} is subtracted from the coefficient of the second term, i.e. that of x^{19}. In general, of course, computers won't store sufficient significant digits to represent 210 to such accuracy. Wilkinson finds that the exact roots for this new polynomial include now ten complex roots with significant imaginary parts. Of the remaining roots, 1,2,3,4 have not changed (to· 10 significant figures), with successively larger roots being more affected—20 becomes 20.8469..., 10 and 11 become 10.095 + .6435 i and its complex conjugate, etc. (see p .418 of Wilkinson). Clearly, one can have trouble with high-degree polynomials no matter how good the numerical methods are.

Complex Arithmetic in C

In this chapter we introduce a complex arithmetic package which make heavy use of the structured data type and the preprocessor of C. We will encounter this package again in the FFT of Chapter 10. It is compatible with the new draft ANSI standard, which provides the definition:

```
struct complex
    { double x,y;
    }
```

and the function cabs.

Complex numbers are represented as a structure consisting of a pair of double floating point numbers. Note that given this definition, arrays can easily be constructed of complex numbers. Then the preprocessor's #define feature is used to produce a number of utility functions for later use. Note that these functions are expanded by the preprocessor before the compiler operates on the code, so that these functions are coded "in-line" without the overhead of subroutine calls. Note also that the complex multiplication CMULT and division CDIV are written in terms of other pre-defined functions for compactness. The functions defined include the four arithmetic operations CADD(), CSUB(), CMULT(), CDIV(), all with three arguments z,x,y, the first being the result. The absolution value function cabs() is defined so that it may be used in a manner similar to the "generic" abs() function that was implemented by the ternary ? : operator combination for real and integer data types. CONJG() performs complex conjugation, (a single argument version, CONJ(), is unused and commented out to avoid problems with preprocessor limits on the number of functions defined in Aztec C). CTREAL() multiplies a complex number by a real number, while CMPLX() forms a complex number from given real and imaginary parts, as does the eponymous FORTRAN function. A variety of functions exist to assign a complex value to another complex variable.

A library of routines to do standard operations on complex variables will also be found. At the end of the listing is cexp(), which returns the value of e^z for z complex. A square root of a complex number is returned by csqrt() (there are of course two square roots for any number; the second may be obtained as the negative of the first), and the principal cut of the logarithm is returned by clog() . The clog() requires the argument, i.e. the angular part of the polar representation of the complex number, supplied by argmnt(). The routine argmnt() returns an angle between 0 and 2π. The comments within the routine detail how to change this to obtain a result between $-\pi$ and π, if that is desired for other purposes. Function polarxy() converts from polar form to rectangular representation of a complex number ($x = $ real part, $y = $ imaginary part).

Muller's Method

In the preceding chapter, we fitted a straight line to the function f(x) at the n-th iterated guess for the solution x[n]. This straight line was tangent to the function at the point x[n], and was extrapolated to its zero intercept to find x[n + 1], the next iterated approximation to the zero of f(x). This procedure involved finding the derivative f '(x). This derivative could be approximated numerically by evaluating f(x + ds) for a small step ds, and differencing. We are in effect then performing a version of the secant rule, the straight line approximating f(x) near x[n] being a secant to the curve at this point.

In Muller's method we abandon straight line fits and instead fit a quadratic to the function. This is of course a complication, and requires that square roots be taken to find the intercept (if any, or perhaps there will be two such intercepts) of the fit quadratic with the x-axis. The interval between the three fit points does not need to be very small, as it should be in determining a tangent. Complex roots are very naturally found, whereas it is somewhat awkward to use Newton's method to treat complex roots. Of the two roots of the quadratic, for numerical reasons it is best to take the root in which the two terms to be added have the same sign, so that there is no loss of precision due to cancellation. This is precisely what was done in Chapter 5 when we discussed Householder's reflection. As a straight line is determined by two points, a quadratic fit needs three. We always use the last three points in the iteration. The program "automatically" generates an initial guess set of points given the user inputs (see below).

Muller's method is not limited to determining polynomial roots, although it will be used for that purpose in our test case. It is not as easily adapted to multi-dimensional problems as the Newton-Raphson iteration.

If more than one root of a polynomial is desired, a "deflation" process must be used similar to the deflation process discussed in Chapter 4, so that the program does not find a previously determined root again. This is easily done. If the root r[i] is known, for i = 0,..., k, we search for roots of the function $F(x) = f(x)/\{(x - r[0])(x - r[1])...\}$. The r[i] roots should no longer be found.

Jenkins-Traub Method

M. A. Jenkins and J. F. Traub (*Numer. Math.* Vol.14, pp. 252-263, 1970 and CACM 419) developed a sophisticated three-stage iteration for finding the zeros of polynomials. As with the Muller method, roots are found one at a time and removed by deflation. The first iteration is similar to classical Bernoulli iteration, and the second stage is the same process but with a shift in origin. The Bernoulli iteration is robust but slow to converge, so a final iteration stage similar to the Newton-Raphson iteration of the previous chapter is used. Bernoulli's method, in effect, converts the root problem into the eigenvalue problem for a matrix with the same characteristic polynomial, and then applies the power method to this matrix. This may also be thought of as interpreting the polynomial as a difference equation, e.g., $x^3 + ax^2 + bx^1 + c = 0$ can be taken as the characteristic equation of the difference equation $y[k+3] = -a\,y[k+2] - b\,y[k+1] - c\,y[k]$ if we assume each step in index multiplies the y value by x. As in the power method, start with an initial guess vector, say y[0]...y[n − 1] = 0, y[n] = 1 and iterate until convergence. See Householder for an extensive treatment of these and other methods.

Program and Test Cases

Muller's Method

Our program is based upon the FORTRAN implementation in Conte and de Boor (see below). In that book, a wide variety of test problems (six examples, polynomials up to eighth degree) are run to demonstrate the talents of Muller's method. Here, we are content to solve a single cubic with real coefficients to obtain the complex roots, Conte and de Boor's example 2.11.

Table 7.1
Functions and Subroutines of Chapter 7

argmnt	Find the argument (in radians) of a complex number
clog	Principal value of the logarithm of a complex number
csqrt	Square root of complex number (only one returned– the other square root is the negative of this)
cexp	Complex exponentiation
polarxy	Convert from polar to rectangular representation of a complex number
muller	Find root(s) of complex function by muller's method
setfr	Subroutine used by muller to provide deflated function
jt	Jenkins-Traub method for polynomial roots
errev	Bounds error for jt() polynomial evaluation
nexth	Finds next shifted polynomial
cauchy	Lower bound of modulus of zeros
calct	Calculates variable shift
fxshft	Fixed shift (2nd stage of method)
noshft	No shift (1st stage of method)
vrshift	Variable shift(3rd stage of method)
polyev	Evaluate polynomial
cmod	Modulus of a complex number
cdiv	Accurate complex division,avoiding overflows
scale	Determines scale factor for coefficients

A variety of changes were made to make the program more suitable for a utility rather than a pedagogical example. The three initial guesses were generated in the book by using the initial guess, which is passed in as an argument, say, g, with g − .5 and g + .5 as the other two guesses. We give the user control over the initial interval between guessed points, here taken as .5, as well as the critical error tolerances.

The reader will note that the integer variable **fnreal** permits forcing the solver to attempt to find only real roots. If this option is invoked, it will apply to all roots. It would not be difficult to make fnreal a vector of values, the i-th applying to the i-th root. We feel this would encumber users too much, as generally they would not want to use the parameter to force real roots, and consequently would not want to set up a vector full of zeros for such a problem.

Jenkins-Traub Method

Our program is based on the published FORTRAN code in CACM Algorithm 419. We have used their more robust version of complex division, similar to that coded in-line in Chapter 4, for maximum accuracy.

Tests have shown that when the machine precision was used as calculated, some compilers produced code which reported failed convergence even though the correct roots were found. For this reason, as well as the possibility that the user might want to obtain less accurate roots more quickly, the program permits the use of a multiplier for the machine precision estimate. In tests on an IBM-PC clone, a multipler of about 7 was required for both TurboC and QuickC; Aztec C apparently fared well with a multiplier of 1. The multiplier was required independently of whether or not the 8087 co-processor was used (in tests with TurboC).

References

S. D. Conte and C. de Boor, *Elementary Numerical Analysis*, (NY: McGraw-Hill, 1972).

G. Dahlquist, A. Bjorck, N. Anderson, *Numerical Methods*, (Englewood Cliffs, NJ: Prentice-Hall, 1974).

A. S. Householder, *Numerical Treatment of a Single Nonlinear Equation,* (NY: McGraw-Hill, 1970).

W. H. Press, B. P. Flannery, S. A. Teukolsky, W. T. Vetterling, *Numerical Recipes*, (Cambridge: University Press, 1986).

Program Listing and Test Problem Output

```
/*
```
Muller's root solver for multiple complex roots of
arbitrary functions.
(from "C Tools for Scientists and Engineers" by L. Baker)

CONTENTS:

double argmt(y,x)
   Returns the argument of the complex number with
   imaginary part y and real part x. Answer
   returned is angle between 0 and 2pi.

clog(x,ans) struct complex *x,*ans;
   returns *ans = complex logarithm of *x

csqrt(x,ans) struct complex *x,*ans;
   returns *ans = complex square root of *x

polarxy(r,angle,x,y)
   converts from rectangular to polar form

printc(x) struct complex *x;
   prints a complex number x

muller
   applies muller's method to find complex roots
   see listing for details

setfr
   called by muller to evaluated the deflated function

cexp(x,ans) struct complex *x,*ans;
   *ans = complex exponential of *x;

main
   driver for test problem

fn

test function whose roots are to be found.

DEPENDENCIES:
  complex.h header file
*/
#include "complex.h"

struct complex   ci,c1,c0,o,o2,ir;

int iterp;/* global to return count used*/

/*
#define min(a,b) (((a)<(b))? (a): (b))
*/
#define max(a,b) (((a)>(b))? (a): (b))
#define abs(x) ((x)? (x):-(x))

double argmt(y,x)
double x,y;
{/* returns answer between 0 and twopi, as needed in
complex principal argument*/
/* caveat- Aztec C returns 0,not + or -halfpi if x=0., y nonzero*/
double ans,ratio,twopi=6.283185307,
    pi=3.14159265358979,halfpi=1.570796327;
double atan(),undef=0.0;/* change if desired*/

if (x==0.){if(y>0.) return(halfpi);
    if(y<0.) return(pi+halfpi);
    return(undef);
    };
/* if -pi to pi: return (halfpi*sign(y));*/
ratio=(y/x);ans=atan(ratio);
/*atan returns answer between -halfpi and halfpi*/
/* now move to correct quadrant between -pi and pi*/
if (ratio>0.){/* ratio, ans>0. */
      if (x>0.) return(ans);/* quadrant I*/
      /* else x<0.,y<0. quadrant III*/
      return (pi+ans);

```
            };
/* else ratio,ans<0.*/
if(x>0.)return(twopi+ans);/*quadrant IV*/
/*else x<0.,y>0., quadrant II*/
return(pi+ans);
```

```
/* if answer bwtn -pi and pi desired: if ans<=pi accept ans unchanged
   else   ans-twopi
   this will affect quadrant III,IV only. change:
       III: pi+ans to ans-pi
        IV: twopi+ans to ans
*/
}
```

```
/*------------ complex logarithm function ---------------*/

clog(x,ans) struct complex *x,*ans;
{
double r,argmt(),sqrt(),log(),angle;
r= sqrt( CNORM(*x) );
angle=argmt(x->y,x->x);
ans->x=log(r);
ans->y=angle;
return;
}
```

```
/* ---------------- complex square root --------------------*/

csqrt(z,ans) struct complex *z,*ans;
{
double x,y,r,sqrt(),argmt(),angle;
r=  sqrt(sqrt( CNORM(*z) ) );
angle=.5*argmt(z->y,z->x);
polarxy(r,angle,&x,&y);
ans->x=x;
ans->y=y;
return;
```

```
}

/* ------- convert from polar to rectangular coordinates---- */

polarxy(r,angle,x,y) double r,angle,*x,*y;
{double sin(),cos();
*x=r*cos(angle);
*y=r*sin(angle);
return;
}

main (argc,argv) int argc; char **argv;
{
double ep1,ep2;
struct complex rts[12],delta;
int i, maxit=20,kn,n,fnreal, fn();
kn=0;n=3;fnreal=0;
ep1=1.e-8;
ep2=1.e-8;
delta.x=.5;delta.y=0.;
for(i=0;i<n;i++){
      rts[i].x=0.;
      rts[i].y=0.;
      };
printf(" in main ");printc( &(rts[0]));printc(rts);printf("\n");
muller(kn,n,rts,maxit,ep1,ep2,fn,fnreal,&delta);
for(i=0;i<n;i++){printf(" root=");
      printc(&(rts[i]));
      printf("\n");
      };


exit(0);
}

/*----------- test function to find zeros (roots) of --------*/

fn(x,ans) struct complex *x,*ans;
```

```
{
/* x^3-x-1. */
struct complex cdum,cdu1,cdu2;
/*printf(" in fn ");printc(x);*/
CLET(cdu1,*x);
CMULT(cdu2,cdu1,cdu1);
CMULT(cdum,cdu1,cdu2);
CSUB(cdum,cdum,cdu1);cdum.x=cdum.x-1.;
CLET(*ans,cdum);
/*printc(ans);printf("\n");*/
return;
}


printc(x) struct complex *x;
{
printf("%f %f",x->x,x->y);
return;
}

/*----------------- muller's method
    based on FORTRAN program of Conte and DeBoor-----------*/

muller(kn,n,rts,maxit,ep1,ep2,fn,fnreal,delt)
int fnreal,n,kn,maxit;
double ep1,ep2; int (*fn)();
struct complex *delt,rts[];
{
double sqrt(),eps1,eps2,real;
int i,j,kount,ibeg,iend,zerodiv,setfr();
struct complex rt,h,delfpr,frtdef,lambda,delta,
cdum,cdu1,delf,dfprlm,num,den,g,sqr,frt,frtprv,*root;

struct complex *kptr,kludge;
/* tolerences*/
eps1= max(ep1,1.e-12);
eps2= max(ep2,1.e-20);
/* skip any previously found roots*/
```

```
ibeg=kn;
iend=kn+n;
CASSN(delta,delt);

/*printf(" muller ");printc(delt);printc(&delta);
printf("\n");
for(i=0;i<n;i++)
   {printf(" roots=");
   root= &(rts[i]);printc(root);printf("rootptr %u",root);
   printf(" \n");
   };
*/
for(i=0;i<iend;i++)
   {
   kount=3;
   /*initial guesses: guess, guess+ and -delta*/
   start: CLET(h,delta);
   root=&(rts[i]);
   /*printf(" rootptr %u",root);printc(root);*/
   CADD(rt, *root,h);
   /*printc(&rt);printf("\n");*/
   setfr(&delfpr,fn,&rt,i,rts,eps2,&zerodiv,&delta);
   if(zerodiv)goto start;
   CSUB(rt,rt,h);
   CSUB(rt,rt,h);
   setfr(&frtprv,fn,&rt,i,rts,eps2,&zerodiv,&delta);
   if(zerodiv)goto start;
   CADD(rt,rt,h);
   setfr(&frtdef,fn,&rt,i,rts,eps2,&zerodiv,&delta);
   if(zerodiv)goto start;
   lambda.x=-.5;lambda.y=0.;

   while(1)
   {
   /* next estimate for root*/
   CSUB(delf,frtdef,frtprv);
   CMULT(dfprlm,delfpr,lambda);
   CLET(cdum,lambda);cdum.x=cdum.x+1.;
```

```
CTREAL(cdum,cdum,(-2.));
CMULT(num,frtdef,cdum);
CTREAL(cdum,lambda,2.);
cdum.x=cdum.x+1.;
CMULT(cdu1,cdum,delf);
CMULT(cdum,lambda,dfprlm);
CSUB(g,cdu1,cdum);
CSUB(cdum,delf,dfprlm);
CTREAL(cdum,cdum,2.);
CMULT(cdu1,cdum,num);
CMULT(cdum,cdu1,lambda);
CMULT(sqr,g,g);
CADD(sqr,sqr,cdum);
if( fnreal && sqr.x<0.) {sqr.x=0.;sqr.y=0.;};
csqrt(&sqr,&sqr);
CADD(den,sqr,g);
real= g.x*sqr.x+g.y*sqr.y;
if (real<0.)
   {CSUB(den,g,sqr);};
if( cabs(den)==0.) {den.x=1.;den.y=0.;};
CDIV(lambda,num,den);
CLET(frtprv,frtdef);
CLET(delfpr,delf);
CMULT(cdum,h,lambda);
CLET(h,cdum);
CADD(rt,rt,h);
if(kount>maxit) goto fini;
while(1)
    {
    kount++;
    setfr(&frtdef,fn,&rt,i,rts,eps2,&zerodiv,&delta);
    if(zerodiv)goto start;
    if( cabs(h)<eps1*cabs(rt) || cabs(frtdef)<eps2) goto fini;
    /*unconverged to desired tolerance*/
    if( cabs(frtdef)<10.*cabs(frtprv)) break; /* compute next estimate*/
    /* diverged cut step size */
    printf(" cutting stepsize\n");
    CTREAL(h,h,.5);
```

```
      CTREAL(lambda,lambda,.5);
      CSUB(rt,rt,h);
      };/* infinite while loop-unconverged*/
   };/* infinite while loop- next estimate for root*/
   fini::root=&(rts[i]);
   /*printf(" befor fini ");printc(&(rts[i]));printc(&(rts[i+1]));
   printf("\n");printf(" %u\n",root);*/
   rts[i].x=rt.x; rts[i].y=rt.y;
}/* loop over desired roots*/
return;
}


setfr(frtdef,fn,rt,i,rts,eps2,zerodiv,delta) int *zerodiv,i;double eps2;
struct complex *rt,*frtdef,rts[],*delta;int (*fn)();
{int j;
double sqrt();
struct complex *root,den,cdum;
*zerodiv=0;
/*printf(" setfr ");printc(rt);printf("\n");*/
(*fn)(rt,frtdef);
/*printf(" in setfr ");printc(rt);printc(frtdef);printf("\n");*/
if(i>0)
   {/*deflate for found roots*/
   for (j=0;j<i;j++)
      {root=&(rts[j]);
      CSUB(den,*rt,*root);
      /*printf(" deflating for root");
      printc( root);printf("\n");*/
      if(cabs(den)<eps2){CTREAL(cdum,*delta,.1);
               root=&(rts[i]);
               CADD(cdum,cdum,*root);
               CLET(*root,cdum);
               *zerodiv=1;
printf(" zero denom. in setfr\n");
               return;
               }
      CDIV(cdum,*frtdef,den);
      CLET(*frtdef,cdum);
```

```
      }
    };/*i>0*/
/*printf(" return from setfr\n");*/
return;
}


/*---------- complex exponential function-------------*/

cexp( x,ans) struct complex *x,*ans;
{
double cos(),sin(),y,z;
struct complex c1,c2;
y = exp ( x->x);
c2.x= cos (x->y);
c2.y= sin (x->y);
CTREAL(c1,c2,y);
/*printf(" cexp ");printc(&c1);printc(x);printf("\n");*/
CLET(*ans,c1);
return;
}
```

```
 in main 0.000000 0.0000000.000000 0.000000
root=-0.662359 0.562280
root=1.324718 0.000000
root=-0.662359 -0.562280
```

```
/*
Jenkins-Traub polynomial root finder
(from "C Tools for Scientists and Engineers" by L. Baker)

CONTENTS: see text

DEPENDENCIES:
    complex.h header file
*/

#include "complex.h"
struct complex     ci,c1,c0,o,o2,ir;

int iterp;/* global to return count used*/

#define abs(x) ((x>0.)? (x) : -(x) )
#define min(a,b) (((a)<(b))? (a): (b))
#define max(a,b) (((a)>=(b))? (a): (b))

double baker;

main (argc,argv) int argc; char **argv;
{
FILE *fopen(),*fileid;
int degree,i,fail;
double x,y,cmod();
float fudge;
struct complex a,b,z,coef[4],ans[3];
/* test problem*/
CMPLX(a,3.,4.);x= cmod(&a);
printf(" test of cmod=%e\n",x);
CMPLX(a,1.,0.); CMPLX(b,0.,1.);
cdivid(&a,&b,&z);
printf(" enter fudge factor for eta");
scanf("%f",&fudge);
baker=fudge;
printf(" eta scaled by %e\n",baker);
printf(" test cdivid=");printc(&z);printf("\n");
```

```
degree=3;
CMPLX(coef[0],1.,0.);
CMPLX(coef[1],0.,0.);
CMPLX(coef[2],-1.,0.);
CMPLX(coef[3],-1.,0.);
jt(coef,degree, ans,&fail);
if(fail)
    {
    printf(" failed\n");
    }
for(i=0;i<3;i++)
    {
    printf(" root=");
    printc(&(ans[i]));
        printf("\n");
    }
exit(0);
}


printc(z) struct complex *z;
{
printf("%f %f",z->x,z->y);
}



#define MAXDEG 50
struct complex p[MAXDEG],h[MAXDEG],qp[MAXDEG]
            ,qh[MAXDEG],sh[MAXDEG];
struct complex s,t,pv;
double are,mre,eta,infin,smalno,base,tempa[MAXDEG],tempb[MAXDEG];
double xx,yy,cosr,sinr;
int nn;

jt(op,degree,zero,fail)
int *fail,degree;
struct complex op[],zero[];
{
double bnd,xxx,scale(),cmod(),sqrt(),cauchy();
```

```c
int i,idnn2,cntl1,cntl2,nm1,conv;
struct complex z;
mcon(&eta,&infin,&smalno,&base);
are=eta;/* factor of 2 my addition*/
mre=2.*sqrt(2.)*eta;
xx=.70710678;
yy=-xx;
cosr=-.069756474;
sinr=.99756405;
*fail=0;
nn=degree+1;

CMPLX(t,-99.,-99.);/* is t initially undefined in fxshft?*/
if (op[0].x==0. && op[0].y==0.)
    {
    *fail=1;
    return;
    }
for(; (op[nn-1].x==0. && op[nn-1].y==0.)&&nn>=0 ;nn--)
    {
    printf(" zero constant term found\n");
    idnn2=degree-nn+1;
    CMPLX(zero[idnn2],0.,0.);
    }
for(i=0;i<nn;i++)
    {
    CLET(p[i],op[i]);
    tempa[i]=cmod(&(p[i]));
    }
bnd=scale(nn,tempa,&eta,&infin,&smalno,&base);
if(bnd!=1.)
    {
    for(i=0;i<nn;i++)
        {
        CTREAL( (p[i]),(p[i]),bnd);
        }
    }
```

```
findzero:
if(nn==1)return;
if(nn<=2)
    {
    cdivid(&p[1],&p[0],&zero[degree-1]);
    CTREAL( zero[degree-1],zero[degree-1],-1.);
    return;
    }
for(i=0;i<nn;i++)
    {
    tempa[i]=cmod(&(p[i]));
    }
bnd=cauchy(nn,tempa,tempb);
for(cntl1=0;cntl1<=1;cntl1++)
    {
    noshft(5);
    for(cntl2=1;cntl2<=9;cntl2++)
        {
        xxx=cosr*xx-sinr*yy;
        yy=sinr*xx+cosr*yy;
        xx=xxx;
        s.x=bnd*xx;
        s.y=bnd*yy;
        fxshft(10*cntl2,&z,&conv);
        if(conv)
            {
            idnn2=degree-nn+1;
            CLET(zero[idnn2],z);
            nn--;
            for(i=0;i<nn;i++)
                {CLET(p[i],qp[i]);
                }
            goto findzero;
            }
        }
    }
*fail=1;
return;
```

```
}


double errev(nn,q,ms,mp,are,mre)
int nn;
struct complex *q;
double ms,mp,are,mre;
{
double ans,e,cmod();
int i;
e=cmod(&(q[0])) * mre/(are+mre);
for(i=0;i<nn;i++)
    {
    e=e*ms+cmod(&(q[i]));
    }
ans=e*(are+mre)-mp*mre;
return(ans);
}


nexth(boolean)
int *boolean;
{
double t1,t2;
int n,nm1,j;
n=nn-1;
/*nm1=n-1;*/
if(*boolean)
    {
    for(j=1;j<n;j++)
        {
        CLET(h[j],qh[j-1]);
        }
    CMPLX(h[0],0.,0.);
    return;
    }
/*else*/
for(j=1;j<n;j++)
    {
```

```
      CMULT(h[j],t,qh[j-1])
      CADD(h[j],h[j],qp[j])
      }
CLET(h[0],qp[0]);
return;
}


double cauchy(nn,pt,q)
double pt[],q[]; int nn;
{
int n,i,nm;
double x,dx,df,log(),exp(),f,xm;
pt[nn-1]*=-1.;
n=nn-1;
nm=n-1;
x= exp(log(-pt[n]))-log(pt[0])/((double)n);
if(pt[nm]!=0.)
    {xm=-pt[n]/pt[nm];
    x=min(xm,x);
    }
repeat:
xm=x*.1;
f=pt[0];
for(i=1;i<nn;i++)
    f=f*xm+pt[i];
if(f>0.)
    {
    x=xm;
    goto repeat;
    }
dx=x;
while( abs(dx/x)> .005)
    {
    q[0]=pt[0];
    for (i=1;i<nn;i++)
        q[i]=q[i-1]*x+pt[i];
    f=q[n];
    df=q[0];
```

```
    for (i=1;i<n;i++)
        df=df*x+q[i];
    dx=f/df;
        x-=dx;
        }
return(x);
}


calct(boolean)
int *boolean;
{
int n,nm1,i;
double cmod();
struct complex hv;
n=nn-1;   nm1=n-1;
polyev(n,&s,h,qh,&hv);
*boolean=  (cmod(&hv)<= are*10.*cmod(&(h[nm1]))) );
if(*boolean)
    {
    CMPLX(t,0.,0.);
    return;
    }
cdivid(&pv,&hv,&t);
CTREAL(t,t,-1.);
return;
}
vrshft(l3,z,conv)
int *conv,l3;
struct complex *z;
{
double cmod(),mp,ms,omp,relstp,r1,r2,sqrt(),errev(),tp;
int boolean,b,j,i;
b=0;
*conv=0;
CASSN(s,z);
for(i=0;i<l3;i++)
    {
    polyev(nn,&s,p,qp,&pv);
```

```
   mp=cmod(&pv);
   ms=cmod(&s);
   if(mp<=(20.*errev(nn,qp,ms,mp,are,mre)) )
       {
       *conv=1;
       CSET(z,s) ;
       return;
       }
   if(i!=0)
       {
       if( !b && !(mp<omp) && (relstp<.05))
             {
             tp=relstp;
             b=1;
             if(relstp<eta)tp=eta;
             r1=sqrt(tp);
             r2=s.x*(1.+r1)-s.y*r1;
             s.y=s.x*r1+s.y*(1.+r1);
             s.x=r2;
             polyev(nn,&s,p,qp,&pv);
             for(j=0;j<5;j++)
                   {
                   calct(&boolean);
                   nexth(&boolean);
                   }
             omp=infin;
             goto skp;
             }
       if(mp*.1 >omp)return;
       }
   omp=mp;
skp:
   calct(&boolean);
   nexth(&boolean);
   calct(&boolean);
   if(!boolean)
       {
       relstp=cmod(&t)/cmod(&s);
```

```
        CADD(s,s,t);
        }
    }
return;
}

fxshft(l2,z,conv)
int l2,*conv;
struct complex *z;
{
int i,j,n,test,pasd,boolean;
double cmod();
struct complex svs,ot,lou;
n=nn-1;
polyev(nn,&s,p,qp,&pv);
test=1;
pasd=0;
calct(&boolean);
for(j=0;j<l2;j++)
    {
    CLET(ot,t);
    nexth(&boolean);
    calct(&boolean);
    CADD((*z),s,t);
    if( (!boolean)&&test && (j!=(l2-1))  )
        {
        CSUB(lou,t,ot);
        if( cmod(&lou)>= .5*cmod(z) )
            {pasd=0;}
        else if (!pasd) {pasd=1;}
        else
            {
            for(i=0;i<n;i++)
                {
                CLET(sh[i],h[i]);
                }
            CLET(svs,s);
            vrshft(10,z,conv);
```

```
                    if(*conv)
                       {
                       return;
                       }
                    test=0;
                    for(i=0;i<n;i++)
                           {
                           CLET(h[i],sh[i]);
                           }
                    CLET(s,svs);
                    polyev(nn,&s,p,qp,&pv);
                    calct(&boolean);
                    }
              }
          else
              {
              }
      }
vrshft(10,z,conv);
return;
}

noshft(l1)
int l1;
{
int n,nm1,i,j,jj;
double xni,cmod(),t1,t2;
n=nn-1;
nm1=n-1;
for(i=0;i<n;i++)
    {
    xni=((double)(n-i))/((double) n);
    CTREAL(h[i],p[i],xni);
    }
for(jj=0;jj<l1;jj++)
    {
    if(cmod(&(h[nm1]))> eta*10.*cmod(&(p[nm1])))
        {
```

```
        cdivid(&(p[n]),&(h[nm1]),&t);
        CTREAL(t,t,-1.);
        for(i=1;i<=nm1;i++)
            {
            j=nn-i-1;
    /*      t1=h[j-1].x;
            t2=h[j-1].y;
            h[j].x=t.x*t1-t.y*t2;
            h[j].y=t.x*t2+t.y*t1;*/
            CMULT(h[j],t,h[j-1]);
            CADD(h[j],h[j],p[j]);
            }
        CLET(h[0],p[0]);
        }
    else
        {
        for(i=1;i<=nm1;i++)
            {
            j=nn-i-1;
            CLET(h[j],h[j-1]);
            }
        CMPLX(h[0],0.,0.);
        }
    }
return;
}


polyev(nn,s,p,q,pv)
int nn;
struct complex *s,p[],q[],*pv;
{/* nested polynomial evaluation*/
int i;
double t; struct complex temp;
CLET(q[0],p[0]);
CLET((*pv),q[0]);
for(i=1;i<nn;i++)
    {
/*    t=pv->x *s->x -pv->y*s->y +p[i].x;
```

```
      pv->y=pv->x*s->y+pv->y*s->x+p[i].y;
      pv->x=t;
*/
      CMULT(temp,(*pv),(*s));
      CADD((*pv),temp,(p[i]));
      CASSN(q[i],pv);
      }
return;
}


mcon(eta,infin,smalno,base)
double *eta,*infin,*smalno,*base;
{
/* will compute eta*/
printf(" entered mcon");
for(*eta=1.; (1.+(*eta))>1.;(*eta)*=.5);
*eta *= baker;/* my modification*/
   printf(" eta=%e\n",*eta);
/*
for(*smalno=1.e-30;*smalno*.5>0;*smalno*=.5)
*/
*smalno=(1.e-30);
      printf(" smalno=%e\n",*smalno);
/* set by hand as some compilers can't handle overflows/underflows*/
*infin=(1.e30);
*base=2.;

printf(" leaving mcon\n");
return;
}


double cmod(x) struct complex *x;
{/* robust but expensive version of cabs()*/
double ans,sqrt(),rpart,ipart,aux;
rpart= x->x; ipart= x->y;
rpart= abs(rpart);
ipart= abs(ipart);
```

```c
if(rpart>ipart)
    {
    aux= ipart/rpart;
    ans=rpart*sqrt(1.+ aux*aux);
    return(ans);
    }
else if (rpart<ipart)
    {
    aux=rpart/ipart;
    ans=ipart*sqrt(1.+aux*aux);
    return(ans);
    }
/*else*/
return (rpart*sqrt(2.));
}

cdivid(a,b,c) struct complex *a,*b,*c;
{/* robust c=a/b*/
double r,d,dummy,infin;
if( b->x==0. && b->y==0.)
    {
    mcon(&dummy,&infin,&dummy,&dummy);
    c->x=infin;
    c->y=infin;
    return;
    }
if (abs(b->x)>=abs(b->y))
    {
    r=b->y/b->x;
    d=1./(b->x + r*b->y);
    c->x=(a->y *r + a->x)*d;
    c->y=(-a->x *r +a->y)*d;
    }
else
    {
    r=b->x/b->y;
    d=1./(b->y + r*b->x);
    c->x=(a->x *r + a->y)*d;
```

```c
    c->y=(a->y *r - a->x)*d;
    }
return;
}


double scale(nn,pt,eta,infin,smalno,base)
double pt[],*eta,*infin,*smalno,*base;
int nn;
{
int i;
double scal,maxx,minn,hi,lo,x,sc,sqrt(),log(),pow();
hi=sqrt(*infin);
lo=*smalno/(*eta);
printf(" hi %e low %e nn %d\n",hi,lo,nn);
maxx=0.;
minn=*infin;
for(i=0;i<nn;i++)
    {
    x=pt[i];
    maxx= max(x,maxx);
    if(x!=0.)minn=min(x,minn);
    }
scal=1.;
if(minn>=lo && maxx<=hi)
    {
    return(scal);
    }
x=lo/minn;
if(x>1.)
    {
    sc=x;
    if( *infin/sc >maxx) sc=1.;
    }
else
    {
    sc=1./(sqrt(maxx)*sqrt(minn));
    }
printf(" before log,pow %e\n",sc);
```

```
i= (int) (log(sc)/log(*base)+.5);
scal= pow(*base, ((double) i));
return(scal);
}
```

```
test of cmod=5.000000e+000
enter fudge factor for eta 10.
eta scaled by 1.000000e+001
test cdivid=0.000000 -1.000000
entered mcon eta=5.421011e-019
smalno=1.000000e-030
leaving mcon
hi 1.000000e+015 low 1.844674e-012 nn 4
root=1.324718 -0.000000
root=-0.662359 0.562280
root=-0.662359 -0.562280
```

CHAPTER 8

B-Spline Interpolation

Chapter Objectives

In this chapter, we present tools to:

- fit data with a particularly useful form of spline curve known as B-splines.

Spline Interpolation

Other chapters in this book, particularly Chapters 4 and 7, allude to a variety of problems associated with high-degree polynomials. In interpolation, they can oscillate wildly between the points at which they match the desired function. The solution is to use low-degree polynomials to interpolate limited regions of the range of the function to be interpolated. In order to make this produce smooth curves at the boundaries of these regions, one matches not merely the function values, but takes care to match slopes as well. This general process is called "spline" interpolation, after the drafter's tool of the same name. Cubic splines are quite popular—as a cubic polynomial has four coefficients, these can be used to match function values and slopes at each end, giving a smooth fit. Forsythe, Malcolm, and Moler (see reference in Chapter 3) present a good discussion of cubic splines as well as a pair of FORTRAN routines that implement cubic spline interpolation. A C implementation may be found in "Curve Fitting with Cubic Splines," by Ian E. Ashdown, *Dr. Dobbs Journal*, p.24, Sept. 1986.

We present here a general method, called "B-splines," that provides a more powerful and flexible formalism for spline applications. The cost, of course, is in program complexity and the consequent computational costs.

B-Splines

B-Splines, or "basis" splines, were originally developed by I. J. Schoenberg, but first became popular when C. de Boor developed a package of FORTRAN routines for their numerical application

The idea behind a spline fit is to approximate a function by a polynomial which is defined piecewise. For example, a cubic spline fit uses cubic polynomials which are defined over distinct, non-overlapping regions. The term "spline" means that the coefficients of the polynomial are chosen so that at the borders when two regions abut not only the values of the fit polynomials are the same, but one or more of the derivatives match as well so that the slope (first derivative), etc., are continuous. For cubic splines, it is possible to match the function values and first derivatives (slopes) at both ends of the interval, resulting in a sufficiently smooth join for most purposes.

The idea behind B-splines is to expand the function in "basis" splines $B(x)$, which are zero over most of the domain to be fit. The $B(x)$ are splines, not simple polynomials—that is, they are different polynomials in different regions. Consider the simplest useful B-splines, the cubic splines. The $B(x)$ will be nonzero in the region between $x[i]$ and $x[i + 3]$; for $x < x[i]$ or $x > x[i + 3]$, $B(x) = 0$. To be continuous, $B(x[i]) = B(x[i+3]) = 0$. The function $B(x)$ can be written for a cubic B-spline as

$$B(x) = A(x - x[i])_+^3 + B(x - x[i+1])_+^3$$
$$+ C(x - x[i+2])_+^3 + D(x - x[i+3])_+^3$$

where $(x - y)_+$ is $x - y$ if $x - y > 0$ and 0 otherwise. Thus, in the leftmost interval, only the term proportional to A contributes, while in the rightmost interval all of the terms contribute. The additional conditions on the derivatives of $B(x)$ at the end of the righmost interval, namely $B'(x[i + 3]) = B''(x[i + 3]) = 0$, result in the B spline being unique up to a normalizing constant which multiplies B. The resultant B-splines are bell-shaped functions which are non-negative (see Fig. 8.1a). B-splines can be defined for higher (odd) degrees but cubic B-splines are generally used in practice.

Beyond the endpoints of the domain, there are fictitious points which are needed to define the B-spline at the edge of the domain. de Boor typically chooses $x[-3] = x[-2] = x[-1] = x[0]$ at the left-hand end, $x[0]$ being the endpoint of the domain, and similarly at the right-hand side (see Fig. 8.1b). The points at which the fit are defined, the $x[i]$, are typically called the "knots" or "breakpoints" of the spline. Often, the knot spacing is uniform within the domain, i.e., $x[i + 1] - x[i] = dx$ is a constant, although this is not necessary.

The process of fitting a function by splines involves determining the coefficients of the splines which satisfy the user-imposed conditions, which are typically to match the specified function and its derivatives on a specified set of points. In order to do this, a spline approximation to the function is built from overlapping B-splines. The first cubic B-spline might

a)

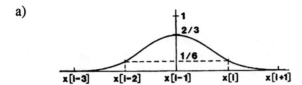

b)

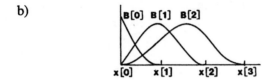

c)

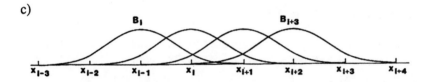

Fig. 8.1. Cubic B-Splines.
a) B-spline at an interior point. b) Near a boundary.
c) Illustrating the range of influence of cublic B-splines.

cover the region from x[0] to x[3]; the next would be defined over x[1] to
x[4], etc. (see Fig. 8.1c). Recall that each cubic B-spline, as defined above,
has one free parameter, its scale factor. Performing the fit requires determining this scale factor. Because at the ends of its range the B-spline takes
on the value 0, there will be three non-zero B-splines contributing to the
value of the sum at each interior point. The linear system which must then
be solved to fit the B-spline approximation to a set of function values is,
then, a tri-diagonal system within the interior of the domain. Because of
the multiple knots at the edges, it is somewhat more complicated at either
end. Such a system is still banded, and so generally can be solved without
the complexity of a full system solver as in Chapter 3.

One interesting feature of B-splines is a locality of influence. The value
of a function to be fit influences only the coefficients of the B-splines
which are non-zero over that interval. Thus, for cubic splines, only four
coefficients are affected. Try this out—intentionally make a "mistake" and
alter one of the fit points, or a boundary condition. It will have no effect
on the coefficients or fit at the other end of the interval.

C Program and Test Case

We employ a test problem discussed by D. Amos in "Computation with
Splines and B-Splines," report SAND78-1968 of Sandia National
Laboratories, March 1979. See also "Constrained Least Square Curve Fit-
ting to Discrete Data Using B-Splines—A User's Guide," by R. J. Hanson,
SAND78-1291, Feb. 1979, for an application of B-splines.

The example involves fitting a cubic spline to the function sin(pi x) in
the interval 0 < x < 1, with uniform dx = .1 . The flexibility of B-splines
allows us to impose the additional conditions that the derivatives of the
function vanish at the endpoints of the interval. This of course cannot
generally be done with cubic splines. It is possible here because the knots
x = 0 and x = 1 are multiple knots, with more than one B-spline contributing to the function and its derivatives here. The cost, of course, is additional coefficients and additional complexity. The linear system to be solved
for the coefficients is no longer simply tridiagonal near the boundaries. In
the *Collected Algorithms from ACM* de Boor has authored Algorithm 546,
Blocksolve, which is a package of FORTRAN routines suitable for matrices
of the form encountered in such spline fits.

The B-Spline package of de Boor is rather general. An array t[] contains the locations of the knots in ascending sequence. If a knot is a multiple breakpoint, it is entered into the t[] array a number of times, the array mult[] holding the multiplicity of each knot. As noted above, the endpoints are typically knots with multiplicities greater than one. There may also be interior knots of greater multiplicity. For example, Amos' report gives an example of fitting to a function which has a discontinuous first derivative. For a cubic spline, the corresponding point must be a knot of multiplicity 3 in order to achieve a discontinuous first derivative.

Assume we are using a spline of polynomials of degree d. The number of coefficients in such a spline is k = d + 1, e.g., 4 in the case of a cubic spline for which d = 3. This parameter k is one of the fundamental parameters in the package and is called the "order" of the spline. Let n be the number of break points or knots, including the endpoints, and nb the number of B-spline coefficients. The variables n,k and nb will be related but the relationship depends upon the multiplicities of the knots used. The knots are stored in order, with multiple knots stored multiple times, in the array t[]. This array must be nb+k long.

The first function interv() of the C package has the name required by the BSPLINE package, but is not based on any similar routine therein. Its purpose is to locate the interval in the t[] array into which the given point x falls. The variable mflag is returned 0 if the point is within the range of the fit, − 1 if x<x[0] and + 1 if x is larger than the largest knot value. In each case, the variable ileft· returns the nearest leftmost point. A binary search procedure is used which repeatedly halves the interval being searched. In this manner, the number of tests which have to be performed is of the order of the logarithm of the number of points in the t[] array, rather than being of the order of the number of points in the array. This can be a considerable saving for a large array.

The remainder of the routines, save for main(), are based on the BSPLINE package. The subroutine bsplvb() calculates the values of the B-splines which do not vanish at the point specified by x. It uses a recurrence relation for evaluation of the B-splines. The subroutine bsplvd() uses bslplv() to calculate the derivatives in addition to the function values. We have conformed to the de Boor package convention in that the argument nderiv to bsplvd() is the value of one plus the highest derivative desired. Each of these routines assumes that the interval in which the point x is located is specified through the integer argument left. Subroutine bvalue() does not make this assumption and uses subroutine interv() to determine this value. The argument jderiv of bvalue() is the highest derivative desired, not one more than the highest derivative desired as was the argument nderiv to bsplvd().

The main program contains much that is general and applicable to most B-spline problems. First, the test function is set up, as arrays yi[] for function values at the corresponding xi[] abscissas. The vector mult[] contains the multiplicity of each knot xi[]. In our case, this is 1 for all interior knots and k for the endpoints. The next nested loop in main sets the t[] array using the xi[] and the mult[]. The boundary conditions and the interior conditions are then imposed as equations which must be satisfied by the fit coefficients, and the linear system solved by the (general) system solver of Chapter 3. If a large set of points were to be fit, it would be a wise idea to use a banded solver to save on time and storage. Because we have n data points at which to match function values, and 2 extra conditions on the vanishing of the derivatives, we have a total nb = n + k − 2 = n + 2 B-spline coefficients to determine. If we had been doing a "usual" spline fit of matching only function values, we would have needed two fewer coefficients, i.e., n, to match n data points. We could have just as easily used conditions on the first derivatives at either endpoint.

Although this example employs equally spaced knots and cubic splines, the packages are general and other choices can be implemented with the subroutines provided. Note that mixing the order of the splines, i.e., using a cubic spline at one end of the range and a quartic at the other, is not something one can easily do. For cubic splines, for example, the knots should be placed where the third derivative is largest (or discontinuous). As with Hastings' procedure, obtain a fit, plot the error curve, i.e., the difference between the fit and the desired function, and either add new knots or move existing ones where the error is largest. Hanson recommends an alternative procedure of starting with a few knots and adding additional knots where the error curve crosses zero between the largest error values.

The de Boor package has various routines to convert from spline approximations to polynomial approximations, etc. Splines may be used in a collocation method to solve differential equations and two-point boundary value problems.

In computer graphics applications, B-splines are used in a variety of ways. Parametric representations are generally used, in which the B-spline is a polynomial in a parameter, say, t, and the x and y locations of a point are given by two different functions of t. As t varies within prescribed limits, the curve is traced out. This generalizes to surfaces in the obvious way. NURBS, or "Non-Uniform Rational B-Splines," are B-spline fits for curves or surfaces in which homogeneous coordinates (x,y,z,w) are fit and projection is used to obtain the spatial coordinates (w,y,z). NURBS are supported by the PHIGS+ (van Dam, 1988) graphics standard. See, for example, Plastock and Kalley for a discussion of the use of B-splines as well as other related methods in computer graphics applications. They will also explain homogeneous coordinates to the uninitiated.

Table 8.1

Functions of Chapter 8

interv() Determines which knots surround the specified point x
bsplvb() Evaluates the basis B-spline functions
bsplvd() Calculates the values of a function and its derivatives given the
          B-spline fit
bvalue() Finds the value of a function at a point given the B-spline fit

(for details of the arguments, see the program listings)

References

Association for Computing Machinery, *Collected Algorithms from ACM (CALGO)*, (NY: ACM, 1983). This is published in four volumes, with the last volume updated periodically.

C. de Boor, *A Practical Guide to Splines*, (NY: Springer, 1978).

R. A. Plastock and G. Kalley, *Computer Graphics*, (NY: McGraw-Hill, 1986) (Schaum's Outline Series).

A. van Dam (Chairman), PHIGS+ Functional Description Revision 3.0, *Computer Graphics*, Vol. 22, 3, July 1988 pp.125-215.

Program Listing and Test Problem Output

(listing begins next page)

```
/* B-spline package
   (based on De Boor's  FORTRAN  package)

test problem: fit sin ( pi*x) for 0<=x<=1
with constraints that the function has zero derivatives at the endpoints;
the test problem uses the linear system solution routines of Chapter 3
to solve for the coefficients  of the fit;
the fundamental B-spline routines do not use the linear system solver
themselves

(from "C Tools for  Scientists and Engineers" by L. Baker)

CONTENTS:
interv
    determines which knots bound the position x

bsplvb
    evaluates the B-spline basis functions

bsplvd
    evaluates function and its derivatives from B-spline fit

bvalue
    returns j-th derivative of function from B-spline fit

main
    test driver

printm
    another version of the matrix printer, determines
    number of values/row from allowed column count.

DEPENDENCIES:
linear systems solver from Chapter 3
*/

#define DOFOR(I,to) for(i=0;i<to;i++)
#define jmax 20
```

```
#define INDEC(i,j,col) [j+(i)*col]
#define min(a,b) ((a)<(b)? (a):(b))
#define max(a,b) ((a)>(b)? (a):(b))

/* determines which interval (between knots) the location x is

   uses binary search

*/

interv(t,nbk,x,left,mflag) int nbk,*left,*mflag;
float x,t[];
{
int i,n,top,btm;
float below,above;
n=nbk-1;/*index of last value in t[]*/
if(x<t[0])
    {*mflag=-1;*left=0;}
else
if(x>=t[n])
    {*mflag=1;*left=n;}
else
    {
    *mflag=0;
    /*search*/
    /* binary search*/
    btm=0;top=n;
    while(1){
       i=(top+btm)>>1;
       below=t[i];above=t[i+1];
/*printf(" top,btm,i %d %d %d\n",top,btm,i);*/
       if( below<=x)
           {
           if(x<above)
               {
               *left=i;
               return;
               }
```

```
            /*x>=above*/
            btm=i;
            }
        else{        /* x<below*/
            top=i;
            }
        }
    }
return ;
}
```

/* evaluates B-spline basis functions */

```
bsplvb(t,jhigh,index,x,left,biatx)
int jhigh,index,left;
float t[],x,biatx[];
{static int j=0; int jp1,i;
static float deltal[jmax],deltar[jmax],saved,term;
/* index=0 start from scratch else j+1 to jout generated*/
/*printf(" bsplvb jhigh %d index %d left %d j %d\n", jhigh,index,left,j);*/
if(!index)
    {
    j=0;
    biatx[0]=1.;
    if(jhigh<2)return;
    }
for( ; j<jhigh-1;j++)
    {
    jp1=j+1;
    deltar[j]=t[left+j+1]-x;
    deltal[j]=x-t[left-j];
/*printf(" x %f t %f %f %f %f\n",x,t[left+j+1],t[left-j],deltal[j],deltar[j]);
*/
    saved=0.;
    DOFOR(i,j+1)
        {
        term=biatx[i]/(deltar[i]+deltal[j-i]);
```

```
      biatx[i]=saved+term*deltar[i];
/*printf(" term=%e saved=%e ans=%e\n",term,saved,biatx[i]);*/
      saved=deltal[j-i]*term;
/*printf(" j=%d,i=%d in b\n",j,i);*/
      }
   biatx[jp1]=saved;
/*printf(" b[%d]=%e\n",jp1,saved);*/
   }
/*printf(" leaving b\n");*/
return;
}




/* calculates values and derivatives of a function
represented by a B-spline
uses bsplvb()
*/


bsplvd(t,k,x,left,a,biatx,nderiv) int k,left,nderiv;
float t[],x,a[],biatx[];
{
double fk,factor,sum;
int i,il,j,jlow,jpmid,kp1mm,ldummy,m,kp1,mhigh,ideriv;
kp1=k+1;
/*printf(" bsplvd k %d,left %d,nderiv %d\n",k,left,nderiv);*/
mhigh= min(nderiv,k);mhigh=max(mhigh,1);
bsplvb(t,kp1-mhigh,0,x,left,a);
/*de Boor uses column ordering of FORTRAN, sends biatx not a*/
if(mhigh==1)
   {
   DOFOR(j,k) biatx INDEC(j,0,k)=a[j];
/*    DOFOR(i,k)printf(" a[%d]=%e\n",i,a[i]);*/
   return;
   }
ideriv=mhigh;
for(m=2;m<=mhigh;m++)
   {
   jpmid=0;
```

```
   for(j=ideriv;j<=k;j++)
       {
       biatx INDEC(j-1,ideriv-1,k)=a[jpmid];
       jpmid++;
       }
   ideriv--;
   bsplvb(t,kp1-ideriv,1,x,left,a);
   }
DOFOR(j,k) biatx INDEC(j,0,k)=a[j];
/*DOFOR(i,k)printf(" a[%d]=%e\n",i,a[i]);*/

jlow=0;
DOFOR(i,k)
   {
   for(j=jlow;j<k;j++)a INDEC(j,i,k)=0.;
   jlow=i;
   a INDEC( i,i,k)=1.;
   }

for(m=2;m<=mhigh;m++)
   {
   kp1mm=kp1-m;
   fk=kp1mm;
   il=left;
   i=k-1;
   DOFOR(ldummy,kp1mm)
       {
       factor=fk/(t[il+kp1mm]-t[il]);

       DOFOR(j,i+1)
          {
          a INDEC(i,j,k)=
            factor*(a INDEC(i,j,k)-a INDEC(i-1,j,k));
          }
       il--;i--;
       }
   DOFOR(i,k)
       {
```

```
        sum=0.;
        jlow= max(i,m-1);
        for(j=jlow;j<k;j++)
            sum+=a INDEC(j,i,k) * biatx INDEC(j,m-1,k);
        biatx INDEC(i,m-1,k)=sum;
/*printf(" biatx[%d][%d]=%f\n",i,(m-1),sum);*/
        }
    }
/*printm(a,4,4,4,4);
printf(" leaving d\n");*/
return;
}


/* ------------------- test driver -------------------*/

main (argc,argv) int argc; char **argv;
{
/* don amos' example 2a- fit spline and check it out */
float xi[11],z,y,x,yi[11],t[17],cm[169],r[13],a[13],vnikx[16];
float work[16],bvalue();/*dimensioned kxk*/
/* CAVEAT  some differences between De Boor's book (1978) and
    previous articles; for example, bsplvd has an extra
    argument, the work array, in the later book.
*/
int pivot[11];
double sin();
int mult[11],interv(),ilft,i,nm1,m,imk,nbk,n,nb,kp1,nm;
int j,it,km1,k,jshift,nderiv,mflag,info;
k=4;n=11;/* cubic spline order k=4, 11 points*/

/*test problem*/
DOFOR(i,n)
    {
    xi[i]= x=i*.1;
    yi[i]=y=sin(x*3.141592653589);
    }

/* the rest of the routine is fairly general*/
```

```
nm1=n-1;
mult[0]=k;
for(i=1;i<nm1;i++) mult[i]=1;
mult[nm1]=k;
j=0;
DOFOR(i,n)
   {
   DOFOR(m, (mult[i]) )
      {
      t[j++]= xi[i];
      }
   }
nb=j-k;
DOFOR(i,nb)
   {
   DOFOR(j,nb) cm INDEC(i,j,nb)=0.;
   }
nbk=nb+k;
km1=k-1;
nderiv=3;/*second deriv b.c. */
ilft=k-1;
printf(" n=%d nb=%d nbk=%d\n",n,nb,nbk);
DOFOR(i,nbk)printf(" t=%f\n",t[i]);
DOFOR(i,n)printf(" mult=%d\n",mult[i]);

bsplvd(t,k,xi[0],ilft,work,vnikx,nderiv);
DOFOR(j,k) cm INDEC(0,j,nb)=vnikx INDEC(j,2,k);
r[0]=0.;
/* rest of equations*/
nderiv=1;
DOFOR(i,nm1)
   {
   x=xi[i];
   interv(t,nbk,x,&ilft,&mflag);
/*printf(" ilft %d mflag=%d x %e\n",ilft,mflag,x);*/
   jshift=ilft-km1+1;
   if(jshift+k >nb )jshift=nb-k+1;
   bsplvd(t,k,x,ilft,work,vnikx,1);
```

```
    DOFOR(j,k)
        {
        it=jshift-1+j;
        cm INDEC(i+1,it,nb)= vnikx INDEC(j,0,k);
/*if (!j)printf(" first it=%d\n",it);*/
        r[i+1]=yi[i];
        }
    }
/*left limits of last two eqns*/
nderiv=3;/*second derivative b.c.*/
jshift=nb-km1;
bsplvd(t,k,xi[nm1],ilft,work,vnikx,nderiv);
DOFOR(j,k)
    {
    it=jshift+j-1;
/*if(!j)printf(" first it=%d\n",it);*/
    cm INDEC(nb-2,it,nb)= vnikx INDEC(j,0,k);
    cm INDEC(nb-1,it,nb)= vnikx INDEC(j,2,k);
    }
r[nb-2]=yi[nm1];
r[nb-1]=0.;/*second deriv.=0*/

/* lufact backsub solve system cm x= r*/
printm(cm,nb,nb,nb,nb);
lufact(cm,nb,nb,pivot,&info);
if(info!=0)printf(" info=%d\n",info);
DOFOR(i,nb)printf("data r=%e\n",r[i]);
backsub(cm,nb,nb,pivot,r);
DOFOR(i,nb)printf("solution=%e\n",r[i]);
DOFOR(i,20)
    {
    x=i*.05;
    y=bvalue(t,r,nb,k,x,0);
    z=bvalue(t,r,nb,k,x,1)/3.14159265358979;/* deriv of sin=cos*/
    printf(" x=%f sin=%f exact=%f cos=%f\n",x,y,sin(x*3.14159265),z);
    }

}
```

```
/* bvalue returns the jderiv-th derivative of a function
represented by a bspline, at any point x within the
range of the fitted function.

uses interv()
*/


float bvalue(t,bcoef,n,k,x,jderiv) int n,k,jderiv;
float t[],bcoef[],x;
{
int i,ilo,nmi,imk,j,jc,jcmin,jcmax,jj,kmj,km1,mflag,nm1;
float fkmj,aj[jmax],dl[jmax],dr[jmax];
if(jderiv>=k)return (0.);
interv(t,n+k,x,&i,&mflag);
if(mflag)return(0.);
km1=k-1;
if(km1<=0)return(bcoef[0]);
jcmin=0;
imk=i-k;  .
/*printf(" i %d,k %d,imk %d\n",i,k,imk);*/
if(imk<-1)
    {
    jcmin=-1-imk;
    DOFOR(j,i+1)dl[j]=x-t[i-j];
    for(j=i;j<km1;j++)
        {
        aj [km1-j-1]=0.;
        dl[j]=dl[i];
/*printf(" j%d i%d aj[%d]\n",j,i,(km1-j-1));*/
        }
    }
else
    {
    DOFOR(j,km1) dl[j]=x-t[i-j];
    }
```

```
jcmax=k;
nmi=n-i;
if(nmi<1)
   {
   jcmax=k+nmi;
   DOFOR(j,jcmax)dr[j]=t[i+j+1]-x;
   for(j=jcmax-1;j<km1;j++)
      {
      aj[j+1]=0.;
      dr[j]=dr[jcmax];
      }
   }
else
   {
   DOFOR(j,km1) dr[j]=t[i+j+1]-x;
   }
/*printf(" jcmin %d max %d\n",jcmin,jcmax);
DOFOR(j,km1)printf(" dr=%f dl=%f\n",dr[j],dl[j]);*/
for(j=jcmin;j<=jcmax;j++) aj[j]=bcoef[j+imk+1];
if(jderiv!=0)
   {
   DOFOR(j,jderiv)
      {
      kmj=km1-j;
      ilo=kmj-1;
      fkmj=kmj;
      DOFOR(jj,kmj)
         {
/*if(ilo<0)printf(" warn1 ilo=%d\n",ilo);*/
         aj[jj]=fkmj*((aj[jj+1]-aj[jj])/(dl[ilo]+dr[jj]));
         ilo--;
         }
      }
   }
if(jderiv!=km1)
   {
   for(j=jderiv+1;j<=km1;j++)
      {
```

```
        kmj=km1-j;
        ilo=kmj;

        DOFOR(jj,kmj+1)
            {
/*if(ilo<0)printf(" warn2 ilo=%d\n",ilo);*/
            aj[jj]-(aj[jj+1]*dl[ilo]+aj[jj]*dr[jj])
              /(dl[ilo]+dr[jj]);
            ilo--;
            }
        }
return(aj[0]);
    }
return(0.);/*for De Smet compiler*/
}


int colpp=48;

printm(a,coln,rown,col,row) int rown,row,col,coln; float a[];
{
    int i,j,ne,btm,top,count;
    putchar('\n');
    btm=top=0;
    ne=colpp/11;
    while(btm<col)
    {
        top=min(col,(btm+ne));
        printf(" printing matrix columns %d to %d\n",btm,(top-1));
        DOFOR(j,row)
        {
            for(i=btm;i<top;i++)
                printf(" %10.2e", a INDEC(j,i,coln) );
            putchar('\n');
        }
        btm+=ne;
    }
    return;
}
```

```
n=11 nb=13 nbk=17
t=0.000000
t=0.000000
t=0.000000
t=0.000000
t=0.100000
t=0.200000
t=0.300000
t=0.400000
t=0.500000
t=0.600000
t=0.700000
t=0.800000
t=0.900000
t=1.000000
t=1.000000
t=1.000000
t=1.000000
mult=4
mult=1
mult=1
mult=1
mult=1
mult=1
mult=1
mult=1
mult=1
mult=1
mult=4
```

```
printing matrix columns 0 to 3
 6.00e+002 -9.00e+002  3.00e+002  0.00e+000
 1.00e+000  0.00e+000  0.00e+000  0.00e+000
 0.00e+000  2.50e-001  5.83e-001  1.67e-001
 0.00e+000  0.00e+000  1.67e-001  6.67e-001
 0.00e+000  0.00e+000  0.00e+000  1.67e-001
 0.00e+000  0.00e+000  0.00e+000  0.00e+000
 0.00e+000  0.00e+000  0.00e+000  0.00e+000
```

```
0.00e+000  0.00e+000  0.00e+000  0.00e+000
0.00e+000  0.00e+000  0.00e+000  0.00e+000
0.00e+000  0.00e+000  0.00e+000  0.00e+000
0.00e+000  0.00e+000  0.00e+000  0.00e+000
0.00e+000  0.00e+000  0.00e+000  0.00e+000
0.00e+000  0.00e+000  0.00e+000  0.00e+000
```
printing matrix columns 4 to 7
```
0.00e+000  0.00e+000  0.00e+000  0.00e+000
0.00e+000  0.00e+000  0.00e+000  0.00e+000
0.00e+000  0.00e+000  0.00e+000  0.00e+000
1.67e-001  0.00e+000  0.00e+000  0.00e+000
6.67e-001  1.67e-001  0.00e+000  0.00e+000
1.67e-001  6.67e-001  1.67e-001  0.00e+000
0.00e+000  1.67e-001  6.67e-001  1.67e-001
0.00e+000  0.00e+000  1.67e-001  6.67e-001
0.00e+000  0.00e+000  0.00e+000  1.67e-001
0.00e+000  0.00e+000  0.00e+000  0.00e+000
0.00e+000  0.00e+000  0.00e+000  0.00e+000
0.00e+000  0.00e+000  0.00e+000  0.00e+000
0.00e+000  0.00e+000  0.00e+000  0.00e+000
```
printing matrix columns 8 to 11
```
0.00e+000  0.00e+000  0.00e+000  0.00e+000
0.00e+000' 0.00e+000  0.00e+000  0.00e+000
0.00e+000  0.00e+000  0.00e+000  0.00e+000
0.00e+000  0.00e+000  0.00e+000  0.00e+000
0.00e+000  0.00e+000  0.00e+000  0.00e+000
0.00e+000  0.00e+000  0.00e+000  0.00e+000
0.00e+000  0.00e+000  0.00e+000  0.00e+000
1.67e-001  0.00e+000  0.00e+000  0.00e+000
6.67e-001  1.67e-001  0.00e+000  0.00e+000
1.67e-001  6.67e-001  1.67e-001  0.00e+000
0.00e+000  1.67e-001  5.83e-001  2.50e-001
0.00e+000  0.00e+000  0.00e+000  0.00e+000
0.00e+000  0.00e+000  3.00e+002 -9.00e+002
```
printing matrix columns 12 to 12
```
0.00e+000
0.00e+000
0.00e+000
```

```
    0.00e+000
    0.00e+000
    0.00e+000
    0.00e+000
    0.00e+000
    0.00e+000
    0.00e+000
    0.00e+000
    1.00e+000
    6.00e+002
data r=0.000000e+000
data r=0.000000e+000
data r=3.090170e-001
data r=5.877852e-001
data r=8.090170e-001
data r=9.510565e-001
data r=1.000000e+000
data r=9.510565e-001
data r=8.090170e-001
data r=5.877852e-001
data r=3.090171e-001
data r=7.932658e-013
data r=0.000000e+000
solution=5.513430e-009
solution=1.047140e-001
solution=3.141421e-001
solution=5.975338e-001
solution=8.224345e-001
solution=9.668300e-001
solution=1.016585e+000
solution=9.668296e-001
solution=8.224345e-001
solution=5.975337e-001
solution=3.141420e-001
solution=1.047140e-001
solution=7.932658e-013
 x=0.000000 sin=0.000000 exact=0.000000 cos=0.999945
 x=0.050000 sin=0.156430 exact=0.156434 cos=0.987710
```

x=0.100000 sin=0.309017 exact=0.309017 cos=0.951005
x=0.150000 sin=0.453979 exact=0.453991 cos=0.891026
x=0.200000 sin=0.587785 exact=0.587785 cos=0.808972
x=0.250000 sin=0.707088 exact=0.707107 cos=0.707122
x=0.300000 sin=0.809017 exact=0.809017 cos=0.587753
x=0.350000 sin=0.890983 exact=0.891007 cos=0.454001
x=0.400000 sln=0.951057 exact=0.951057 cos=0.309000
x=0.450000 sin=0.987663 exact=0.987688 cos=0.156438
x=0.500000 sin=1.000000 exact=1.000000 cos=-0.000000
x=0.550000 sin=0.987663 exact=0.987688 cos=-0.156439
x=0.600000 sin=0.951056 exact=0.951056 cos=-0.309000
x=0.650000 sin=0.890983 exact=0.891007 cos=-0.454000
x=0.700000 sin=0.809017 exact=0.809017 cos=-0.587753
x=0.750000 sin=0.707088 exact=0.707107 cos=-0.707122
x=0.800000 sin=0.587785 exact=0.587785 cos=-0.808973
x=0.850000 sin=0.453979 exact=0.453990 cos=-0.891026
x=0.900000 sin=0.309017 exact=0.309017 cos=-0.951004
x=0.950000 sin=0.156430 exact=0.156435 cos=-0.987710

Chapter 9

Adaptive Quadrature

Chapter Objectives

In this chapter you will find tools to:

- integrate a function adaptively, i.e., with the number of function evaluations controlled by error estimates.

Numerical Integration

This chapter and the next are devoted to the problem of "quadrature," i.e., the integration of a known function. In this chapter, we present an adaptive method, one that estimates its own error and refines its estimate of the solution if that error exceeds a specified tolerance.

We assume that the function, say f(x), is known for any value of x within the range of integration. If this is not the case, e.g., if we are working with tabulated data or other measurements, the interpolation methods discussed below and in Chapter 6 can be used to provide such a function.

Occasionally, "cubature" (double integration) or other multiple integration is required. This may be accomplished recursively by defining a function, say F(x), as the integral of f(x,y), and computing the integral over x of F. In FORTRAN, one has to exercise care in doing this as many implementations of FORTRAN do not support recursion. One could find the program "daisy-chaining" infinitely. This is not a problem in C. Indeed, the program for adaptive quadrature we will present is itself recursive.

Quadrature

Numerical integration is more often ancillary to solving another problem. In the finite-element and moment methods discussed above, it often is not possible to obtain analytic integrals of the weighting functions and the expansion functions over the element, necessitating a numerical approach. A particular example of this is in antenna theory. The expressions for expansion functions may be supplied by, for example, the Geometrical Theory of Diffraction or some related approximation method. Even when these expressions are analytic, they are not simple. Numerical integrations must then be performed to determine the coefficients in the system to be solved. The functions to be integrated are often tricky in such cases—for example, the current near the edge of a perfectly conducting plane which is diffracting an incident wave has a singularity. The singularity is weak and integrable, but can cause headaches if not properly accounted for. Similar problems arise in mechanics, where one typically has to set up a mass matrix **M** and a stiffness matrix **K** for the elements in a finite-element model.

Perhaps less often, an integral is (excuse the pun) an integral part of the problem. An example is a transport problem, such as that of radiation, neutrons, etc. The radiation intensity I is a scalar function of position and direction (and also frequency in the case of radiation, or energy in the case of neutrons, etc.; see, e.g., Kourganoff for an introduction to the essentials). The moments of the function I at a point are the integrals over direction, weighted by powers of the direction cosine with a fixed direction. The mean intensity E is proportional to the integral of I over direction, i.e., the zeroth moment (different authors use different factors in the definition of E). The flux vector **F** is the vector composed of the first moments of I with the direction cosines with respect to the three axes of the coordinate system. The second and higher moments follow similarly, the second moments similar to the inertia tensor in mechanics. The interaction of the radiation field with matter is dependent upon functions of E, for example, and **F** is often either a boundary condition, or the principal result of interest at some point, or both. In treating such problems, one does not solve for I and then do the integrals to find the moments—rather, integration formulas are at least implicit in the solution procedure. In particular, Gaussian quadrature forms the basis of the P-N method of transport theory.

Explicit use of integration is less likely in the social sciences. The important statistical functions are either tabulated or related to well-studied integrals (e.g., the beta function or the error function) for which there are good approximate fits. It may be necessary to perform integrals numerically if your work strays from the beaten path, however.

Newton-Cotes Formulae and Simpson's Rule

In what follows, assume we wish to integrate the function f(x) from x[min] to x[max]. We will evaluate f at the points x[i], at which points it takes on the values f[i].

In a nutshell, quadrature formulas are all derived by performing some fit to the function f over a range of x (an interpolation method), in which the integral of the fitting function can be analytically determined. Very often, the function fit to the data is a polynomial of some kind. This is because polynomials may easily be integrated once their coefficients are known. The drawback is that polynomials are notorious for oscillating wildly between the interpolation points if they are of high degree. Consequently, in numerical analysis, interpolating polynomials are often quadratics or cubics, with quartics or quintics used sparingly and higher degrees almost never. Better results are obtained by using lower-degree polynomials to fit smaller regions, as applied below and in Chapter 8 where spline interpolation is discussed.

The term "Newton-Cotes formula" (or "rule") applies to an integration method which assumes that the data points x[i], at which the function f(x) is to be evaluated and fit to the integrable interpolation function, are equally spaced in x, and that a polynomial of lowest order is to be interpolated through these points. For example, if the individual ranges we integrate over are the intervals between successive x[i], treating two points at a time, we interpolate through them with a straight line. (Each of these non-overlapping regions into which we have broken the full range of integration is called a "panel." For linear interpolation, the panel will extend from x[i] to x[i+1]; for quadratic interpolation we will interpolate through the function values for the three points x[i],x[i + 1],and x[i + 2], etc.) This produces a trapezoid whose area (integral) is

$$(x[i + 1] - x[i])*(f[i] + f[i])/2$$

(the base times the average height). Unless the function we are integrating is a linear function over the entire range to be integrated, it will not be sufficiently accurate to use the above formula with   x[1] = x[min] and x[2] = x[max]. There are two possible ways to get a closer approximation to the integral. We can go to a higher-order interpolating polynomial. This will give us more freedom—a straight line is determined by two points, but a quadratic requires three points to determine it, etc. Thus we will have to evaluate the function at more points. Alternatively, we can subdivide the range of integration and apply the above rule to each part. Such methods are termed "composite." The interpolating straight line segments will then deviate less from the function, in general. If we do so, we obtain the trapezoidal rule by summing this formula over the entire range to be integrated. Each interior point i contributes to the integral twice, once when it's on the right-hand side of an interval and once when it's on the left. Furthermore, we have by assumption

$$h = x[i + 1] - x[i]$$

is a constant. The integral is then

$$h/2\{f(x[min]) + 2f(x[min + h]) + 2f(x[min + 2h]) + ... + 2f(x[max - h]) \;\; +f(x[max])\}$$

In Simpson's rule, we use a panel with two intervals and interpolate a quadratic. The resultant formula (to be derived below) for the panel is

$$h/3\{f(x) + 4f(x + h) + f(x + 2h)\}$$

which produces, on summing over the panels, the composite formula

$$h/3\{f(x[min]) + 2f(x[min] + h) + 4f(x[min] + 2h) + 2f(x[min] + 3h)... + f(x[max])\}$$

with the alternating pattern of coefficients 2, 4, 2, 4,... at interior points. Note that Simpson's rule requires the use of an even number of intervals, and an odd number of function evaluations. Note that h is the width of one interval, or one-half the width of the full panel.

The next Newton-Cotes rule—for panels with 3 intervals—is called "Simpson's 3/8 rule," and is exact for cubics. Next is Bode's rule, with four intervals and five function evaluations, and which is exact for functions that are quintic polynomials. Formulas for these, and the next six formulae of the same type, may be found in chapter 25 of Abramowitz and Stegun. These formulae, which include the values at the endpoints of the panel, are called "closed type." Formulae for open-type Newton-Cotes formulas are also give, e.g., for a panel with two intervals and one interior point, we have the "midpoint rule"

$$2hf(x[min + h])$$

or with three intervals, and hence 2 interior points:

$$3h/2(f[min + h] + f[min + 2h])$$

or for four intervals

$$4h/3(2f[min + h] - f[min + 2h] + 2f[min + 3h]).$$

Table 9.1 summarizes the properties of the lowest-order Newton-Cotes formulae. Note the exceptional accuracy of Simpson's rule; for the same
order of accuracy as Simpson's 3/8 rule, we get away with one less function evaluation. Although we interpolate with parabolas, i.e., quadratic or
second degree curves, the formula is actually exact for cubics! It is for this
reason the Simpson's rule is an attractive choice upon which to base an
adaptive integration scheme.

Table 9.1

Newton-Cotes Formulae

Rule name	Exact for polynomials of degree n = error order h^n	
Trapezoidal	1	3
Simpson's	3	5
Simpson's 3/8	3	5
Bode's	5	7

Here h is the stepsize.
The error term is proportional to the $(n - 1)$th derivative of the function to
be integrated (at some point in the range of integration).

Derivation of Simpson's Rule

Let $y = A^2 x + Bx + C$ be our fit to the function to be integrated, f[x] at
$x[i] = i h, i = 0, 1, 2$. Then $f[0] = C$, and

$$f[1] = Ah^2 + Bh + f[0]$$

$$f[2] = 4Ah^2 + 2Bh + f[0]$$

We can then solve for A and B:

$$A = (f[0] + f[2] - 2f[1])/2h^2$$

$$B = (2f[1] - 3f[0]/2 - f[2]/2)/h.$$

The area under y from 0 to 2h is $8Ah^3/3 + 2Bh^2 + 2Ch$ which is
$(h/3)\{f[0]+2f[1]+f[2]\}$

Consider now the cubic $y = Dx^3$. The area under it over the interval from 0 to 2h is $4Dh^4$. We find that $f[0] = 0, f[1] = Dh^3, f[2] = 8Dh^3$. Simpson's rule gives the area $12Dh^4/3 = 4Dh^4$, which is exact. Because integration is a linear process, as Simpson's rule is exact for any quadratic and for the simple cubic, it will be exact for the sum, i.e., the general cubic.

The adaptive Simpson quadrature routine is designed to take advantage of this underserved good fortune by applying Simpson's rule repeatedly to the integration of troublesome functions.

Hermite Interpolation and Other Methods

Various special purpose methods exist for treating integrands with known properties, or integrands that are known to be relatively well-behaved. For example, if the derivative of the function is known or can be easily and economically evaluated (without numerical differencing), so-called "Hermite-interpolation methods" may be used. An example is the "corrected trapezoidal rule"

$$h/2(f[min] + f[min + h]) + h^2/12(f'\ [min]\text{-}f'\ [min + h])$$

where $f'\ [x]$ is the derivative of f evaluated at x.

The Clenshaw-Curtis method deserves mention as a sort of "semi-adaptive" method. It is suitable for integrands which are continuous—if the function is suspected of being pathological, this method should not be used. If it is appropriate, however, it should generally be more economical in terms of the number of function evaluations required for a given accuracy. The method interpolates the function by the use of Chebyshev (or Tchebyshev, or any alternative spelling) polynomials, relying on the Fast Fourier Transform technique (see Chapter 10) to optimize the calculation.

Romberg extrapolation is another "semi-adaptive" method, which uses the error estimate of the integration scheme, coupled with integral evaluations for a number of different step sizes, to estimate the integral in the limit of zero stepsize. It is also suitable for non-pathological integrals.

Adaptive Quadrature

In adaptive quadrature, we allow the program to estimate the error in the result and compare it to a user-defined error criterion. If that is satisfied, the result is accepted. If not, the program attempts to generate a more accurate answer. We will see similar adaptive techniques used in the IVP solvers in Chapters 10 and 11, where the timestep has been adjusted based upon the difference in two different computations of the "same" solution.

Adaptive quadrature is completely analogous. We estimate the integral in two ways, and if there is sufficient agreement we accept the result. Typically, what is done is to obtain the second result by subdividing the interval more finely, e.g., dividing it in half and using the same formula as used on the whole interval to treat the subintervals, summing the result and comparing it with the answer for the single-interval subdivision. The adaptive quadrature method used here does exactly that. It uses recursion, so that the accuracy of that interval is checked for accuracy, etc. In the routine used here, which is based upon the method of Algorithm 145 of the *Collected Algorithms from ACM* (see Chapter 8 for reference) by W. M. McKeeman, the formula used for the individual interval is Simpson's rule, and if the error criterion is not satisfied, the region is trisected and the three sub-regions are integrated and summed. Note that the use of recursion concentrates the effort of the routine on regions where the effort should be concentrated. We use a recursive routine, which is quite natural in C. The recursion can be simulated by a "stack" data structure, for example, and Algorithm 182 is a "nonrecursive" version of the method. This removal of recursion has to be done for methods in FORTRAN, which until the most recent versions did not support recursion. It may or may not be more efficient, depending upon how well the compiler optimizes recursive calls compared to how well it handles the non-recursive code. Forsythe, Malcolm, and Moler present a non-recursive FORTRAN program for adaptive quadrature, QUANC8. It is based upon the Newton-Cotes formula for 8 points rather than Simpson's rule.

The coding is fairly straightforward, with some exceptions. First, note that if we evaluate the area of a region by Simpson's rule, we have to evaluate the function at the endpoints of the region. If we decide to subdivide the region and recompute the area of the subdivided regions, we can re-use the values determined at the endpoints of that region. This accounts for the fact the values of the functions at the endpoints of the region of integration are sent in as parameters to the integration routine, so that they need not be re-evaluated. Note also that the depth of recursion is limited; this prevents the routine chasing its tail ad infinitum on a difficult problem. The parameter eta is a fractional error tolerance, the ratio of the absolute value of the difference in the estimates of the integral to absarea, which is the integral of the absolute value of the function. In the original published version of the algorithm, McKeeman multiplied the error estimate variable eps by 1/3, which would be justified if the error were uniformly distributed over the three subintervals. However, this rarely happens for any integral which requires adaptive quadrature, and in the certification of the algorithm, also by McKeeman, it was recommended that this be changed to dividing eps by 1.7 (i.e., the square root of 3), i.e., multiplying eps by .58. This value must be viewed as a "rule-of-thumb" value. Particularly nasty integrals probably require a smaller divisor, i.e., a more gradual reduction of eps. The level limit might also be subject to change (in the original published version, this was set at 7 rather than 20).

The Program and Test Case

McKeeman publishes a fairly stringent test, namely that of the integral of $f(x) = 1/\mathrm{sqrt}(\mathrm{abs}(x))$ in the interval from -9 to 1000, with eps $= 1$

We have used a simple quadratic, to test that the exact result which we would expect from Simpson's rule is obtained.

Note that 19 function evaluations have been used to generate this result. Adaptive quadrature should generally be reserved for "tricky" integrals (those with singularities or rapid changes in the function), or as a check on results obtained by more economical methods.

The error estimates with eps should be taken with a very large grain of salt. The error estimate is based upon comparison of approximate results, so it is itself approximate. In the case of quadrature, if there is significant cancellation of terms in the integral, i.e. if $f(x)$ is rapidly oscillating in sign, the fractional error in the integral can be larger than might be expected. (We might mention Filon's method at this point, for integrating functions multiplied by sin x or cos x. A brief discussion of Filon's method, with references to caveats on its use, can be found in the book by Abramowitz and Stegun, *Handbook of Mathematical Functions*).

Table 9.2 lists the subroutines of this chapter.

Table 9.2

Programs of Chapter 9

adsimp   Adaptive Simpson Quadrature

References

M. Abramowitz and I. A. Stegun, *Handbook of Mathematical Functions, (Washington, D. C.:GPO, 1964)*.

V. Kourganoff, *Basic Methods in Transfer Problems*, (NY: Dover, 1962).

Program Listing and Test Problem Output

(listing begins next page)

```
/*
adaptive integration routine
uses Simpson's rule adaptively
(from "C Tools for Scientists and Engineers" by L. Baker)

CONTENTS:

adsimp
    adaptively computes integral of function

simp
    recursively applies simpson's rule

main
    test driver

funct
    function to be integrated

DEPENDENCIES:
NONE
*/

/*#include "libc.h"
#include "math.h"
*/
#define abs(x) ((x)?(x):-(x))
#define max(a,b) ((a)>(b)?(a):(b))
int level,maxlev,levmax,feval;

double adsimp(a,b,eps,f) double a,b,eps,(*f)();
{
double simp(),aa,epss,absarea,ans,fa,fb,fm,range,est;
levmax=1;
feval=3;
level=1;
maxlev=20;
aa=a;epss=eps;
```

```
absarea=1.;
est=1.;
range=b-a;
printf(" adsimp\n");
fa=(*f)(a);
fb=(*f)(b);
fm=(*f)( 5*(a+b)) *4.;
/* printf(" intergrand fa,fb,fm %e %e %e\n",fa,fb,fm)*/;
ans=simp(aa,range,fa,fm,fb,absarea,est,epss,f);
return(ans);
}


double simp(a,da,fa,fm,fb,area,est,eps,f)
double a,da,fa,fm,fb,area,est,eps,(*f)();
{
double absarea;
double funct();
double dx,x1,x2,est1,est2,est3,f1,f2,f3,f4,sum,epss,norm=.588;
absarea=area;
/*printf("simp %e %e %e %e %e \n %e %e %e %d\n"
,a,da,fa,fm,fb,absarea,est,eps,level);*/
dx=.333333333*da;
epss=eps*norm;
x1=a+dx;
x2=x1+dx;
f1=4.*(*f)(a+.5*dx);
f2=(*f)(x1);
f3=(*f)(x2);
f4=4.*(*f)(a+2.5*dx);
/*
f1=4.*funct(a+.5*dx);
f2=funct(x1);
f3=funct(x2);
f4=4.*funct(a+2.5*dx);
*/
feval+=4;
est1=(fa+f1+f2)*dx*.166666666666;
est2=(f2+fm+f3)*dx*.166666666666;
```

```
est3=(f3+f4+fb)*dx*.166666666666;
absarea=area-abs(est)+abs(est1)+abs(est2)+abs(est3);
sum=est1+est2+est3;
level++;
levmax= max(level,levmax);
if ( ((abs(est-sum)> eps*absarea)||(est==1.)) && level<maxlev)
    sum= simp(a,dx,fa,f1,f2,absarea,est1,epss,f)
       +simp(x1,dx,f2,fm,f3,absarea,est2,epss,f)
       +simp(x2,dx,f3,f4,fb,absarea,est3,epss,f);

level--;
return(sum);
}


main(argc,argv) int argc;char **argv;
{
double funct();
double a,adsimp(),b,eps,ans;
a=0.;
b=1;
eps=.001;
ans=adsimp(a,b,eps,funct);
printf (" fini\n");
printf(" area=%e max depth=%d\n function evaluations=%d\n"
,ans,levmax,feval);
exit(0);
}


double funct(x) double x;
{
return(x*x);
}


 adsimp
 fini
 area=3.333333E-1 max depth=3
 function evaluations=19
```

CHAPTER 10

Fourier Transforms

Chapter Objectives

In this chapter we will present tools to:

-compute the Fast Fourier Transform (FFT) of an array of numbers.

We will discuss the theory of the method and how it generalizes to other transforms of interest.

A Caveat

If you have not used the FFT before, you may be surprised by the result that it gives you. There are many pitfalls involved in numerical Fourier analysis in general and the FFT in particular. For example, an errata appeared in *Physical Review Letters,* vol. 56, no.16, 21 April 1986, p. 1757,1986, referring to "an error in the interpretation of the coefficients from the Fourier-transform algorithm..." which occurred in a paper which appeared approximately four years earlier (*Phys. Rev. Lett.* vol. 48,p. 677,1982). The authors involved were not neophytes but highly experienced and respected workers in the field. The error magnified the discrepancy between simple theory and computation, and the original paper put forward a model to account for this discrepancy. With the growth rates doubled, the simple theory and computational results are in good agreement, considering the uncertainties in such computations. We will try to point out the major pitfalls in the use of the Fast Fourier Transform and supply methods to avoid them.

In what follows, all of the variables should be assumed to be complex numbers.

Fourier Analysis and Its Uses

We can view the Fourier Transform as a simple expansion of a function f(t) in terms of a sum of exponentials, i.e.,

$$f(t) = \Sigma \; a[n] \exp \; (\; i \; \omega \; n \; t) \tag{1}$$

With coefficients simply related to the a[n], we can represent the terms on right-hand side as sums of sin(ωnt) and cos (ωnt). Note that we are not expanding in some arbitrary exponents, but rather the exponents are integer multiples of iωt, and that the exponents are imaginary. Notice that we must in general include positive and negative values of n. Because of this form of the expansion, the function f(t) is implicitly assumed to be a periodic function of t, f(t + T) = f(t), where T = $2\pi/\omega$.

We have named the independent variable t because, most often, f is a function of time. The multiples of the fundamental angular frequency W, i.e., nW, are the higher harmonics. It is often useful to analyze the behavior of electrical circuits in terms of their behavior for various frequencies, i.e., for imposed signals which have a time dependence of the form exp(iωt). The behavior of typical circuit components, such as capacitors and inductors, is simply described for such signals. The circuit equations become simple algebraic equations rather than differential equations for such an exponential (sinusoidal) signal. Circuits can often be characterized effectively for study as rational functions of frequency, called "transfer functions."

It is natural to discuss the "electromagnetic spectrum." The term "spectrum" refers to the frequency-domain behavior, i.e., the distribution of a[n] as a function of n. In the limit where we consider infinitesimally small W, so that the sum becomes an integral, we have a Fourier integral, and the discrete a[n] become a continuous function F(ω) (the discrete variable n corresponds to a frequency nω where in F(ω) we use ω to denote a continuous independent variable rather than a specific fundamental frequency W) called the "Fourier Transform of f(t)." Dealing with f(t) is called working in the "time-domain", while analyzing the same system by studying the properties of F(ω) is called working in the "frequency domain."

In optics, the simple action of focusing an image produces the Fourier Transform of the imaged object in the focal plane. This is part of the reason for the value of the Fourier Transform in optics. It is often used in laser resonator analysis. Recent interest in optical computing turns this relationship on its head by contemplating the use of a lens to "calculate" the Fourier Transform, rather than using the Fourier Transform to calculate the properties of an optical system. The standard reference on this subject is by J. Goodman. A succinct introduction may be found in Chapter 10 of Nussbaum and Phillips. As in electrical systems, in which the assumption of a single-frequency (monochromatic in optics terms) "driving" or forcing of the system permits great simplification, the use of the Fourier Transform in optics permits the definition of the optical transfer function and the modulation transfer function, analogous to the transfer functions in electronics.

Even for systems which are not fundamentally periodic, e.g., stochastic systems, it is often useful to consider their properties in "frequency domain." In part, this is probably due to characteristics of the measuring apparatus. One often hears of "white" noise (a stochastic signal which is independent of frequency, i.e., the magnitude of the a[n] are apparently all the same) or "colored" noise ("red" noise would be more intense at low frequencies, "blue" noise at high).

The Fourier Transform is useful in a number of signal processing applications. For example, the Fourier Transform of the convolution of two functions is the product of the Fourier Transform of those two functions. Therefore, we can transform each function, form the product, and take the inverse transform to obtain the convolution. A similar result may be obtained for the correlation of two functions, or the autocorrelation of a function (its self-correlation). The convolutions and correlations are important in a variety of signal analysis procedures, such as linear predictive coding and spectral estimation.

Our purpose is to determine the a[n] knowing f(t). Of particular interest is the situation in which we are given the values of f(t) measured periodically, i.e., f(m dt) for a fixed timestep dt and positive integral values of m = 0,1,...M. (Note again that f(t) will be implicitly assumed periodic, i.e., f(0) = F(Mdt). When we consider possible pitfalls to Fourier analysis, this will be significant.) It is to this special case of periodic measurements of f(t) that the remainder of the chapter is devoted. Technologically, this is the situation of most interest. Conversely, it is of most interest in such cases to consider the a[n], i.e., the Fourier coefficients for multiples of a fixed frequency, giving equal intervals of the F(ω) in frequency domain. We will assume that there are N data points in the time domain, i.e., that f(n dt) is known for n = 0,...N − 1. We will then be able to solve for N coefficients a[n], i.e., for F(ω) where ω = m/T, m = 0,..., N − 1, (T = $2\pi/(N - 1)$).

In situations where the frequencies of interest span a very broad range, this is not so useful, and the technique of the Fast Fourier Transform may not be of value. An old-fashioned "slow" Fourier Transform in which the points are spaced, say, logarithmically in frequency, may be more appropriate.

The function F(ω) for ω = mW, or, equivalently, a[n], may be found by multiplying the equation (1) through by exp(− imkWt) where k is an integer, and summing over k, using the properties of the exponentials to give us the relation (see Flanders)

$$a[n] = \Sigma\, f(m\,dt) \exp(-\,i\,nmWt)$$

For each of the a[n], we have have a sum over N terms to calculate. Even assuming that all of the necessary exponentials have been calculated previously and tabulated, we will have N floating-point multiplications and additions to perform for each a[n], or about $2N^2$ floating-point multiplications for the whole calculation (remember, we are dealing with complex numbers). If we have merely one thousand data points, this is a million floating-point multiplications required. This is probably prohibitively expensive, due to the scaling with the square of N.

The FFT

The so-called "Fast Fourier Transform" (FFT) is an efficient method of calculating the coefficients a[n], or equivalently F(w). Note that if we think of the calculation in terms of F(w), it is being fixed only at discrete points. It created a sensation in 1965 when J. W. Cooley and J. W. Tukey announced it, as it made computations which were previously believed to be prohibitively expensive practical. Since that time it has been found that the underlying ideas were embodied in a number of papers, including work by C. F. Gauss!

The basic idea is to exploit the facts that $\exp(a + b) = \exp(a)\exp(b)$ and that $\exp(2\pi\,i) = 1$. Using these two facts together, we find that many of the N^2 terms in calculating the a[n] are the same. If we cleverly arrange the calculation so that these terms are only calculated once, we can economize greatly.

Define $q = \exp(iWt)$. One approach, discussed fully in Flanders and in Press et al. (see reference in Chapter 7) is to break the terms in (1) for f(m dt) into odd and even powers of q. The sum of even powers is the Fourier transform of a[0],a[2],... while that of the odd powers is that of a[1],a[3],... multiplied by q^m. If N = 2K, then each sum contains K terms. However, we only have to calculate half as many sums because either sum for any m is the same as that sum for $m' = m + K$. This follows from the fact that $q^K = 1$, which must hold assuming we have N points with an equal number of positive and negative frequencies in the Fourier expansion. By this means we can cut the number of floating-point calculations in half. If N is a power of 2, we do this factorization recursively, cutting the effort down by a factor of 2 each time. The cost then becomes proportional to N log N, which increases much more slowly with N and makes calculations involving thousands of points quite reasonable.

The preceding paragraph describes the "radix 2" FFT. There are many variants possible which do not require the number of points N to be a power of 2. See Blahut for an exhaustive (and exhausting) compilation of the many variants on the FFT.

An alternative way to view the FFT is via matrices. Consider the FFT for N = 4, which by definition is

$$
\begin{pmatrix} a[0] \\ a[1] \\ a[2] \\ a[3] \end{pmatrix} = \begin{pmatrix} q^0 & q^0 & q^0 & q^0 \\ q^0 & q^1 & q^2 & q^3 \\ q^0 & q^2 & q^4 & q^6 \\ q^0 & q^3 & q^6 & q^9 \end{pmatrix} \begin{pmatrix} f(0) \\ f(dt) \\ f(2dt) \\ f(3dt) \end{pmatrix}
$$

Using the fact that $q^4 = 1$, we have

$$
\begin{pmatrix} a[0] \\ a[1] \\ a[2] \\ a[3] \end{pmatrix} = \begin{pmatrix} 1 & 1 & 1 & 1 \\ 1 & q & -1 & -q \\ 1 & -1 & 1 & -1 \\ 1 & -q & -1 & q \end{pmatrix} \begin{pmatrix} f(0) \\ f(dt) \\ f(2dt)) \\ f(3dt) \end{pmatrix}
$$

The crucial trick is to interchange the second and third rows. If we do this, we can factor the matrix as the product of two matrices

$$
\begin{pmatrix} a[0] \\ a[2] \\ a[1] \\ a[3] \end{pmatrix} = \begin{pmatrix} 1 & 1 & 0 & 0 \\ 1 & -1 & 0 & 0 \\ 0 & 0 & 1 & q \\ 0 & 0 & 1 & -q \end{pmatrix}
$$

$$
\begin{pmatrix} 1 & 0 & 1 & 1 \\ 0 & 1 & 0 & 1 \\ 1 & 0 & -1 & 0 \\ 0 & 1 & 0 & -1 \end{pmatrix} \begin{pmatrix} f(0) \\ f(dt) \\ f(2dt) \\ f(3dt) \end{pmatrix}
$$

Whereas our original matrix required sixteen complex multiplications, the new matrix requires only two involving the complex variable q (although additional multiplications by -1 are required). This is at the cost of rearranging the a vector. It turns out (see the references cited above, and also Brigham) that the desired rearrangement of the indices of the vector **a** can be achieved by reversing the order of the bits in the index of **a**. Thus, in our example, 0 and 3 remain unchanged, while 2 (10 in binary) and 1 (01 in binary) exchange places. We refer you to Brigham and Flanders for the details, but, briefly, this comes about because first a "perfect shuffle" is performed to separate the odd and even terms in the sum, then each of these halves is again shuffled, etc. For a discussion of the FFT from this point of view, see, e.g., Sedgwick.

Pitfall: What Answer Does the FFT Give?

The test program below produces the FFT of the decaying exponential function $f(t) = \exp(-t)$. This is the example Brigham gives at the start of his Chapter 9. Notice that we set the value of $f(0) = .5$, not 1. This is because, as noted above, $f(t)$ should be a periodic function, and the value at $f(0)$ should be the same as that at $f(T)$. Since the latter is essentially zero, the value at $f(0)$ should be the average of zero and one. This fine point is not of crucial significance.

Now consider the answers. The Fourier transform of $f(t)$ should be $1/(1+j\omega)$, monotonically decreasing as w increases. But the real part of the FFT result decreases to the midway point and then increases. The explanation is simple. The negative frequency components are in the array, too, and the order in which they appear may be a surprise. The smallest (in magnitude) frequencies occur at the ends of the array, increasing toward the center (see Brigham).

Note that if you have a frequency domain function and wish to transform back to time domain, you must "fold" the function midway in the array and invert the sign of the imaginary part for $n < N/2$. Otherwise, you will not get a real function as the answer (see the section on real and causal functions below). To get the FFT to agree numerically with the Fourier Transform, it must be scaled (i.e., multiplied) by the time period being transformed. Similarly, the inverse transform must be scaled by the frequency increment between points.

Pitfall: Aliasing (Time-Domain)

Aliasing refers to the fact that different Fourier components, when sampled periodically, can appear to be other frequencies. This may give rise to contributions to a frequency component which actually arise from another component.

Suppose we were using the FFT to analyze an optical system, say an aperture. By the comments above concerning the periodic nature of the function being transformed, the FFT will actually be that of an infinite, periodic array of slits (a diffraction grating, in effect). The effect is illustrated in Figure 10.1. If the diffraction pattern of one of the "images" of the slit

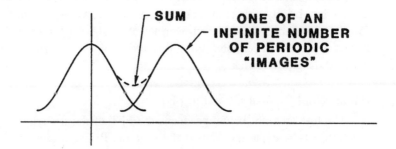

Fig. 10.1: How aliasing arises.

overlaps another, its high-frequency components (the "tails" of the diffraction pattern shown) overlap the neighboring pattern, resulting in a spurious contribution to the edges of the pattern of the individual slit.

The cure to this problem is to put appropriate "guard" zones, whose value for $f(t)$ is zero, at the periphery of the actual function $f(t)$ to be transformed. This moves the images apart until the overlap is negligible. How many guard cells are needed, of course, depends upon the problem, but it is often a significant number, say half of the number of "real" data points. Similar protection must be used when the FFT is employed for the purpose of a convolution or correlation (including autocorrelation) of a function which is not periodic.

Pitfall: Aliasing (Frequency-Domain)

There is another, possibly more subtle way for aliasing to introduce error into a calculation. Suppose, for example, we have Fourier transformed a function with a nonzero component $\sin(5\omega t)$, but have only used sampling points at the periodicity of $4\omega t$. Because $\sin(5\omega t) = \sin(4\omega t)\cos(\omega t) + \cos(4\omega t)\sin(\omega t)$, at these sampling points $\sin(4\omega t) = 0$, and $\cos(4\omega t) = 1$, so $\sin(5\omega t) = \sin(\omega t)$, i.e. a function of the form $A\sin(5\omega t)$ or $A\sin(\omega t)$, will contribute exactly the same. The functions are indistinguishable, insofar as the sampling at the 4ω frequency is concerned. Thus, the unresolved frequency component at 5ω will produce an apparent signal at ω.

This is in fact the same aliasing mechanism as discussed under the heading "time domain" aliasing. The "images" in the figure are in frequency domain. The periodicity is now $T = \pi/\omega$, where ω is the frequency resolution of the FFT. There is a lost factor of 2 in this expression due to the requirement to sample at twice the frequency of the maximum frequency component of the signal, in order to obtain phase as well as amplitude information (i.e., tell the sines from the cosines). This is called the "Nyquist frequency" (see Brigham).

There are two possible treatments to the problem of frequency-domain aliasing. The first is, as in time-domain aliasing, to move the images further apart until the overlap can be ignored. For frequency-domain aliasing, this requires sampling at or above the Nyquist frequency. Such sampling may be prohibitively expensive, or may not be possible if the data is already taken and presented for analysis as a fait accompli. In such a case, an anti-aliasing filter may be used. The idea is simply to remove the dangerous high-frequency components, which we do not have sufficient resolution to usefully analyze but which can cause errors. This can either be done when the data is taken (i.e., a low-pass filter is inserted in the system) or a smoothing to remove the troublesome frequencies may be done on the data, if it has sufficient resolution. If such aliasing occurs during the measurement itself, it is of course difficult to correct a posteriori.

Real and Causal Functions

Advantage may be taken of known characteristics of the functions to be transformed, under various circumstances. For example, if the function to be transformed is real, the "Fast Hartley Transform" may be employed, cutting the computational effort in half. This is discussed fully in Bracewell, and the FORTRAN code presented there provides the basis for our implementation in C of the FHT. Note that the normalization convention used by Bracewell differs from that used for the FFT, so a scaling conversion is performed to permit ease of comparison of the results.

Note that, if $f(t)$ is real, its transform $F(\omega)$ must satisfy $F(-\omega) = F^*(\omega)$, where $*$ denotes the complex conjugate. This results in the behavior of our sample problem, where, for $F = R + iX$, we have $R(\omega) = R(-\omega)$ and $X(\omega) = -X(-\omega)$.

Causal functions, i.e., those for which $f(t) = 0$ for t, are often of interest for signal processing. The term "causal" invariably means that $f(t)$ is assumed real as well. In such cases, the real and imaginary parts of F are related by the Hilbert Transform. Physicists may recognize the Hilbert Transform as the Kramers-Kronig relation(s). Unfortunately, the relationship between the functions R and X through the Hilbert is sufficiently complicated that the computational burden cannot be reduced by this. Given observed X and R, one can check the consistency, however, assuming the $f(t)$ is causal.

One often sees the frequency spectrum specified by IFI. The phase information, i.e., the relationship of R and X at any ω, is lost. It is not possible to uniquely determine the f which gave rise to a given IFI, even if the function f is causal. However, there are standard forms, such as the "Bode minimum phase" f, which can be constructed. If F is a transfer function for an electrical network, then it may be shown, for example, that if the network is a ladder network, then the time-domain response of the network must be given by the minimum phase f.

The Program and Test Cases

The program employs the complex arithmetic package developed in Chapter 7 to compute the FFT of the test problem from Brigham discussed above. The inverse FFT is then computed to confirm the accuracy of the calculation. The program is similar to the PASCAL program of Flanders (see above). Advantage has been taken of the shift operation in C to produce the bit-reversed indices for a[n]. In addition, the computation of the powers of the exponential (w in the program, q in the text) has been placed in an auxiliary routine so that it need not be calculated each time. The vector of powers required for the inverse transform is merely the complex conjugate of those for the direct transform. Thus, one set of evaluations of the exponential function will suffice for all FFTs—direct and inverse—for the given N. The calculation of log N is performed in integer arithmetic rather than being a required input variable. Note carefully that the function fft() does not "know" if it is doing a direct or inverse FFT. To do an inverse FFT, supply the wi[] array instead of the w[] array, and divide the results by N. (This is the usual normalization convention. Sometimes, the results of both direct and inverse transforms are divided by the square root of N for symmetry.)

Table 10.1

Functions of Chapter 10

log2	Computes the base-2 logarithm of an integer (assumes integer result)
fftinit	Initialize fft
bitr	Perfom bit reversal for FFT
fft	Compute Fast Fourier Transform
fhtinit	Initialize FHT
fht	Compute Fast Hartley Transform

References

R. E. Blahut, *Fast Algorithms for Digitial Signal Processing*, (Reading,MA: Addison-Wesley, 1986).

R. N. Bracewell, *The Fourier Transform and Its Applications*, (NY: MGraw-Hill, second edition 1986).

E. O. Brigham, *The Fast Fourier Transform*, (Englewood Cliffs, NJ: Prentice-Hall, 1974).

H. Flanders, *Scientific Pascal*, (Reston, VA: Reston Publ., 1984).

J. Goodman, *Introduction to Fourier Optics*, (NY: McGraw-Hill, 1968).

A. Nussbaum and R. A. Phillips, *Contemporary Optics for Scientists and Engineers,* (Englewood Cliffs, NJ: Prentice-Hall, 1976).

R. Sedgewick, *Algorithms*, (Reading, MA: Addison-Wesley,1983).

Program Listings and Test Problem Output

(listing begins next page)

```
/*  fast Fourier transform (FFT)
(from "C Tools for Scientists and Engineers" by L. Baker)

CONTENTS:

log2
    integer log to base 2 of an integer power of two
bitr
    do bit reversal for FFT array addressing
fftinit
    initialize arrays for given size (n) fft
fft
    perform FFT
printc
    print complex number
main
    test driver

DEPENDENCIES:
complex.h header file required

*/

#include "complex.h"
#define twopi 6.283185307

int iterp;/* global to return count used*/

#define max(a,b) (((a)>(b))? (a): (b))
#define abs(x) ((x)?  (x):-(x))
#define DOFOR(i,to) for(i=0;i<to;i++)

main(argc,argv) int argc;char **argv;
{int i,ii,nh,n=16;
double invn,exp(),dt=.25,omega,realpt,imagpt;
struct complex w[32],wi[32], data[32];
nh=n>>1;
DOFOR(i,n)
```

```
    {
    CMPLX(data[i], exp(-dt*(i)),0.);
    };
/* caveat*/ data[0].x=.5;/*not 1. see text*/
printf(" before transform:\n");
DOFOR(i,n){printc(&(data[i])) ;printf("\n");}
invn=1./n;
fftinit(w,wi,n);
/*(printf(" w factors:\n");
DOFOR(i,n){printc(&(w[i])) ;printc(&(wi[i])) ;printf("\n");}\*/
printf(" transformed:\n");
fft(data,w,n);
DOFOR(i,n){printc(&(data[i])) ;printf("\n");}
printf(" scaled by T=n*dt and compared to analytic answer:\n");
DOFOR(i,n)
    {
    ii= (i-nh)<0  ? i : i-n ;
    omega= twopi*ii/(n*dt);
    realpt= 1./(1.+omega*omega);
    imagpt= -realpt*omega;
    printf(" %f %f  %f %f\n", dt*data[i].x,dt*data[i].y,realpt,imagpt);
    }
/* inverse FFT*/
fft(data,wi,n);
printf(" transformed back and scaled by d(frequency)=1/n:\n");
DOFOR(i,n)
    {
    CTREAL(data[i],data[i],(invn));
    printc(&(data[i]));printf("\n");
    }
exit(0);
}

int bitr(k,logn) int k,logn;
{
int ans,j,i;
ans=0;
j=k;
```

```
DOFOR(i,logn)
   {
   ans=(ans<<1)+(j&1);
   j=j>>1;
   }
return(ans);
}


int log2(n) int n;
{
int i;
i=-1;/* will return -1 if n<=0 */
while(1)
   {
   if(n==0)break;
   n=n>>1;
   i++;
   }
return(i);
}

printc(x) struct complex *x;
{
printf("%f %f",x->x,x->y);
return;
}

fftinit(w,wi,n) int n; struct complex w[],wi[];
{
int i;
double realpt,imagpt,cos(),sin();
double factr,angle;
factr=twopi/n;
DOFOR(i,n)
   {angle=i*factr;
    realpt=cos(angle);imagpt=sin(angle);
    CMPLX(w[i],realpt,imagpt);
```

```
      CMPLX(wi[i],realpt,(-imagpt)));
      }
return;
}


fft(x,w,n) int n; struct complex w[],x[];
{
int n1,logn,i,j,k,l,l1,logl,exponent,p;
struct complex s,t,a,b;
logn=log2(n);
n1=n>>1;
j=logn-1;
/* transform*/
k=0;
DOFOR(logl,logn)
   {
   do{
   DOFOR(i,n1)
      {
      p=bitr((k>>j),logn);
      l=k+n1;
         CONJG(s,w[p]);
         CMULT(t,s,x[l]);
         CSUB(x[l],x[k],t);
         CADD(x[k],t,x[k]);
         k++;
      };/* dofor i*/
   k+=n1;
   }while (k<n);
k=0;
j--;
n1=n1>>1;
}


/*reorder*/
for(i=1;i<n;i++)
```

```
    {
    k=bitr(i,logn);
    if (i>k)
        {
        /*exchange i,k elements*/
        CLET(s,x[i]);
        CLET(x[i],x[k]);
        CLET(x[k],s);
        }

    };

return;
}
```

before transform:
0.500000 0.000000
0.778801 0.000000
0.606531 0.000000
0.472367 0.000000
0.367879 0.000000
0.286505 0.000000
0.223130 0.000000
0.173774 0.000000
0.135335 0.000000
0.105399 0.000000
0.082085 0.000000
0.063928 0.000000
0.049787 0.000000
0.038774 0.000000
0.030197 0.000000
0.023518 0.000000
transformed:
3.938010 0.000000
1.143903 -1.746777
0.373174 -1.070216
0.181974 -0.699026
0.111059 -0.475893
0.078526 -0.320685
0.062163 -0.199640
0.054256 -0.096066
0.051880 0.000000
0.054256 0.096066
0.062163 0.199640
0.078526 0.320685
0.111059 0.475893
0.181974 0.699026
0.373174 1.070216
1.143903 1.746777
scaled by T=n*dt and compared to analytic answer:
0.984503 0.000000 1.000000 -0.000000
0.285976 -0.436694 0.288400 -0.453018

0.093294 -0.267554 0.092000 -0.289025
0.045493 -0.174757 0.043091 -0.203062
0.027765 -0.118973 0.024705 -0.155223
0.019631 -0.080171 0.015953 -0.125293
0.015541 -0.049910 0.011133 -0.104922
0.013564 -0.024017 0.008203 -0.090200
0.012970 0.000000 0.006293 0.079077
0.013564 0.024017 0.008203 0.090200
0.015541 0.049910 0.011133 0.104922
0.019631 0.080171 0.015953 0.125293
0.027765 0.118973 0.024705 0.155223
0.045493 0.174757 0.043091 0.203062
0.093294 0.267554 0.092000 0.289025
0.285976 0.436694 0.288400 0.453018
transformed back and scaled by d(frequency)=1/n:
0.500000 -0.000000
0.778801 -0.000000
0.606531 -0.000000
0.472367 0.000000
0.367879 0.000000
0.286505 0.000000
0.223130 0.000000
0.173774 -0.000000
0.135335 0.000000
0.105399 0.000000
0.082085 0.000000
0.063928 -0.000000
0.049787 -0.000000
0.038774 -0.000000
0.030197 -0.000000
0.023518 -0.000000

```
/*
Discrete Fast Hartley Transform
based upon BASIC code in 2nd revised edition of R. N. Bracewell's
"The Fourier Transform and Its Applications" (McGraw-Hill,1986)
various modifications have been made to reduce storage required
(transform is done in place, unlike Bracewell) and reduce
computation (e.g., cos and sin only computed for n/4 + 1 values,
not n as in Bracewell).
(from "C Tools for Scientists and Engineers" by L. Baker)

CONTENTS:

log2
    returns integer logarithm to base 2 of integer (power of two assumed)

fhtinit
    intializes arrays of sines and cosines needed for FHT

fht
    do FHT.  fhtinit need be called oncefor multiple xfms of
    arrays if size unchanged.

main
    test driver.

DEPENDENCIES:
NONE
*/
#define min(a,b) (((a)<(b))? (a): (b))
#define max(a,b) (((a)>(b))? (a): (b))
#define abs(x) ((x)? (x):-(x))
#define DOFOR(i,to) for(i=0;i<to;i++)
#define INDEX(i,j) [j]
/* above def is same as for 1-d array on index j only*/

main(argc,argv) int argc;char **argv;
{int i,n=16,l,log2();
double invn,exp();
```

```
int m[256];
double dt=.25,f[256],r[256], w[256],wi[256],x[256];
n=8;/* bracewell testcase*/
DOFOR(i,n){
   f[i]= i+1;
   };
DOFOR(i,n){printf(" input %e ",f[i]) ;printf("\n");}
fhtinit(w,wi,m,n,256);
fht(f,r,x,w,wi,m,n);
printf(" warning- FFT results unscaled by T for ramp test case\n");
printf(" Fourier Tranform  Hartley Transform\n(Real Pt.)    (Imaginary)\n");
DOFOR(i,n){printf(" %e %e %e",r[i],x[i],f[i]) ;printf("\n");}
n=16;
DOFOR(i,n){
   f[i]= exp(-dt*(i));
   };
f[0]=.5;
DOFOR(i,n){printf(" input %e\n",f[i]) ;}
fhtinit(w,wi,m,n,256);
fht(f,r,x,w,wi,m,n);
invn=16.*dt;/*scaling for FT*/
printf(" decaying exponential: FT scaled\n");
printf(" Fourier Tranform  Hartley Transform\n(Real Pt.)    (Imaginary)\n");
DOFOR(i,n){ r[i]*=invn;x[i]*=invn;
         printf(" %e %e %e\n",r[i],x[i],f[i]);
         }
exit(0);
}


int log2(n) int n;
{
int i;
i=-1;/* will return -1 if n<=0 */
while(1)
   {
   if(n==0)break;
   n=n>>1;
   i++;
```

```
    }
return(i);
}


#define twopi 6.283185307

int cols,logn,n2,n4,log1;

fhtinit(c,s,m,n,columns) int n,m[],columns;
    double c[],s[];
{
int i,log2(),l;
double cos(),sin(),con,angl;
cols=columns;
con=twopi/n;
m[0]=1; logn=log2(n);log1=logn-1;
n2=n>>1;n4=n2>>1;
DOFOR(i,logn)
    {
        m[i+1]=(m[i])<<1;
    }
;
angl=0.;
DOFOR(i,n4+1)
   {c[i]=cos(angl);s[i]=sin(angl);
   angl+=con;
        }
return;
}



fht(f,r,x,c,s,m,n) int n,m[];
double x[],r[],c[],s[],f[];
{
double temp,temp2,temp3,temp4,temp1,invn;
int t,u,i,j,k,l,l1,d,e,ss,so,s2,exponent,p;
invn=1./n;
/*reorder, i.e.,permute */
```

```
if(logn>1)
{
j=-1;i=-1;
do   {
   do{
   i++;
   k=logn;
   do   {
            k--;
            j-=m[k];
       }while(j>=-1);
   j+=m[k+1];
   }while(i<=j);
   temp=f[i+1];
      f[i+1]= f[j+1];
      f[j+1]=temp;
   } while(i<n-3);
};
/* transform*/
/*2 element DHT unrolled inner loop*/
for(i=0;i<=n-2;i+=2)
   {
   temp= f[i];
   temp2=f[i+1];
   f[i]=temp+temp2;
   f [i+1]= temp-temp2;
      }
l=1;
if(logn!=1)
{
l=2;
/*4 element DHT unrolled inner loop*/
for(i=0;i<=n-4;i+=4)
   {
   temp= f[i];
   temp2=f [i+2];
   temp3=f [i+3];
   temp1=f [i+1];
```

```
   f [i]=temp+temp2;
   f [i+1]= temp1+temp3;
   f [i+2]=temp-temp2;
   f [i+3]=temp1-temp3;
      }
/*remaining loop*/
}
if(logn>2)
{
ss=4;
u=log1;
for(l=2;l<logn;l++)
   {
      s2=ss<<1;
      u--;
      so=m[u-1];
      for(k=0;k<n;k+=s2)
         {
         i=k;
         d=i+ss;
         temp= f[i];
         temp2=f [d];


         f [i]=temp+temp2;
         f [d]=temp-temp2;
         l1=d-1;
         for (j=so;j<=n4;j+=so)
            {
            i++;
            d=i+ss;
            e=l1+ss;
            temp= f[d]*c[j]+f[e]*s[j];
         temp2=f[d]*s[j]-f[e]*c[j];
         temp3=f[i];
         temp1=f[ l1];
         f[i]=temp3+temp;
         f[d]=temp3-temp;
```

```
            f[l1]=temp1+temp2;
        f[e]=temp1-temp2;
                    l1--;
                }
            e=l1+ss;
        }
    ss=s2;
    }
}
f[0]*=invn;
/*dft*/
r[0]=f[0]/*+ f INDEX(l,0)*/;
x[0]=0.;
for(i=1;i<=n2;i++)
    {
        temp2=f[n-i]*invn;
        temp= f[i]*invn;
        r[i]= (temp2+temp)*.5;
        x[i]= (temp2-temp)*.5;
        f[n-i]=temp2;
        f[i]= temp;
    }
/* reflect for other components of Fourier Transform*/
for(i=n2+1;i<n;i++)
    {
    j=n-i;
    r[i]=r[j];
    x[i]=-x[j];
    }
return;
}
```

input 1.000000E0
input 2.000000E0
input 3.000000E0
input 4.000000E0
input 5.000000E0
input 6.000000E0
input 7.000000E0
input 8.000000E0
warning- FFT results unscaled by T for ramp test case
Fourier Tranform Hartley Transform
(Real Pt.)   (Imaginary)
4.500000E0 0.000000E0 4.500000E0
-5.000000E-1 1.207106E0 -1.707106E0
-5.000000E-1 5.000000E-1 -1.000000E0
-5.000000E-1 2.071067E-1 -7.071067E-1
-5.000000E-1 0.000000E0 -5.000000E-1
-5.000000E-1 -2.071067E-1 -2.928932E-1
-5.000000E-1 -5.000000E-1 -2.244904E-11
-5.000000E-1 -1.207106E0 7.071067E-1
input 5.000000E-1
input 7.788007E-1
input 6.065306E-1
input 4.723665E-1
input 3.678794E-1
input 2.865048E-1
input 2.231301E-1
input 1.737739E-1
input 1.353352E-1
input 1.053992E-1
input 8.208499E-2
input 6.392786E-2
input 4.978706E-2
input 3.877420E-2
input 3.019738E-2
input 2.351774E-2
decaying exponential: FT scaled
Fourier Tranform Hartley Transform
(Real Pt.)   (Imaginary)

9.845025E-1 0.000000E0 2.461256E-1
2.859758E-1 -4.366942E-1 1.806675E-1
9.329362E-2 -2.675540E-1 9.021190E-2
4.549346E-2 -1.747565E-1 5.506250E-2
2.776464E-2 -1.189732E-1 3.668446E-2
1.963139E-2 -8.017116E-2 2.495063E-2
1.554076E-2 -4.990996E-2 1.636268E-2
1.356402E-2 -2.401650E-2 9.395132E-3
1.296997E-2 0.000000E0 3.242492E-3
1.356402E-2 2.401650E-2 -2.613119E-3
1.554076E-2 4.990996E-2 -8.592298E-3
1.963139E-2 8.017116E-2 -1.513494E-2
2.776464E-2 1.189732E-1 -2.280214E-2
4.549346E-2 1.747565E-1 -3.231577E-2
9.329362E-2 2.675540E-1 -4.356509E-2
2.859758E-1 4.366942E-1 -3.767960E-2

CHAPTER 11

Systems of Differential Equations

Chapter Objectives

In this chapter you will find C tools to:

-implement the Runge-Kutta-Fehlberg (RKF) class of methods for integrating systems of ordinary differential equations (ODEs) as part of an initial value problem (IVP)

-implement the popular 5th order version of the RKF method.

The theoretical basis of these methods will be discussed, as well as the concept of stiffness. (Another integrator suitable for stiff systems will be found in the next chapter.)

Numerical Treatment of Differential Equations

Next to ·solving systems of equations, solving systems of differential equations is probably the most frequent numerical chore for an engineer or physical scientist. Strictly speaking, a set of differential equations by themselves does not constitute a problem to be solved—that system must be augmented with various additional specifications, called in general "boundary conditions."

In this chapter and the next, we discuss methods for solving systems of ordinary differential equations (i.e., those with a single independent variable) within the context of an "initial value problem" or IVP. In the next chapter, so-called "stiff" systems are treated in detail.

How Initial Value Problems Arise

Implicit in the term "initial value problem" is the notion that the independent variable is time. In an IVP, we know the state of the system at the earliest time, say $t = 0$, and wish to determine the subsequent evolution of the system.

Any system of ordinary differential equations may be converted to a system of first-order differential equations through the introduction of new dependent variables representing derivatives of other dependent variables. As a simple example, the harmonic oscillator equation ($'$ denotes a derivative)

$$x'' + x = 0$$

may be written as the system

$$y = x'$$

$$y' + x = 0$$

Assuming we have put all of our equations in this form, we should have a problem with N equations, N dependent variables, and N initial conditions. If we do not, we either have too many or too few of something, and consequently either a non-unique solution or no solution at all. There are exceptions to this rule (if the equations involved are nonlinear or possess singularities), but as a general rule one needs equal numbers of equations, variables, and initial conditions.

IVPs arise often because natural laws are often easily and intuitively expressible as specifications of rates of change. Newton's law $F = ma$ is an example. It's really a second-order differential equation, if we assume that the motion is confined to one particle in one dimension, and that the force F is given. In three dimensions, one would have a similar equation for each of three components, giving a sixth-order system for a single particle. For a system involving many particles, merely write the system for each particle's acceleration and (velocity)

$$a = F/m = v'$$

$$x' = v$$

where x is the particle's position and v its velocity (view these as vectors if you wish, or else write similar equations for y and z and corresponding velocity components u and w). This system is not just of academic interest. It is solved for problems involving orbital mechanics and astrodynamics. It is used in particle code simulations of electron devices (klystrons, relativistic diodes, etc.).

Other applications of the IVP come to mind—circuit solvers, for example. The voltage across an inductor is given by $V - L i'$, a first-order differential equation. The charge on a capacitor is given by $q = CV$, or, differentiating and using the fact that $i = q'$, $i = C V'$. These relationships are used with Kirchhoff's laws to obtain ODE's that describe the circuit. That system of ODE's is then solved, almost invariably as an IVP with t = 0 when the "switch" is first closed and power is applied to the circuit.

Simulation of system evolution does not have to be limited to physical systems, such as systems of particles. When simulation using ODE's is employed, it is usual to call the process "continuous" simulation, as opposed to "discrete event" simulation. Discrete event simulation generally applies to models of queues and inventories, where the events are things such as "arrival of customer," "dispatching of order," "arrival of shipment," etc. Continuous models involve, for example, the simulation of flow processes, e.g., the draining or filling of a reservoir, the action of a servomechanism, etc.

Continuous simulations are also of use beyond the physical sciences. What Keynes called a "marginal propensity" was nothing more than a derivative, that is, a rate of change. In econometric models, it is not infrequent to see a modeling assumption such as "the rate of change of the gross national product is proportional to the investment rate." If we introduce a relationship such as: "The gross national product at any time is equal to the sum of investment, consumption, and government spending," then, along with relationships giving consumption and government spending, we could model the economy with a system of ODEs. Thus, while economists tend not to use the typical mathematical terms like derivative, they often are discussing ODEs. Population models, such as those involving predator-prey relationships, are typically ODE systems.

The independent variable need not be time. For example, in beam theory the independent variable may be the longitudinal coordinate along the beam, and the dependent variable the perpendicular displacement of the beam at that point. Chapter 38 of Volume II of the *Feynman Lectures on Physics* gives a concise introduction to the theory, deriving the approximate equation

$$z'' = F/YI$$

where z is the deflection, F the force, YI the "stiffness" of the beam (I the moment of inertia of the cross section and Y the Young's modulus).

If the ODE's and the IVP involving them are linear in the dependent variables, then the system is easily represented with matrix algebra in the form $\mathbf{d} = \mathbf{Ax} + \mathbf{F}$, where $\mathbf{d}$ is a vector of derivatives, $\mathbf{x}$ is the vector of dependent variables, $\mathbf{A}$ a coefficient matrix, and $\mathbf{F}$ a term representing external forcing of the system. The initial conditions can then be written as x[t = 0] =x[0], where x[0] is a given vector. Writing the system in this manner brings out the relationship of the IVP to the problems discussed in the previous section of this book. If we set d =0, we have Ax + F = 0, i.e. an algebraic system as discussed in chapter 3. This represents the equilibrium problem, i.e. the determination of states in which the system will remain in if achieved. If, further, F = 0, we will in general have only the trivial solution x =0, unless the matrix A is rank deficient. If the coefficients of A are functions of a parameter, we can determine the parameter values for which such nontrivial solutions of the homogenous problem are possible—this is the eigenvalue problem. If the independent variable is time, then we are finding resonant frequencies at which the system (in the absence of dissipation) will "ring" at forever. In the case of beam theory, such an eigenvalue generally gives us a critical value for the buckling of the beam, i.e., a point a which no (additional) forcing produces an (arbitrarily large) displacement.

Numerical Treatment of IVP's

Having considered why one might want to solve IVP 's, let us now turn to how one can go about it. There is a huge variety of methods to choose from. In this chapter we will consider one family of methods, the Runge-Kutta-Fehlberg formulas, and concentrate specifically on the 4th-order member of that family. The basic tradeoff in the choice of any method for solving an IVP is the number of function evaluations per timestep, balanced against the size of the timestep allowable to achieve a desired tolerance. We want a method that automatically monitors how well it is doing, and that cuts or increases the timestep accordingly. The RKF family provides this ability to estimate the local error (defined below) of approximation and to adjust the timestep according. This property of the method to adapt itself to the problem is very useful and was met before in Chapter 9 when we discussed adaptive quadrature techniques.

Stiffness

There is one potential stumbling block—the so-called "stiff" problem. The term "stiff" seems to be derived from the idea of a stiff spring, which corresponds to a large spring constant K in the harmonic oscillator equation $x'' + Kx = 0$ (Hooke's law for this problem would be $F = - (K)^{1/2} x$). Actually, the terminology is somewhat misleading. A large K corresponds to a large frequency, i.e., a short timescale for the variation of x. Stiff problems are problematic not so much because they involve short timescales, but rather because they involve disparate timescales. One of the equations in the system may have a variable which can change on a very short time-scale, while the other variables evolve much more slowly. To get to an answer, i.e., a final equilibrium state, requires carrying out the integration of the system to those longer time-scales, but to do so limited by the timescale of the rapid reaction would be prohibitively expensive.

The nature of the difficulty is illustrated in Fig. 7.1. Consider the simple first order IVP $y' = - Ay (A > 0), y(t = 0) = 1$, whose solution is $y = 1 - \exp(- At)$. There is nothing pathological or difficult about solving this equation by itself. But if we use too large a step in the independent variable t, we can have embarrassing results. If we used a simple integration scheme such as Euler's method, i.e., we wrote

$$y(t + dt) = y(t) - Ad\,t\,y(t) = y(t)(1 - Adt)$$

and we would need to use very small values of Adt to get an accurate solution. Otherwise, if $Adt > 1$, we would have instead the diverging oscillation, the results getting progressively worse. If y represented, say, the concentration of a chemical reactant or some other intrinsically positive quantity, this behavior would be extremely embarrassing very quickly. Now, if we only had this one equation to solve, the limitation dt 1/A might be easy to live with—indeed, we would have to keep dt of this order if we wanted

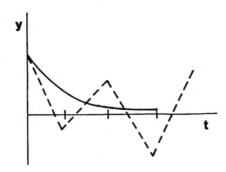

Fig. 7.1: Divergent numerical oscillation

to have an accurate depiction of the evolution of y. If this were a system of one equation, finding the detailed behavior of y would probably be the reason we were solving the system in the first place, so we would want to live with dt on the order of 1/A. But if we were studying the behavior of a number of chemicals reacting together, we might not want to have the timestep constrained by the most rapid reaction. The detailed history of the reactants on such a short timescale might safely be approximated, while still obtaining the correct result for the behavior of the system on much longer timescales.

There are a number of ways around such a difficulty, and these will be discussed in the next chapter. The methods given here will often do quite well on moderately stiff problems, but can give uneconomically small timesteps on truly stiff problems. If this happens, try using the routines in the next chapter on the problem. Stiff problems can arise in a number of ways. Often, systems of chemical reactions have widely disparate rates, giving rise to stiff problems. Orbital dynamics can give rise to stiff problems as well, as will be discussed further below.

Runge-Kutta Methods

We will discuss in this chapter only simple "single-step" methods for treating IVPs; in the next chapter, multistep, predictor-corrector, and multi-value methods will be discussed as a prerequisite to understanding the methods required for stiff systems. One advantage of single-step methods is that they are "self-starting," i.e., that they may be used with no modification from the outset at $t = 0$ to determine the solution at $t = dt$. Multistep methods typically require values at times such as $t - dt$, which don't exist for the first step. Usually, these are generated using a simple method, e.g., Euler's (see below), with very small timesteps. Another attractive feature of single-step methods is that it is relatively inexpensive to change the time step dt with such methods, compared to multistep methods. It has been stated that multistep methods are more efficient for similar accuracy (see Shoup), but this statement is probably based on Runge-Kutta methods without Fehlberg's improvements. Forsythe, Malcolm, and Moler argue on p. 129 of their book (see Chapter 3 for full reference) that for non-stiff problems and moderate accuracy requirements, the RKF methods are just as economical and more convenient.

In what follows, we will assume that the independent variable is time, and talk of timesteps. There is no change, except perhaps in terminology, if the independent variable is not time but some other variable.

Faced with a differential equation of the form

$$y' = f(y,t)$$

(for a system of differential equations y and y' may be viewed as N-dimensional vectors in which case f is a vector of functions) we have two decisions to make when developing a discrete approximation suitable for computation:

1) *how to model the derivative y'*

2) *how to model the "effective" mean value of f*

Because we will in general have a nonlinear problem in which the functions f are functions of the dependent variables y, the right-hand sides of these equations cannot be predicted, and errors in the determination of y' will then feed back on future determinations of y' through errors in later evaluations of the f. This leads to a distinction between local error and global error. The local error is that made in going from y[t] to y[t + dt], assuming y[t] were known exactly. It is in general composed of the truncation error, which is the error of approximation due to the finiteness of dt, and the roundoff error, due to the finite precision of the computer arithmetic. We will in general assume that the latter is small compared to the former. Because the local errors will not merely accumulate but will in general make the y inaccurate, the global error, the difference between the computed y[t + dt] and the exact y[t + dt], is worse than otherwise expected.

The simplest method is Euler's method, which may be considered a "first order" Runge-Kutta method. For an assigned timestep dt, y' is taken as (y[t + dt] − y[t])/dt and f as f(y[t],t), where t and y[t] are known. We can then easily solve for the unknown quantities as

$$y[t + dt] = y[t] + dt\, f(y[t],t).$$

The basic problem with this approach is that to get acceptable accuracies, dt has to be very small in general, resulting in many evaluations of the function f. The approximations made are only first order in dt, i.e., we can expect local errors which are second order in dt. These accumulate into global truncation errors which are first order in dt. In what follows, we will attempt to obtain higher-order accuracy in our approximation formulas. This will result in improved economy through the use of larger time-steps. Just how much of an improvement results depends on how costly the evaluation of f is. Note that we will be evaluating f more times per timestep, but the problem will require fewer timesteps to achieve similar accuracy at the same end time.

The general approach for Runge-Kutta methods is to look for formulae of the form

$$y[t + dt] = y[t] + dt\{af(y[t],t) + bf(y[t] + c*dtf(y[t],t)),t + ddt)+...\}.$$

Note that this can be rewritten as

$$y_1 = f(y[t],t)\,dt$$

$$y_2 = f(y[t] + cy_1, t + d\,dt)$$

$$y[t + dt] = y[t] + dt\{ay_1 + b\,y_2 + ...\}.$$

In this simple version we have stopped at two function evaluations, for y_1 and y_2, and we have four constants, a, b, c, d to choose. We make 2 function evaluations per dependent variable per timestep. If we expand the variable $y[t + dt]$ in a Taylor series about $y[t]$, and match powers of dt, we achieve the three constraints: $a + b = 1, bc = bd = 1/2$. We can still choose, say, a to be anything, with the values of the other parameters following from that choice. What Erwin Fehlberg did was, first, put more effort into the optimal determination of these constants than did anyone before him, and, second, show how to economically compute two estimates of $y[t + dt]$. These could then be compared for an estimate of the (local) error. For example, the typical textbook choice is

$$a = b = 1/2 \quad c = d = 1$$

Fehlberg refers to this method as the "modified Euler-Cauchy method" in his paper "Low-Order Classical Runge-Kutta Formulas with Stepsize Control and their Application to Some Heat Transfer Problems," NASA Tech. Report TR R-315, July 1969. This method is given as "Runge-Kutta method of order 2" in Conte and de Boor and is given in C. F. Gerald. It is not a "straw man" that I am setting up to knock down easily. The total truncation error is of the order $(y_1 - y_2)dt/2$. This is second-order accuracy, as the difference $y_1 - y_2$ may be expected to be of order dt for small dt. The analogous formula derived by Fehlberg (which uses three function evaluations) has an error of order $(y_3 - y_1)/512$. Thus, we are doing approximately 256 times better (although at the cost of an additional function evaluation in this case). In most cases, this is a favorable exchange.

The formulae given by Fehlberg in that case give as the two estimates of $y[t + dt]$:

$$y_1 = f(y[t], t)$$
$$y_2 = f(y[t] + y_1/2, t + dt/2)$$

$$y_3 = f(y[t] + y_1/256 + y_2\ 255/256)$$

$$y[t+dt] = y[t] + dt\{y_1/512 + y_2 255/256 + y_3/512 \}$$

and also $y[t+dt] = y[t] + dt\{ y_1/256 + y_2\ 255/256 \}$.

The beauty of these formulae is as follows:

1) *The second formula for y[t+dt] re-uses the function evaluations used by the first, so there is no "wasted" evaluations of f, and*

2) *The coefficients in the second formula, 1/256 and 255/256, add up to one, and are identical to the coefficients used in the evaluation of y_3.* This has been craftily designed by Fehlberg with the result that, on the next step, we need not re-evaluate the new $y_1 = f(y[t' = t + dt], t' = t + dt)$ but can take over the result for y_3 from the previous timestep. Hence, for a large number of timesteps, we will save a function evaluation per time-step! Fehlberg uses the same trick for his so-called second- and third-order formulae.

Note that in practice, rather than evaluate both versions of $y[t + dt]$, only the latter (which we will reuse as described above) is evaluated, and we evaluate the difference of the two "predictions" for $y[t + dt]$.

Fehlberg's fourth-order formula, which we shall implement, does not use this device to save a function evaluation by reusing one from the previous step. This higher-order formula appears to be generally considered to be the best compromise between order (number of function evaluations per timestep) and size of timestep permissible. For functions f that are either extremely simple and cheap, or very costly, one should probably use a higher or lower order method, respectively. A mildly stiff problem would probably do better with a higher-order formula, although one should probably use the multivalue methods of the next chapter for a truly stiff problem.

For the 4th-order formula, we have

$$y_1 = f(y[t], t)$$

$$y_2 = f(y[t] + dt\ y_1/4, t + dt/4)$$

etc. (see code listing or references below) with

$$y[t + dt] - y[t] = dt\{...\}$$

where $\{...\}$ is

$$16/135 \ y_1 + 6656/128453 \ y_3 + 28561/56430 \ y_4 - 9/50 y_5 + 2/55 y_6$$

or

$$25/216 \ y_1 + 1408/2565 y_3 + 2197/4104 y_4 - 1/5 y_5$$

which give a local error term of the form

$$dt\{ -1/360 y_1 + 128/4275 y_3 + 2197/75240 y_4 - y_5/50 - 2/55 y_6\}$$

The first formula for $y[t + dt]$ has a fifth-order order local error, the latter a fourth order local error, giving us a fifth order accurate (local error) method, which Fehlberg calls RK4(5) but which is typically referred to as RKF45 (see, e.g., Forsythe, Malcolm, and Moler), which is a fourth-order method in terms of global accuracy. The error term compares favorably to Kutta's and Sarafyan's results (the latter's are contained in Fehlberg's paper referenced above). Kutta's method is

$$y_1 = f(y[t],t)$$

$$y_2 = f(y[t] + y_1 dt/2, t + dt/2)$$

$$y_3 = f(y[t] + y_2 dt/2, t + dt/2)$$

$$y_4 = f(y[t] + dt \ y_3, t + dt)$$

$$y[t + dt] - y[t] = dt/6\{y_1 + 2y_2 + 2y_3 + y_4\}$$

(see also Conte and de Boor and Gerald, each cited above), which has error terms between one and two orders of magnitude larger.

How do we control the stepsize? "Simply" by comparing the (local) error with a user specified tolerance—if we haven't achieved a sufficiently accurate solution, we try again with the timestep cut. If we have to cut the timestep too much, the system is judged to be stiff.

Formulae of higher and lower orders

A RK3(4) (also called RKF34) method given by Fehlberg is

$$y_1 = f(y[t],t)$$

$$y_2 = f(y[t] + 2/7\,dt\,y_1, t + 2/7\,dt)$$

$$y_3 = f(y[t] + dt\{77/900 y_1 + 343/900\,y_2\}, t + 7/15\,dt)$$

$$y_4 = f(y[t] + dt\{805/1444 y_1 - 77175/54872 y_2 + 97125/54872 y_3\},$$
$$t + 35/38\ dt)$$

$$y_5 = f(y[t] + dt\{79/490 y_1 + 2175/3626 y_3 + 2166/9065 y_4\}, t + dt)$$

with $y[t + dt] - y[t] = dt\{...\}$ with $\{...\}$ given by

$$229/1470 y_1 + 1125/1813 y_3 + 13718/81585 y_4 + y_5/18$$

or

$$79/490 y_1 + 2175/3626 y_3 + 2166/9065 y_4$$

Note that one reuses the last calculated value of f as the first value y_1 for the subsequent step. Similarly, the RK2(3) or RKF23 method is

$$y_1 = f(y[t],t)$$

$$y_2 = f(y[t] + dt/4 y_1, t + dt/4)$$

$$y_3 = f(y[t] + dt\{-189/800 y_1 + 729/800 y_2\}, t + 27/40\,dt)$$

$$y_4 = f(y[t] + dt\{214/891 y_1 + y_2/33 + 650/891 y_3\}, t + dt)$$

with $y[t + dt] - y[t] = dt\{...\}$ where $\{...\}$ is

$$533/2106 y_1 + 800/1053 y_3 - y_4/78$$

or

$$214/891 y_1 + y_2/33 + 650/891 y_3$$

Higher-order methods can be found in an earlier paper by Fehlberg, NASA TR R-287, October 1968. See also his article in *Computing*, vol. 6, p. 61, 1970. Fehlberg did not have the last word, however, and higher-order methods were developed by J. H. Verner and presented in *SIAM J. Numerical Analysis*, vol. 15, p. 722, 1978. The article by B. Thomas in *BYTE*, page 191, April 1986, presents his methods for fifth and seventh order in tabular form. It is much more likely, I think, that you might wish to go to lower order than to higher order. Also, there are some typographical errors in Thomas' article. The coefficient in the RK4(5) method which should be 28561/56430 is erroneously given as 285161/56430. In Figure 3, step 8, it states an operation should be performed for x = 0 when in fact it should be performed for x not equal to zero. The negative signs in Tables 7 and 8 should be omitted.

Program and Test Case

The RKF45 program has a long and noble history. This particular implementation in FORTRAN was developed by L. Shampine and H. A. Watts of Sandia Laboratories, and presented in Forsythe, Malcolm and Moler (see reference in Chapter 3). It is a tried-and-true implementation which we have not monkeyed with to any great degree. We did modularize it somewhat in that we have extracted from the main body of the routine the code that is specific to the RK4(5) scheme. The global integer parameter norder and the global coefficient arrays would have to be changed for another order scheme to be used. Parameter norder is used when the timestep is to be changed to estimate how large an alteration is to be made, based on the theoretical error properties of the RKF scheme of that order. In addition, for the lower order schemes in which the last function evaluation of one step is saved to be the first evaluation of the next step, the input variable iflag could be used to "remember" whether the value is saved or whether it need be recalculated (it would have to be passed to the replacement of subroutine feval). The values of the final functions are in the work array, addressed as array ff INDEC(5,i,neq) for $i = 0,...$ (neq $-$ 1) where there are neq equations.

The parameters in the argument list to rkf are:

neq   the number of equations to be solved in the system.

y   the dependent variables (a vector).

t   pointer to float variable: on input:
           the time at the beginning of the timestep;
           on output: the time reached by rkf.

tout   pointer to floating point variable. on input:
            the desired time at the end of the timestep.

relerr,abserr   the error tolerance in the dependent variables; the code
            attempts to keep the local error in y[i] less than (in absolute
            magnitude)relerr*y[i] + abserr.

flag   pointer to integer; on input:
            set equal to + 1 to start the problem; set to − 1 forces the
            code to attempt to integrate from t to tout in a single step;
            on output:

            2 normal step.

            − 2 successful single step.

            3 error tolerance too small. relerr increased.

            4 more than 3000 derivative evaluations were needed;
            integration not successfully completed.

            5 integration not completed because abserr was zero and
            relerr was too small; either alter abserr or use the one
            step method.

            6 integration not completed because minimum stepsize did
            not alow sufficient accuracy; Increase error tolerance.

            7 rkf is probably inefficiently applied to the problem—
            use the one-step mode.

            8 invalid input parameters—correct them.

work,iwork   work arrays used by the program; iwork must be
            dimensioned at least 5 for rkf, and work must be at least
            3 + (norder + 2)*neq

f   pointer to a function of the form f(t,x,xdot) which returns a
            vector sized neq for the right-hand sides of the equations of
            the system, i.e. the time derivatives of the x[].

Some of the error codes in iflag require discussion. If iflag = 4 or 7 then rkf is probably inappropriate for the problem. The error tolerance might be set too low to be practical. These warning are not fatal. If iflag is 5 or 6 the problem is somewhat more serious, and the error tolerances must be changed, or another method used. It is possible that the problem is too stiff for the solver if one of these warnings, particularly iflag = 6, arises. If the subroutine rkf has returned with iflag = 3 or 4, recalling it with iflag unchanged will cause it to proceed. Otherwise, if iflag is 5, 6, or 7, iflag must be reset to 2 before rkf is recalled or it will terminate. It should be clear that iflag must be checked for an error condition by the calling routine!

The "smallest possible stepsize" is set in rkf as a number related to the precision of the arithmetic used, multiplied by the absolute value of the time at the start of the timestep. Clearly, this is somewhat of a "rule of thumb," since we can alter this minimum step merely by shifting the time origin. Nonetheless, if an iflag = 6 return occurs, it is likely that either the problem is stiff or a singularity on the solution is being approached, and a close look at the results to the current state is warranted. Similarly, the iflag = 4 return is a "rule of thumb" based upon experience. Change or ignore these criteria if you believe you have something better, but not just out of a desire to be different. The sample test problems give the user a choice between an harmonic oscillator with user-specified spring constant, and the mildly stiff problem discussed by Gear as well as in the books by Forsythe, Malcolm and Moler and by Press et al. (references in Chapters 3 and 7, respectively). This problem (see the code listing) has as right hand sides two linear combinations of the dependent variables. The solution is a sum of damped (negative) exponentials, $x[1] = 4 \exp(-t) - 3 \exp(-1000\,t)$ and $x[2] = -2\exp(-t) + 3\exp(-1000\,t)$. The timescales differ by a factor of 1000 for the two components of the solution, resulting in a stiff problem. In our tests, RKF45 did surprisingly well on this problem. The same test problem is used to test our stiff method in the next chapter. The main program will print the exact answers for comparison to the numerical results.

None of the books mentioned above work an example with this problem, with only Gear presenting a solver appropriate for stiff problems. Instead, Forsythe et al. did present as a test case an orbital mechanics problem. Such many-body problems, with each particle interacting gravitationally with the others, can easily become a stiff problem. What happens is two of the particles make a close approach, become a tightly bound binary system, and subsequently rotate about their common center of mass. The orbital period of the two members of this system can be very much shorter than the time-scale of evolution of the system as a whole. One way to treat such a stiff system is to recognize the binary system for what it is, and simply replace it by one object whose mass is the sum of the masses of the objects in the system. From the point of view of the many-body system being simulated, the gravitational field of this combined object will almost exactly equal that of the binary system (which, if orbiting rapidly, will average its own field to a close approximation to that of a single point). While a later close approach to the system might result in its dissolution, this is not typical, so our "fudge" to remove the stiffness of the system should work out very well in practice. This "fudge" or "heuristic" for treating stiffness can be generalized, as will be discussed in the next chapter.

Note that, unless the user specifically requests the program to do so (by setting iflag $= -1$ at the start of the problem, and permitting it to remain -2 for the other steps), the code will not simply do a single step with timestep dt = tout $-$ t, but will generally try smaller steps if it feels that it needs to do so. Therefore, do not compare results from rkf() with another code by simply specifying the difference tout $-$ t and comparing accuracy. The only fair comparison would be to compare computer time used to achieve results of similar precision. When this is done, it will be seen that, on the stiff problem, the solver stiff2() of the next chapter is considerably better than rkf().

As an alternative test problem, the simple harmonic oscillator is offered. We present examples with this option as well.

The stiff problem was handled successfully on a Kaypro II (Z80 processor) using Aztec C as well as on an IBM PC clone using Aztec C86, either with or without the use of the 8087 math coprocessor chip. The values of u26 and eps differ for each of these cases, reflecting the different floating point precisions. Table 7.1 lists the programs contained in this chapter. No routines or headers from other chapters are required—these codes are "stand-alone."

Table 11.1

Programs of Chapter 11

rkf	Body of Runge-Kutta-Fehlberg integrator
error	Computes error term for RKF method
feval	Computes terms for RKF method
sign	Analog of FORTRAN sign transfer
isign	" " " " " for integers

References

R. P. Feynman, R. B. Leighton, M. Sands, *The Feynman Lectures in Physics*, (Reading, MA: Addison-Wesley, 1963,1964,1965).

C. W. Gear, *Numerical Initial Value Problems in Ordinary Differential Equations*, (Englewood Cliffs, NJ: Prentice-Hall, 1971).

T. E. Shoup, *Numerical Methods for the Personal Computer*, (Englewood Cliffs, N.J.: Prentice-Hall, 1983), p.131

Program Listing and Test Problem Output

(listing begins next page)

```
/*
Runge-Kutta-Fehlberg integrator for
    system of Ordinary Differential Equations
    (Initial Value Problems) non-stiff to mildly stiff
    general order; RKF45 i.e. RK4(5) parameters supplied
(from "C Tools for Scientists and Engineers" by L. Baker)


CONTENTS:

rkf()
    Runge-Kutta-Fehlberg integrator. General order.
    (see text for qualifications of this statement)

feval()
    evaluates steps
error()
    evaluates error term


sign()    similar to FORTRAN routine for sign transfer
isign()   ditto


DEPENDENCIES:
ftoc.h header file
*/
#include "ftoc.h"
/*#include "math.h"*/
#define iabs(x)  (((x)>=0)? (x):-(x))
/* C ordering but with k*/
#define INDEC(i,j,k) [j+(i)*(k)]
/* ------ global variables to remember eps, u26,etc between calls of rkf*/
float u26,eps,crit,criti;
double order,iorder;

/* The constant order is the only scheme dependent parameter
in RKF; other parameters are globals used by error and feval
the functions to evalute the error terms and the intermediate
```

derivatives. order should be set to m=n+1, e.g. 5 for RKF45*/

int norder=5;

/* subroutine rkf for general Runge-Kutta-Fehlberg integrations*/

```
rkf(neq,y,t,tout,relerr,abserr,iflag,work,iwork,f)
Int Iwork[],neq,*iflag; int (*f)();
float *t,*tout,y[],abserr,relerr,work[];
/* NB that relerr and abserr are float variables,t and tout pointers
     to float variables.
*/
/* iwork must be dimensioned at least 5, work at least 3+7*neq for rkf45*/
/* generally work must be 3+neq*(2+norder) norder=5 for rkf45*/
{
int base,*nfe,*kop,*init,*kflag,*jflag,hfaild,output,k,maxnfe=3000;
int i,mflag,gflag,coln;
float *h,*yp,*ss,s,*ff,*savre,*savae,a,dt,ee
,eeoet,esttol,et,hmin,remin=1.e-12,rer,scale,tol,epsp1,ypk;
/* FORTRAN code had two unused variables: ae and toln */
float sign(),error();
double pow();
/*assign to work-this will enable different ODE's to be solved
simultaneously by passing in different work, iwork vectors*/

coln=neq;
/* set pointers to work areas*/
nfe= iwork;
base=1;
kop= &(iwork[base++]);
init=&(iwork[base++]);
kflag=&(iwork[base++]);
jflag=&(iwork[base++]);
base=neq*(1+norder);
yp=work;
ff=work;
ss=&(work[base]);
base+=neq;
```

```
h=&(work[base++]);
savre=&(work[base++]);
savae=&(work[base]);
/* valid input? */
mflag= iabs(*iflag);

if(neq<1 || relerr<0. || abserr<0.
|| mflag==0 || mflag>8 ||((*t==*tout) && (*kflag!=3)))
    {*iflag=8;
    return;}
gflag=0;
if (mflag==1)
   {/*first call set precision limit*/
   eps=1.;
   while(1)
      {
      eps=eps*.5;
      epsp1=eps+1.;
      if(epsp1<= 1.)break;
      }
   u26=26.*eps;
   /*printf(" u26,eps %e %e\n",u26,eps); 8087: eps=5.96e-8*/
/* now set the limits to stepsize change-these depend upon
the parameter order, and are larger for larger orders */
   order=(double) norder;
   iorder= 1./(order);
   crit =pow(9., order);
   criti=pow( (.9/order),order);/* make sure 5 here is order*/
   /* crit= 59059., criti=1.889568e-4 for rkf45*/
   }
else
   {

        if ( *iflag==3 || (mflag==2 &&(*init==0 || *kflag==3)) )
           {gflag=1;goto next;}
        if(*iflag==4||(*kflag==4&&mflag==2))
           {*nfe=0;if(mflag!=2)gflag=1;goto next;};
        if((*kflag==5 && abserr==0.)||
```

```
                (*kflag==6 && relerr<*savre && abserr<*savae))
                    {/* unrecoverable serious pblm*/
                    printf(" iflag=5,6,7,8 not properly handled by user\n");
                    *iflag=9;return;
                    }
        };
next:
if(gflag){*iflag=*jflag;if(*kflag==3)mflag=iabs(*iflag);}

*jflag=*iflag;
*kflag=0;
*savre=relerr;
*savae=abserr;
rer=2.*eps+remin;
if(relerr<rer)
    {
    relerr=rer;
    *iflag=*kflag=3;
    return;
    };
gflag=0;
dt=*tout-*t;
if(mflag==1)
    {/* initialize*/
    *init=0;
    *kop=0;
    a=*t;
    gflag=1;
    (*f)(a,y,yp);
    *nfe=1;
    if(*t==*tout){*iflag=2;return;}
    };/* mflag==1*/
if(*init==0||gflag)
    {
    *init=1;
    *h=abs(dt);
    /*toln=0.; In FORTRAN version but not used*/
    DOFOR(k,neq)
```

```
      {
      tol=relerr*abs(y[k])+abserr;
      if(tol> 0.)
          {
          /*toln=tol; in FORTRAN but not used*/
          ypk=abs(yp[k]);
          if( ypk* pow((double)*h,order)>tol) *h=pow((tol/ypk),iorder);
          }/*if tol */
      }    /*do*/
   if(tol<=0.)*h=0.;
   ypk=max(abs(dt),abs(*t)) ;
   *h= max(*h, u26*ypk);
   *jflag= isign(2,*iflag);
   }/* if int ==0*/

*h=sign(*h,dt);
/* too many output requests?*/
if ( abs(*h)>=2.*abs(dt)) (*kop)++;
if(*kop==100){*kop=0;*iflag=7;return;}

if(abs(dt)<= u26*abs(*t))
   {
   DOFOR(k,neq) y[k]+=dt*yp[k];
   a=*tout;
   (*f)(a,y,yp);
   (*nfe)++;
   *t=*tout;
   *iflag=2;
   return;
   }
output=0;
scale=2./relerr;
/*ae=scale*abserr; not used- in FORTRAN*/
while(1) /* infinite loop over steps*/
{
hfaild=0;
hmin=u26*abs(*t);
dt=*tout-*t;
```

```
if( abs(dt)<2.*abs(*h))
   {
   if(abs(dt)<=abs(*h)){output=1;*h=dt;}
   else *h=.5*dt;
   }

if(*nfe>maxnfe)
   {
   *iflag=*kflag=4;return;
   };
step:
feval(f,neq,y,*t,*h,ff,ss);
DOFOR(i,neq) ff INDEX(1,i)=ss[i];
(*nfe)+=norder;
/* error ok?*/
eeoet=0.;
DOFOR(k,neq)
   {
   et=abs(y[k])+abs(ff INDEX(1,k) );
   if(et<=0.){*iflag=5;return;}
   ee= abs(error(k,ff,coln));
   eeoet=max(eeoet,ee/et);
   };
esttol=abs(*h)*eeoet*scale;
if(esttol>1.)
   {/*step failed*/
   hfaild=1;
   output=0;
   s=.1;
   if(esttol<crit )s=.9/pow((double)esttol,iorder);
   *h=s* *h;
   if(abs(*h)>hmin)goto step;
   *iflag=*kflag=6;
   return;
   };
/*successful step*/
(*t)+=*h;
DOFOR(k,neq) y[k]=ff INDEX(1,k);
```

```
a=*t;
(*f)(a,y,yp);
(*nfe)++;
s=5.;
/* power is .2= 1/5 for 4th-5th order scheme
crit= 9**(1/power) criti=(.9/5)**(1/power) */
if(esttol> criti ) s=.9/pow((double)esttol,iorder);
if(hfaild)s=min(1.,s);
*h=sign(max(hmin,s*abs(*h)),*h);
if(output) {*t=*tout;*iflag=2;return;};
if(*iflag<=0){*iflag=-2;return;}
};/* end while loop- loop back for next step*/

}


/* coefficients for RKF45 4-5th order scheme*/

   double e[6]={0.0027777777,0.0, -0.0299415,-0.0291998,0.02
                               , 0.036363636};
   double a[6] = { 0. , .25 , .375 , .9230769 , 1. , .5 } ;
   double c[6]={.1157407,.0,.5489278,.5353313,-.2,0.};
   double b[6][5]={0.,0.,0.,0.,0.,.25,0.,0.,0.,0.,
    .09375,.28125,0.,0.,0.,.8793809,-3.2771961,3.3208921,0.,0.,
    2.0324074,-8.,7.1734892,-.2058966,0.,
    -.29629629629,2.,-1.3816764,.4529727,-.275};
/* note that the zeros in b are merely placeholders to simplify indexing
-not used in calculations*/


float error(k,ff,coln)
int k,coln; float *ff;
{
  int i;
  double sum;
sum=0.;
DOFOR(i,(norder+1))sum+= e[i]* ff INDEX(i,k);
return(sum);
}
```

```
/* compute terms in RKF steps */

feval(f,neq,y,t,h,ff,s)
int neq; float y[],t,h,ff[],s[];
int (*f)();
{
int i,j,m;
double x;
DFOR(j,2,(norder+1))
    {
    DOFOR(i,neq)
      {x=0.;
      DOFOR(m,j)
          x+=b[j][m]*  ff INDEC(m,i,neq);
      s[i]= x*h+ y[i];
      }
    x=t+a[j]*h;
    (*f)(x,s,&(ff INDEC(j,0,neq)) );
    }
DOFOR(i,neq)
    {
    x=0.;/* note that c[5]=0. */
    DOFOR(j,norder)x+= c[j]* ff INDEC(j,i,neq);
    s[i]=h*x+ y[i];
    }
return;
}

isign (to,from) int to,from;
{
int sign;
if (from>=0)sign=1;
if (from<0)sign=-1;
return( abs(to)*sign);
}

float sign (to,from) float to,from;
```

```
{
float sin;
if (from>=0)sin=1.;
if (from<0)sin=-1.;
return( abs(to)*sin);
}
```

```
/* test driver for

    RKF45 Runga-Kutta-Fehlberg integrator for
    system of Ordinary Differential Equations
    (Initial Value Problems)
    non-stiff to mildly stiff
(from "C Tools for Scientists and Engineers" by L. Baker)


DEPENDENCIES:
ftoc.h header file required
/*
#include "libc.h"
#include "math.h"
*/
#include "ftoc.h"

int problem; float ksq;

main (argc,argv) int argc; char **argv;
{
double sin(),cos(),exp(),sqrt();
float a,b,time,x[8],tout,t,u,v;
int f();float abserr,relerr,work[200],dt;
int i,j,iwork[25],ibug,neq,iter;
x [0]=x[1]=1.;t=0.;
ibug=1;neq=2;
for (i=0;i<1000;i++)
abserr=.001;relerr=.01;
printf(" enter dt");scanf("%f",&dt);
printf(" enter 0 for harmonic osc 1 for stiff\n");
scanf("%d",&problem);
if(!problem)
    {printf(" enter square of spring constant\n");
    scanf("%f",&ksq);
    x[1]=0.;
    a=sqrt((double)ksq);
    }
```

```
printf(" Time x1(Calculated) x1(Exact) x2(Calculated) X2(Exact)\n");
for(i=0;i<100;i++)
  {
  tout=t+dt;neq=2;
  rkf(neq,x,&t,&tout,relerr,abserr,&ibug,work,iwork,f);
  if(ibug>2){printf(" ibug=%d\n",ibug);exit(0);};
  time=t;
  t=tout;/*bumpt t*/
  if ((i % 10)==0    || (i<5) )
    {
    if(problem)
        {
        a=exp(-time);b=exp(-1000.*time);
        u= 4.*a-3.*b;
        v=-2.*a+3.*b;
        }
    else
        {
        b=time*a;
        u=cos((double)b);
        v=-a*sin((double)b);
          }
    printf(" %f %f %f %f %f\n",time,x[0],u,x[1],v);
    };
  };
exit(0);
}


/*------------ right-hand sides of ODE'S--------------------*/

f(t,x,xdot) float t,x[],xdot[];
{float u,v;
u= x[0];
v= x[1];
if(problem==0)
   {
   xdot[0]=v;
   xdot[1]=-ksq*u;
```

```
    }
else
    {
    xdot[0]= 998.*u+1998.*v;
    xdot[1]=-999.*u-1999.*v;
    }
return;
}
```

enter dt .05
enter 0 for harmonic osc 1 for stiff
0
enter square of spring constant
1.

Time	x1(Calculated)	x1(Exact)	x2(Calculated)	X2(Exact)
0.050000	0.998750	0.998750	-0.049979	-0.049979
0.100000	0.995004	0.995004	-0.099833	-0.099833
0.150000	0.988771	0.988771	-0.149438	-0.149438
0.200000	0.980067	0.980067	-0.198669	-0.198669
0.250000	0.968912	0.968912	-0.247404	-0.247404
0.550000	0.852525	0.852524	-0.522687	-0.522687
1.050000	0.497571	0.497571	-0.867423	-0.867423
1.550000	0.020796	0.020795	-0.999784	-0.999784
2.049999	-0.461071	-0.461072	-0.887363	-0.887363
2.549999	-0.830052	-0.830053	-0.557685	-0.557685
3.049998	-0.995808	-0.995808	-0.091467	-0.091466
3.549998	-0.917755	-0.917755	0.397145	0.397146
4.049997	-0.615005	-0.615004	0.788523	0.788524
4.549999	-0.161678	-0.161677	0.986843	0.986844

enter dt .01
enter 0 for harmonic osc 1 for stiff
1

Time	x1(Calculated)	x1(Exact)	x2(Calculated)	X2(Exact)
0.010000	3.959537	3.960063	-1.979437	-1.979963
0.020000	3.920065	3.920795	-1.959667	-1.960397
0.030000	3.885784	3.881782	-1.944893	-1.940891
0.040000	3.843771	3.843158	-1.922191	-1.921579
0.050000	3.805195	3.804918	-1.902736	-1.902459
0.110000	3.574208	3.583337	-1.782539	-1.791668
0.210000	3.249930	3.242337	-1.628761	-1.621168
0.310000	2.952858	2.933788	-1.485963	-1.466894
0.410000	2.657840	2.654601	-1.330539	-1.327301
0.510000	2.401938	2.401983	-1.200946	-1.200991
0.610000	2.164270	2.173404	-1.077568	-1.086702
0.710000	1.966569	1.966578	-0.983280	-0.983289
0.810000	1.779166	1.779433	-0.889449	-0.889717
0.909999	1.607824	1.610098	-0.802776	-0.805049

enter dt .02
enter 0 for harmonic osc 1 for stiff
1

Time	x1(Calculated)	x1(Exact)	x2(Calculated)	X2(Exact)
0.020000	3.921461	3.920795	-1.961064	-1.960397
0.040000	3.857060	3.843158	-1.935482	-1.921579
0.060000	3.766207	3.767058	-1.882678	-1.883529
0.080000	3.692584	3.692465	-1.846350	-1.846233
0.100000	3.619435	3.619350	-1.809760	-1.809675
0.220000	3.205029	3.210075	-1.599991	-1.605038
0.420000	2.628188	2.628187	-1.314094	-1.314094
0.620000	2.151779	2.151778	-1.075889	-1.075889
0.820000	1.761728	1.761727	-0.880864	-0.880864
1.020000	1.442381	1.442380	-0.721191	-0.721190
1.219999	1.180922	1.180921	-0.590461	-0.590461
1.419999	0.966857	0.966857	-0.483429	-0.483428
1.619999	0.791596	0.791596	-0.395798	-0.395798
1.819999	0.648104	0.648104	-0.324052	-0.324052

CHAPTER 12

Stiff Systems of Differential Equations

Chapter Objectives

In this chapter you will find tools to:

-efficiently integrate systems of ordinary differential equations (ODEs) which are "stiff." This will enable the solution of initial value problems containing such systems.

The general concept of implicit methods will be discussed. These methods are of importance in treating partial differential equations, for example.

What are Stiff Systems of ODEs?

You probably haven't looked at the previous chapter if you are reading this subheading. If so, please read the section in Chapter 11 on stiffness. We will consider in this chapter how to solve IVPs involving such systems. If at any point in this chapter the terminology is unfamiliar, rereading the preceding chapter will be helpful.

Heuristic Methods for Stiff Systems

We discussed in the preceding chapter a many-body problem involving mutually gravitating point masses, how such a system might become stiff, and a simple "fix." The basics of that approach were:

1) *Recognize what portion of the system is "stiff", i.e., varying on a short timescale relative to all else*

2) *Treat that system specially, ignoring its time dependence by averaging over that short timescale in order to determine its role in the system as a whole*

Consider the other common type of stiff system, a set of chemical reactions. A reaction that has much faster reaction rates than the other causes the chemical species whose concentration's derivative is determined to quickly come to equilibrium with the concentrations of the "slower" species at the given moment. Thus, it is often possible to replace that stiff equation by an algebraic equation by setting the derivative to zero, and solving the remainder of the system. There are a number of difficulties in converting this attractive idea into an algorithm. First, the program must decide which equations should be regarded as stiff and given such special treatment. Next, we must solve the algebraic equation in conjunction with the remainder of the ODEs, which may not be easy. In fact, some approaches to solving nonlinear equations treat the equations as ODEs, i.e., the non-linear equation f = 0 is solved by regarding it as de/dt = f, where e is a dummy error term, and we try to integrate the IVP so defined from our initial guess to a state in which de/dt = e = 0. The utility of this approach is therefore strongly dependent upon the nature of the system of ODEs and whether the "stiff" terms can be easily solved if converted to algebraic equations. Such heuristic methods are probably not of general usefulness, and we will not consider them further.

Multivalue Methods

C. W. Gear (see reference in Chapter 11) uses the term "multivalue method" to denote methods which use more than one value of each dependent variable. Often, these methods use values defined at previous timesteps, in which case they are called multistep methods. An example would be the Adams-Bashford method

$$y[t + dt] = y[t] + dt/24\{55f[t] - 59f[t - dt] + 37f[t - 2dt] - 9f[t - 3dt]\}$$

In what follows, let us simplify notation by assuming a fixed value for dt, denoting t as the 0th step, t − dt as the − 1 step, etc. The formula is derived by fitting a cubic through the four values of f from − 3 to 0 and integrating the extrapolated cubic from 0 to 1. This method gives a local truncation error proportional to the fifth power of dt, yet it requires only one function evaluation per timestep—compare this to the RKF45, which requires six function evaluations. However, the error term is proportional to the fifth derivative of y and can be quite large. In practice, the Adams-Bashford method is improved at the cost of an additional function evaluation by using the value of y[1] obtained not as the "final" value but only as a "prediction" or estimate of y[1]. That value is then corrected by the result found from fitting a cubic through the four f values from − 2 to 1, evaluating f at 1 using the predicted value of y. The corrected y is then

$$y[1] = y[0] + dt/24\{9f[1] + 19f[0] - 5f[- 1]+f[- 2]\}$$

If we stop at this point, we have what is known as the "Adams-Moulton method." One can instead iterate on the correction formula, for example, if the difference between the predicted and corrected y[1] is unacceptably large. Such predictor-corrector methods are very economical and, until the reduced errors of the Fehlberg and Verner versions of the Runge-Kutta methods, were preferred for most problems over the single step methods. They have the difficulty, mentioned in chapter 11, that they are not self-starting; at t = 0 we have no y[– 1],etc. to work with.

The methods we have considered so far have been explicit, i.e., we have known all of the y values required for the evaluation of f. The value of y[1] was supplied by the predictor in the Adams-Moulton method. For stiff systems, it is desirable to use an implicit method, i.e., a formula in which the derivative of y at 1 is written in terms of a backward difference formula involving the values of y at 1 and previous steps, such as in the corrector step of the Adams-Moulton method, but solving this equation self-consistently rather than using a predicted value. (Note that the possibility of iteration mentioned above is a crude version of this.) Because f will generally be a nonlinear function of y, this will involve solving a nonlinear algebraic equation. However, we should have a good guess for that value in, for example, the predicted value for y[1]. Instead of simple iteration, however, a more rapidly convergent method for the solution of the non-linear equation is used, such as the Newton-Raphson iteration discussed in Chapter 6. Such implicit methods can be designed to have the property known as A-stability (see Gear, referenced in Chapter 11, Dahlquist et al., Chua and Lin), which means roughly that if the problem at hand has only solutions with decaying exponential terms (not growing), then the solutions of the discretized equations will similarly decay. Gear has pioneered such methods, and his DIFSUB program (in FORTRAN) may be found in his book and in the *Collected Algorithms of the ACM*. These methods, being multivalue methods, are not self-starting. The typical implementation mimics a self-starting code by using a simple self-starting scheme the first few calls (with a very small dt) until there are a sufficient number of timesteps to proceed with the multivalue method.

Interestingly, Dahlquist has shown (see Gear, or Dahlquist et. al. as referenced in Chapter 7) that to gain stability in a method we may have to sacrifice accuracy in the sense that the schemes with the highest order of truncation error achievable for the number of terms in the difference for-mula will not be stable. Thus, implicit schemes based on a Newton-Cotes type of formula might work better, particularly for stiff problems, than ones based on a scheme similar to Gaussian quadrature. See the references just mentioned, or Isaacson and Keller.

Implicit Methods and Stability

To illustrate the relationship between stability and implicit methods, consider the IVP of the ODE $y' = -ky$ with the initial condition $y[t = 0] = 1$. The exact solution is $y = \exp(-t)$. First, consider the simplest explicit method, namely Eulers

$$\frac{y[t + dt] - y[t]}{dt} = -ky[t]$$

This may be solved to give $y[t + dt] = y[t]\{1 - kdt\} = y[t]\{1 - a\}$ where $a = kdt$. Note that for $a > 1$ the solution for y oscillates in time from timestep to timestep. For $a > 2$, the results are catastrophically bad. The solution is "overstable." It oscillates in sign with ever increasing amplitude. It is as if the scheme knows it is wide of the mark, and tries to bring the solution back to zero, but overshoots with ever-worsening effect. Now consider the simplest implicit method

$$\frac{y[t + dt] - y[t]}{dt} = -\frac{k\{y[t] + y[t + dt]\}}{2}$$

If we introduce $b = kdt/2$, we find $y[t + dt] = y[t]\{(1 - b)/(1 + b)\}$. We now get an solution oscillating with sign for $b > 1$, which corresponds to $a > 2$, so we have delayed this problem by a factor of two in timestep. The solution is never of increasing amplitude, however. It won't, of course, decay with the correct amplitude if kdt is large—we didn't guarantee accuracy with an implicit scheme—but it will not go disastrously unstable.

Program and Test Case

The program we present for solving stiff systems is based on the algorithm of R. K. Brayton, F. G. Gustavson, and G. D. Hachtel, "A New Efficient Algorithm for Solving Differential-Algebraic Systems Using Implicit Backward Differentiation Formulas," *Proc. IEEE,* vol. 60, p. 98,1972. These authors state that, among other things, their methods are superior to Gear's method if the timestep dt is varying rapidly.

The paper of Brayton et. al. does not include a code listing. The program here is based on a FORTRAN implementation by Dr. W. R. Zimmerman. In his implementation, the method is of fixed order, namely second order. In the works of Brayton et. al. and Gear the order as well as the timestep varied automatically. There is a tradeoff both in code complexity and overhead versus the possibility of increased timesteps and hence greater efficiency.

The code input parameters are as follows:

t   a vector of size 4; the last element, t[3], should be the current time

x   a matrix of values of the dependent variable with the first index the variable number (ranging from 0 to neq-1), and the second index ranging from 0 to 3

delt   on input: pointer to the desired timestep dt. on output, returns dt used.

deltmn   pointer to minimum allowable timestep dt.

deltst   pointer to dt used to start the integration (should be small compared to expected typical timestep dt.

deltmax   pointer to maximum timestep dt allowable

emax   pointer to error criterion used for timestep control; the code will accept a step if the maximum absolute value of the $dx[i]/(abs(x[i]) + deltax)$ (evaluated for each of $i = 0,..., neq - 1$) is less than emax.

deltax   pointer to variable used in convergence test above; it is used to prevent division by zero if x[i] should be zero.

deltbx   pointer to a variable used similarly to deltax to prevent spurious divisions by zero; in the case of deltbx, this is in the numerical differentiation of f with respect to the x[i] to determine the Jacobian matrix used in the Newton-Raphson iteration (see Chapter 6).

acc   pointer to a variable which limits the maximum fractional change of a variable per Newton-Raphson iteration. deltax is again used to prevent spurious divisions by zero; the value used in the code is conservative but there may be applications in which it should be increased or decreased.

pivot   integer array used as work space in the Newton-Raphson solution (which employs the linear system solver of

Chapter 2); must be dimensioned at least neq

work   workspace array, must be dimensioned at least
$\max(3,\text{neq})^3 + 3$ neq

There were some minor changes from the FORTRAN implementation of Zimmerman. A global error criterion was converted to the more familiar local error constraint, similar to criteria used in rkf(). In addition, the step acceptance criterion and the change to delt based upon the error criterion were slightly changed for greater efficiency. Finally, some minor refinements were introduced in the code.

The test problem is the same (mildly) stiff problem of Chapter 11, due to Gear and discussed in Forsythe et al. and Press et. al. (see chapters 11, 7 and 3 for full references). Note that it would not be fair to naively compare results from stiff2() and rkf() because the latter may not be using as its timestep tout − t but may be "subcycling" with smaller steps. The true comparison would be that of comparable achieved accuracy (not merely similar error criterion) versus computer time expended.

Because the method is multistep and not self-starting, a simple Euler step is included for the first few steps, which use as their timestep the value deltst. This value should be small, near the minimum timestep specified or possibly less. The stiff solver does appear to have a "self-healing" property in problems with decaying solutions in that even if the results from the initial Euler steps appear inaccurate, there is some recovery of accuracy later. This cannot be guaranteed in general, however. Another self-starting method, such as a version of RKF, might be used instead.

Table 12.1 lists the subroutines in the solver package. Function pown() is used to supply only the very lowest integral powers of a number.

Table 12.1

Programs of Chapter 12

stiff2	Integrate stiff ODE IVP system
pown	Supply x^n for n between 0 and 2 inclusive

References

L. O. Chua and P.-M. Lin, *Computer Aided Analysis of Electronic Circuits*,(Englewood Cliffs, NJ: Prentice-Hall, 1972).

G. Dahlquist, A. Bjorck, N. Anderson, *Numerical Methods*, (Englewood Cliffs, NJ: Prentice-Hall, 1974).

Program Listing and Test Problem Output

```
/*
stiff IVP-ODE solver
based on method Brayton, Gustavson, Hachtel as implemented by
Zimmerman second-order method only
(from "C Tools for Scientists and Engineers" by L. Baker)

DEPENDENCIES:
ftoc.h header file required
uses the linear system solver from Chapter 3
*/
#include "ftoc.h"
#define INDEC(i,j,col) [j+(i)*col]
main (argc,argv) int argc; char **argv;
{
double exp();
float a,b,time,x[8],t[4],delt,deltmn,deltmx,u,v,emax;
int f();
static float deltax=1.e-6,deltbx=.01,acc=.001;
float deltst,work[100];
int i,j,pivot[3],ibug,coln=4,iter;
x INDEX(0,3)=x INDEX(1,3)=1.;time=0.;iter=1;
ibug=0;
printf(" enter ibug>0 for debug info from stiff2\n");
scanf("%d",&ibug);
printf(" ibug=%d\n",ibug);
t[0]=t[1]=t[2]=t[3]=0.0;
printf(" enter delt,deltmn,deltmx,deltst,emax\n");
scanf("%f %f %f %f %f",&delt,&deltmn,&deltmx,&deltst,&emax);
printf(" delt %f min %f max %f st %femax %f\n"
,delt,deltmn,deltmx,deltst,emax);
printf(" Time x1(Calculated) x1(Exact) x2(Calculated) x2(Exact) dt\n");
for (i=0;i<200;i++)
{
t[3]=time;
/*printf(" calling stiff2 %f %f %f %f\n",delt,deltmn,deltmx,emax);*/
stiff2(t,x,&iter,2,&delt,&deltmn,&deltst,&deltmx,&emax,&ibug,f
,deltax,deltbx,acc,pivot,work);
time=t[3];
```

```
if (ibug>0)printf(" WARNING- ibug=%d\n",ibug);
if (ibug==5)ibug=0;/* reset */
if ((i % 10)==0    || (i<5) ){
   a=exp((double)-time);b=exp((double)-1000.*time);
   u= 4.*a-3.*b;
   v=-2.*a+3.*b;
printf(" %f %f %f %f %f %f\n",
time,u,x INDEX(0,3),v,x INDEX(1,3),delt);
   };
};
exit(0);
}


f(x,t,xdot,neq) int neq; float t,x[],xdot[];
{float u,v;int coln=4;
u= x INDEX(0,3);
v= x INDEX(1,3);
xdot[0]= 998.*u+1998.*v;
xdot[1]=-999.*u-1999.*v;
return;
}



stiff2(t,x,iter,neq,delt,deltmn,deltst,deltmax,emax,ibug,f
,deltax,deltbx,acc,pivot,work)
/* pivot must be dimensioned at least neq, work max(3,neq)**2+3neq;
see text for details of other input parameters
note that t is a vector of length 4 with t[3] the current time
and x is a matrix of the dependent variables; x[i][3] is the
i-th dependent variable at the current time, both on entry and exit
*/
int pivot[],neq,*ibug,*iter; int (*f)();
float t[],x[],*delt,*deltmn,*deltst,*deltmax,*emax,
                  deltax,deltbx,acc,work[];
{
int base,nlist=1000,norder=2,ierr1=0,newton=20,
                  iredmx=10,lerr=0,isflag=0;
int coln,nn,ired,i,j,k,npow,iflag,info;
```

```c
/* will modify so that a,xdot,xdot1,xp pivot point to sections of
   a single work array passed in*/
float *a,alpha[3],sum,gamma[3],*xdot,*xdot1,*xp,pown(),delx,erm;
float w1,detold,detnew,w2,w3,w4,ww5,ddx;
float dum; float xnorm;int lufact(),backsub();
coln=3;a=work;base=max(3,neq);base=base*base;
xdot= &(work[base]);base+=neq;
xdot1= &(work[base]);base+=neq;
xp= &(work[base]);
/*shift arrays*/
if (*delt<=0.){
     *delt=*deltmn;
     printf(" bad delt input to stiff2, reset to %f\n",*delt);
         };
if(*emax<=0.)
   {
   printf(" bad emax=%f\n",*emax);
   return;
   }
for (i=0;i<neq;i++)
   {
   x INDEC(i,0,4)= x INDEC(i,1,4);
   x INDEC(i,1,4)= x INDEC(i,2,4);
   x INDEC(i,2,4)= x INDEC(i,3,4);
   };
t[0]=t[1];t[1]=t[2];t[2]=t[3];

if( (*iter-norder)<=1)
   {/* start by Euler steps at (small) delst */
   *delt=*deltst;
   t[3]=t[2]+ *delt;

   (*f)(x,t[3],xdot,neq);
   for (i=0;i<neq;i++) x INDEC(i,3,4)= x INDEC(i,2,4)+*delt*xdot[i];
   (*iter)++;
/*detold just for diagnostics printed by stiff2*/
   detold=*delt;
   return;
```

```
    }

if((*iter-norder)>=2)
   {
redo:    for(ired=0;ired<iredmx;ired++)
      {
      if((*ibug)>0){printf("ired %d delt %f ibug %d\n"
            ,ired,*delt,*ibug);};
      t[3]=t[2]+*delt;
      /* predictor*/
      nn=norder+1;
      coln=3;
      for (k=0;k<nn;k++)
         {
         gamma[k]=0.;
         if(!k)gamma[k]=1.;
         dum=((t[3]-t[2-k]) / (*delt) ) ;
/* pulled out of loop-dum is independent of i*/
         for(i=0;i<nn;i++)
            {
            a INDEX(i,k)=pown(dum,i);
            };
         }/* for k*/;
         lufact(a,coln,nn,pivot,&info);
         if(info){printf(" bad matrix 1in stiff2\n");
               *ibug=1; return;};

         backsub(a,coln,nn,pivot,gamma);
      for(k=0;k<neq;k++)
         {
         sum=0.;
         for(i=0;i<nn;i++)
            {
            sum+=gamma[i]*x INDEC(k,2-i,4);
            }
         xp [k]=sum;
         x INDEC(k,3,4)=xp[k];
         } /* for k */
```

```
      /* prepare for iteration*/
      nn=norder+1;
      for (k=0;k<nn;k++)
         {
         alpha[k]=0.;
         if(k==1)alpha[k]=1.;
dum=((t[3]-t[3-k]) / (*delt) );
/*similarly moved out of loop*/
      for (i=0;i<nn;i++)
            {
         a INDEX(i,k)=pown(dum,i);
         };
      }/* for k*/;

      lufact(a,coln,nn,pivot,&info);
      if(info){printf(" bad matrix 2in stiff2\n");
         *ibug=2;return;};

      backsub(a,coln,nn,pivot,alpha);
       coln=neq;

      /* Newton-Raphson iteration*/
      for (j=0;j<newton;j++)
         {/*zerom(a,neq,neq);not needed*/
         (*f)(x,t[3],xdot,neq);
         for (k=0;k<neq;k++)
            {
            w4= x INDEC(k,3,4);
            ddx=deltbx*w4;
            x INDEC(k,3,4)=w4-ddx;
            (*f)(x,t[3],xdot1,neq);
            x INDEC(k,3,4)=w4;
            ww5=0.;
            if (ddx!=0.)ww5=*delt/(ddx*alpha[0]);
            for(i=0;i<neq;i++)
               {
               w2=0.0;
               if(i==k)w2=1.;
```

```
            w3=ww5*(xdot[i]-xdot1[i]);
            w4=w2+w3;
            /* a= 1+Jacobian */
            /* no need to zero a, or add to itself*/
            a INDEX(i,k)=w4;
            }
        }/*end k*/
    /* rhs vector calc*/
    for (k=0;k<neq;k++)
        {
        sum=0.;
        for (i=1;i<nn;i++)
        sum+=alpha[i]* x INDEC(k,3-i,4);
        xdot[k]=-x INDEC(k,3,4)
        -(sum+*delt*xdot[k])/alpha[0];
        }/*end k*/
    lufact(a,coln,neq,pivot,&info);
if(info){printf(" bad matrix 3 in stiff2\n");
    *ibug=4;return;};

        backsub(a,coln,neq,pivot,xdot);
    /*advance state vector*/
    delx=0.;
    xnorm=0.;
    ddx=0.;
    iflag=0;
for (i=0;i<neq;i++)
        {
        ddx=abs(xdot[i]);
        xnorm=abs(x INDEC(i,3,4))+deltax;
        w1=ddx/xnorm;
        if(w1>acc)iflag=1;
        x INDEC(i,3,4)+=xdot[i];
        if(w1>delx)delx=w1;
        }/*i*/
    if((*ibug)>0)
    {printf(" j %d, delx %f acc %f ibug %d\n"
    ,j,delx,acc,*ibug);};
```

```
          if(iflag!=1)goto convg;
          /* else continue iteration*/
          }/* for j Newton-Raphson*/
     /* no convergence in NR- cut delt and repeat or exit*/
     if( *delt<= *deltmn) { isflag=1;
          if((*ibug)>0)printf("dt<dtmin at" ,t[3]);
                }
     *delt=*delt*.25;
     if(isflag>=1)goto goodbye;
     *delt= max(*delt,*deltmn);
   };/* end iteration ired */
     /* warn about outerloop nonconvergence*/
     printf(" outer loop stiff2 nonconvrg\n");
convg:
     erm=0.;
     for (i=0;i<neq;i++)
        {
        ddx= abs( xp[i]-x INDEC(i,3,4));
        xnorm= abs( x INDEC(i,3,4) ) +deltax;
        w1=ddx/(xnorm*(t[3]-t[2-norder]));
        if(w1>erm)erm=w1;
        }
/* erm is   now  (x[predictor]-x[corrector])/{t-t}/x-norm:
compared to Henrici local trunc. error, need to mult by dt
and xnorm-this is a relative local trunc error if we mult by
dt*/
   erm= erm* (*delt);
     if (erm>= .25* *emax && erm<= *emax*4.) goto goodbye;
     if (erm < *emax*.25) {*delt=2.* *delt;/* was 4.*/
            *delt= min(*delt,*deltmax);
           /* alternatively, set iflag-rather
              than exit*/
              goto goodbye;};
     if (erm> *emax*4.)
        {if( *delt <= *deltmn)goto goodbye;
        *delt=*delt*.5;
        }
     *delt= max(*delt,*deltmn);
```

```
      *delt= min(*delt,*deltmax);
   if((*ibug)>0)printf(" redoing in stiff2 error= %f %f\n",erm,*emax);
      goto redo;
goodbye:
      w1= *deltmax;
      if(erm>0.)w1=*delt* *emax/erm;
      detnew= min(w1, (2.* *delt) );
      *delt=detnew;
      *delt= max(*delt,*deltmn);
      *delt= min(*delt,*deltmax);
(*iter)++;    }/* end of if  iter-norder>=2 (90 in FTN)*/
detold=*delt;
return;
}



float pown(x,n) int n; double x;
{float ans,power;
if (!n) return (1.);
if(n==1)return (x);
power=x*x;
/* as only need up to n=2, will not do binary decomp of n*/
if(n==2)return(power);
if(n==3)return(power*x);
printf(" pown n=%d>3\n",n);
return (1.);/* should never get here*/
}
zerom(a,n,m) int n,m; double a[];
{int i,k;
k=n*m;
for (i=0;i<k;i++) a[i]=0.0;
return;
}
```

```
            stfode
enter ibug>0 for debug info from stiff2
0
ibug=0
enter delt,deltmn,deltmx,deltst,emax
.01 .001 .1 .001 .1
delt 0.010000 min 0.001000 max 0.100000 st 0.001000emax 0.100000
Time x1(Calculated) x1(Exact) x2(Calculated) x2(Exact) dt
0.001000 2.892364 3.996000 -0.894363 -1.998000 0.001000
0.002000 3.586002 3.992004 -1.589998 -1.996002 0.001000
0.003000 3.838657 3.988012 -1.844648 -1.994006 0.001000
0.004000 3.929085 3.984025 -1.937069 -1.992013 0.004000
0.008000 3.967121 3.968120 -1.983057 -1.984060 0.016000
0.488000 2.455411 2.452420 -1.227706 -1.226210 0.100000
1.488000 0.903295 0.898926 -0.451648 -0.449463 0.100000
2.488000 0.332304 0.329496 -0.166152 -0.164748 0.100000
3.487999 0.122248 0.120775 -0.061124 -0.060388 0.100000
4.487998 0.044973 0.044269 -0.022486 -0.022135 0.100000
5.487997 0.016544 0.016227 -0.008272 -0.008113 0.100000
6.487996 0.006086 0.005948 -0.003043 -0.002974 0.100000
7.487995 0.002239 0.002180 -0.001120 -0.001090 0.100000
8.487996 0.000824 0.000799 -0.000412 -0.000400 0.100000
9.488000 0.000303 0.000293 -0.000152 -0.000146 0.100000
10.488004 0.000111 0.000107 -0.000056 -0.000054 0.100000
11.488008 0.000041 0.000039 -0.000021 -0.000020 0.100000
12.488011 0.000015 0.000014 -0.000008 -0.000007 0.100000
13.488015 0.000006 0.000005 -0.000003 -0.000003 0.100000
14.488019 0.000002 0.000002 -0.000001 -0.000001 0.100000
15.488023 0.000001 0.000001 -0.000000 -0.000000 0.100000
16.488026 0.000000 0.000000 -0.000000 -0.000000 0.100000
17.488029 0.000000 0.000000 -0.000000 -0.000000 0.100000
18.488033 0.000000 0.000000 -0.000000 -0.000000 0.100000

C:\FOR>
```

Chapter 13

Plotting Scatter Diagrams and Functions

"The purpose of computing is insight, not numbers."—(R. Hamming)

" Computers are long on the ability to generate numbers, and short on insight."—(L. Baker)

Chapter Objectives

In this chapter, we present a program which is probably both one of the shortest and one of the most useful in this book. Acknowledging the difficulty of having the computer provide the insight, we fall back on the adage "one picture is worth a thousand words" and let the user supply the insight. It is generally easier to be insightful with a graph than with a table of numbers.

Quick and Dirty Plots

This program is purposely not sophisticated. We wish it to be as portable as possible, producing readable graphs on most any terminal screen or line printer. We wish to plot both continuous functions and scatter diagrams of points with this program. We want gaps in the data to show up clearly rather than being supplied by some interpolation routine in a plausible but potentially misleading fashion. For preliminary data analysis, this is essential. For publication-quality graphs, you will have to take this program's output to a drafter or else use a more sophisticated routine (see discussion below).

Program And Test Case

The test driver plots a simple parabola of $y = x^2$. Function splot() is the plotting routine. Its arguments are two floating point arrays, x[] and y[], representing the points (or function) to be plotted, and the number of points supplied. The former is the horizontal axis or abscissa, the latter the vertical or ordinate. For compatibility with most screens and line printers, the program limits the horizontal line length actually printed to 78 characters (otherwise, we would sometimes get "screwy" graphs on screens that automatically "wrap" on the 80th character per line). For similar reasons the height of the graph is limited to 20 lines.

First, splot() scales the graph, detecting constant functions in the process. Then, the graph is printed, line by line. The entire array y[] is searched for points which may be in any given line, i.e., between the values of the variables ytop and ybtm. Values of y[] at or sufficiently close to the minimum value are plotted "on" the abscissa.

The auxiliary routine setl() is used to plot the labels at the vertical limits of the graph. Subroutine plotl() outputs an individual line. The subroutine unclob() ensures that NULL characters are printed as spaces; on different screens, they do different things. (In normal operation NULLs should not be present in the lines to be plotted.)

It might be argued that the points to be plotted should be sorted in ordinate, so that the entire array need not be searched each time. The flaw in this logic is that while we will be searching the array 20 times, or 20N pairs of tests on ordinates, the sorting will cost us some factor times N log N tests. As we expect N to often be much larger than 20, and since sorting is not cheap, we think that in this case simplicity is also efficiency.

The plot is not beautiful. There are gaps noticeable for small x values because only 40 data points are plotted, although there are more points on the abscissa.

As noted above, this is a "bare bones" routine. There are numerous modifications and options that come to mind for improving this program. Some might be:

1) *More numerous and more sophisticated labels.* Periodic tick marks can be placed on the axes. The graph itself, and the axes, can be given titles.

2) *The option of plotting more than one function.* This is most easily done, perhaps, by replacing n with a count of relations (functions or sets of points) to be plotted, along with an array of the count of points in each one, and a similar array with the character to be plotted for each. This would require one additional loop encompassing the plotting within splot(), indexing over the function count.

3) *For plotting orbits, maps, etc., it would be useful to force the scaling such that horizontal and vertical scales were specified (particularly equal).* If an orbit were a circle, it should look circular, not elliptic. This would not be portable, in general. Some experimentation with the screen at hand or the plotter will be needed to get the best approximation to account for the

aspect ratio of the device. Things will look different on the screen and the printer, in all likelihood.

4) *Continuous lines, smoothed and interpolated, can be drawn and peri-odically labeled with a specified character or perhaps a more sophisticated label.* We approach the level of publication quality with this suggestion. As noted above, there are reasons for eschewing such sophistication in preliminary data analysis. Furthermore, such a program would not be suitable for scatter plots. The method used by splot() of separating points into ranges of ordinates no longer makes sense, as there will be as many such groups as the resolution of the plotting medium. For such high resolution plotting, it is more effective to draw curves between point pairs. The easiest method would be to draw straight lines between points. These lines could then be plotted with Bresenham's algorithm (see Chapter 15). The mapping to the logical address space of a pixel on the screen from an x,y pair can be done just as in splot(), namely by determining scale factors as embodied in dx and dy within splot(). More sophisticated interpolation, based on splines, is a popular alternative for producing smooth curves. (As remarked above, you should probably be sure that your first look at the data has not been so thoroughly massaged.) The resultant spline curve fits will have to be broken down into line segments to be plotted. See Chapter 8 above on the use of B-splines. While these can be used, it might be more economical to use simple cubic splines designed to match function values and first derivatives at the endpoints of each interval (refer to Chapter 8 for a discussion and references).

I would be interested to hear from readers with suggestions, improvements, etc.

Table 13.1

Programs of Chapter 13

splot()	Produces simple plot of y vs x arrays
plotl()	Plots a line on the raster output device
setl()	Clears line of plot
setl()	Ssets line to background character
unclob	Insures line is blank

Program Listing and Test Problem Output

(Listing begins next page)

```
/* simple line printer plotting package
(from "C Tools for Scientists and Engineers" by L. Baker)

CONTENTS:
splot
    plots point set
setl
    initializes contents of a row of the plot
plotl
    plots a row
unclob
    ensures no premature NULLs in row to be plotted

DEPENDENCIES:
NONE
*/
#define max(a,b) (((a)>(b))? (a):(b))
#define min(a,b) (((a)<(b))? (a):(b))

#define NLINES 20

main(argc,argv) int argc;char **argv;
{
float y[100],x[100],z;int i,j;
for(i=0;i<40;i++)
    {
    x[i]=i;y[i]=i*i;
    }
splot(x,y,40);
exit(0);
}


setl(line,n,chr)
char chr,*line; int n;
{
int l;
for (i=0;i<n;i++) line[i]=chr;
```

```
return;
}

plotl(line,n) char line[];int n;
{
line[n]='\000';
printf("%s\n",line);
return;
}

splot(x,y,n) float x[],y[];int n;
{
float xmax,ymax,xmin,ymin,dx,dy,ytop,ybtm,ybar,dxi;
int k,i,j;
char line[81],label[17];
xmin=xmax=x[0];
ymin=ymax=y[0];
for(i=1;i<n;i++)
    {
    xmin= min(xmin,x[i]);
    xmax= max(xmax,x[i]);
    ymin= min(ymin,y[i]);
    ymax= max(ymax,y[i]);
    }

dy=(ymax-ymin)/NLINES;
dx=(xmax-xmin);
dxi=50./dx;
if( dx==0 || dy==0)
    {printf(" plot range=%f domain=%f\n",dx,dy);
        return;
    }

setl(label,19,' ');
label[18]='\000';/* make sure label is NULL terminated*/

ytop=ymax;
ybtm=ytop-dy;
```

```
for (i=0;i<NLINES;i++)
   {if(i<(NLINES-1))setl(line,80,' ');
    else setl(line,80,'-');
    line[19]='|';
    for(j=0;j<n;j++)
        {
        if( y[j]>yhtm && y[j]<-ytop)
            {k=(x[j]-xmin)*dxi+19;
             line[k ]='X';

            }/*if*/
        };/*for*/
if(i==0){sprintf(label,"%10.2f",ymax);
   strncpy(line,label,10);
   unclob(line,12);
   }
else if (i==(NLINES-1))
   {sprintf(label,"%10.2f",ymin);
   strncpy(line,label,10);
   unclob(line,12);
   };
   plotl(line,78);
   ytop-=dy;
   ybtm-=dy;
   }/* end of loop over lines*/
setl(line,80,' ');
/* x values print*/
sprintf(label,"%10.2f",xmin );strncpy(&(line[15]),label,10);
sprintf(label,"%10.2f",xmax);strncpy(&(line[65]),label,10);
plotl(line,78);
return;
}

unclob(line,kt) int kt; char line[];
{int i;
for (i=0;i<=kt;i++)
   {
   if(line[i]=='\000')line[i]=' ';
```

}

}

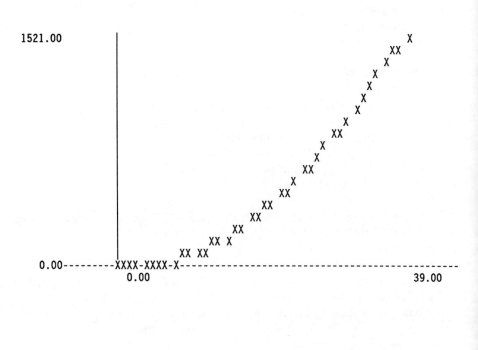

```
/* COMPLEX.H header file
 * use for complex arithmetic in C
 * see MULLER.C for support functions such as
   csqrt(),clog(),cexp(),argmt(),polarxy()
(from "C Tools for  Scientists and Engineers" by L. Baker)

DEPENDENCIES:
NONE
*/


struct complex { double x;
     double y;} ;
double d;/* dummy*/


/* for below, X,Y are complex structures, and one is returned*/

#define CMULTR(X,Y) ((X).x*(Y).x-(X).y*(Y).y)
#define CMULTI(X,Y)  ((X).y*(Y).x+(X).x *(Y).y)
#define CDRN(X,Y)  ((X).x*(Y).x+(Y).y*(X).y)
#define CDIN(X,Y)  ((X).y*(Y).x-(X).x*(Y).y)
#define CNORM(X) ((X).x*(X).x+(X).y*(X).y)
/*#define CNRM(X) (X->x*X->x+X->y*X->y)
*/
#define CDIV(z,nu,de) {d=CNORM(de);z.x=CDRN(nu,de)/d;z.y=CDIN(nu,de)/d;}
#define CONJG(z,X) {(z).x=(X).x;(z).y=-(X).y;}
/*#define CONJ(X) {(X).y=-(X).y}
*/
#define CMULT(z,X,Y) {(z).x=CMULTR((X),(Y)); (z).y=CMULTI((X),(Y));}
#define CADD(z,X,Y) {(z).x=(X).x+(Y).x;(z).y=(X).y+(Y).y;}
#define CSUB(z,X,Y) {(z).x=(X).x-(Y).x;(z).y=(X).y-(Y).y;}
#define CLET(to,from) {(to).x=(from).x;(to).y=(from).y;}
#define cabs(X) sqrt((X).y*(X).y+(X).x*(X).x)
#define CMPLX(X,real,imag) {(X).x=(real);(X).y=(imag);}
#define CASSN(to,from) {to.x=from->x;to.y=from->y;}
#define CTREAL(z,X,real) {(z).x=(X).x*(real);(z).y=(X).y*(real);}
#define CSET(to,from) {to->x=(from).x;to->y=(from).y;}
```

Index

About the Author

Louis Baker, Ph.D., is a senior researcher at Mission Research Corporation in Albuquerque, New Mexico. Prior to this, he held positions at Sandia National Laboratories and the Naval Research Laboratory in Washington, D.C. Dr. Baker has written numerous articles on electromagnetic field propagation, computer interfacing, A.I., and computer simulation.